THE JOHNS HOPKINS UNIVERSITY STUDIES IN
HISTORICAL AND POLITICAL SCIENCE

Under the Direction of the Departments of History,
Political Economy, and Political Science

Series LXXX   Number 1
   (1962)

THE ROAD TO NORMALCY
THE PRESIDENTIAL CAMPAIGN AND ELECTION OF 1920

THE ROAD TO NORMALCY

THE PRESIDENTIAL CAMPAIGN AND ELECTION OF 1920

By
WESLEY M. BAGBY

BALTIMORE
THE JOHNS HOPKINS PRESS
1962

© 1962 by The Johns Hopkins Press, Baltimore 18, Md.
Printed in the United States of America by
J. H. Furst Company
Library of Congress Catalog Card Number: 62–14361

This book has been brought to publication with the assistance of a grant from the Ford Foundation.

PREFACE

The election of 1920 was one of the most momentous in American history, with great impact on both foreign and domestic policies. One result was American rejection of membership in the League of Nations. Another was the reversal of the Progressive Movement.

The last presidential election before World War I, that of 1912, in which Taft, Wilson, and Roosevelt all championed reform, was a high point of the Progressive Movement. Eight years later, in sharp contrast, the election marked the " advent of the conservative reaction." Wartime social and intellectual trends were so parallel to the political reaction that the relationship may profitably be examined.

I wish to acknowledge the help of Professor Allan Nevins of Columbia University, Dr. Arthur S. Link of Princeton University, Dr. Festus P. Summers and Dr. John A. Caruso of West Virginia University, and Dr. Donald S. Barnhardt of San Francisco State College, all of whom have read the manuscript in various stages of its preparation. Mr. Homer Cummings and Mr. Will Hays, who were national chairmen of the Democratic and Republican parties in 1920, were most helpful and generous with their time. I also wish to thank Mr. Francis H. McAdoo for permitting access to the William Gibbs McAdoo Papers, and Mr. Ray Baker Harris for allowing me to use his collection of Warren G. Harding materials. Miss Katherine Brand and Dr. C. Percy Powell of the Manuscripts Division of the Library of Congress gave much friendly and conscientious aid, and I wish to thank those who have been generous in permitting the quotations which are acknowledged in the footnotes.

W. M. B.

CONTENTS

	PAGE
PREFACE	7
INTRODUCTION	13

I. REPUBLICAN PRECONVENTION POLITICS

Roosevelt's Successor: General Leonard Wood	25
Hiram Johnson	31
Frank O. Lowden	33
Warren G. Harding	36
Herbert Hoover	42
Calvin Coolidge	45
Henry Cabot Lodge	46
William C. Sproul	47
Henry Allen	48
Butler, Hughes, Taft, and Pershing	48
Republican Primaries	49
The Campaign Fund Investigation	52

II. DEMOCRATIC PRECONVENTION POLITICS

Wilson, a Third Term, and the "Solemn Referendum"	54
William Gibbs McAdoo	63
A. Mitchell Palmer	71
James M. Cox	73
William Jennings Bryan	76
Dark Horses	78

III. THE REPUBLICAN NATIONAL CONVENTION

The Lines Are Drawn at Chicago	79
Smoke-filled Rooms	85
The Smoke Clears	92
Reaction	96
The Coolidge Stampede	100

IV. THE DEMOCRATIC CONVENTION

The Democrats Espouse Principles	102
The Democratic Nominations	110
Wilson's Third Term Bid	117
The Selection of Franklin D. Roosevelt	120

V. THE CAMPAIGN

The Republican Battle Plan	123
Battle Lines of the Democracy	127
The Scandal of " Slush Funds "	132
Harding Beclouds the League Issue	134
Cox, Wilson, and a League Crusade	141
Progressivism	146
Wilsonism	150
The " Liquor Issue "	151
The Woman Vote	152
Race	152
Hyphenated Americans	153
Labor	155
The Press	155
The Recession	156
The Demand for Change	157
Predictions	158
The Returns	159
Interpretations	160
The Defeat of Progressivism	161
NOTES	168
INDEX	191

THE ROAD TO NORMALCY
THE PRESIDENTIAL CAMPAIGN AND ELECTION OF 1920

INTRODUCTION

The 1920 election was unusually decisive. Coming two years after the end of World War I, it answered two important questions, one in domestic and the other in foreign policy. The first was whether America would resume the Progressive Movement after its interruption by the war. The second was whether United States foreign policy would continue to reflect the idealistic internationalism that contributed to entry into the war and to the creation of the League of Nations. Both answers were negative, but the story of how they were made is no less instructive. This study describes the process and attempts to analyze the factors that contributed to these momentous shifts in national policy.

THE PROGRESSIVE MOVEMENT

In a favorable setting of abundant resources, indulgent government, prosperous farmers, good wages, and a continent-wide market, American industry grew more rapidly after the Civil War than that of any other nation. Value added by manufacturing, somewhat over one-half billion dollars in 1869, multiplied to nearly $5½ billion by 1899 and almost doubled again to $9½ billion by 1914. In addition to a rising standard of living, this massive industrialization brought certain social dislocations.

Large corporations prevailed over small businesses, and the growing industrial output came to be produced by an ever diminishing number of giant corporations. Over 80 per cent of the production of twenty-six products such as tobacco, sugar, whisky, matches, and lead, and over 70 per cent of steel fell under the control of single corporations. John D. Rockefeller's Standard Oil gained control of 90 per cent of America's oil refining. Furthermore, banking groups found that they could exercise invisible government over even vaster segments of the national economy. By 1913 J. P. Morgan's group was represented on the board of 112 corporations.

This centralization of control over industry occurred because it rationalized economic processes, was more efficient, and therefore more profitable than myriad small, desperately competing enterprises. In some cases it resulted in lower prices. But consolidation had other consequences that seemed to threaten the American free-enterprise and democratic system.

Such giant corporations were in a position to hold their prices far above costs, to set low prices to producers of raw materials, and effectively to combat labor's demands for higher wages. Consequently, the benefits of America's industrialization flowed largely to businessmen, particularly big-businessmen, and income became ever more unequally distributed. By 1910 one per cent of the population owned 47 per cent of the nation's wealth.

It soon became evident that such inequalities of property could produce civil inequities, and that great wealth could exert great political power. By bribery, and by financing newspapers and political parties, the great financial interests were often able to sway public policy to their private gain, and to the detriment of the common man. Thus, in a Jefferson-Jackson nightmare come to life, centralization of control of the nation's economy into the hands of a few threatened not only free enterprise but democracy itself.

The "Progressive Movement" is a name given to the great wave of reform that dominated the American scene from 1901 through 1917. The reformers had two main goals. First, they sought political reforms which would make the government more democratic and more responsive to the common man. Once this was achieved, they would use governmental power to protect the common man from exploitation by big business, and as an "instrument of social welfare."

The most striking feature of the Progressive Movement was its wide pervasiveness. Progressives were numerous in all classes, all sections of the country, and in both major parties. Farmers and workingmen naturally favored progressivism because it backed most of the demands of the old Populist party and the labor unions. But these groups, though numerous, were unable to take the concerted action necessary to win political power. Essential to the success of the Progressive Movement was the conversion of a large section of the middle and upper income groups to the cause of reform.

Many small-businessmen feared the trusts that threatened to destroy them, and some big-businessmen felt that moderate social legislation was necessary to head off a dangerous growth of radicalism among the workers. But, important also were the idealists who enlisted middle-class support for the movement in the name of humanitarianism. In the churches arose a social gospel movement that taught that the ethical sayings of Jesus should be accepted as a practical guide in political, economic, and social matters. Charles M. Sheldon's social gospel novel, *In His Steps,* became an outstanding best seller, and Walter Rauschenbusch, whose *Christianity and the Social Crises* was published in 1907, became the most influential theologian among the younger generation. Social workers, after Jane Addams of Hull House, went into the slums to help some of the casualties of the economic system, and incidentally educated in social service the squadrons of idealistic youngsters who flocked to their aid. Repudiating proletarian dictatorship and maintaining that socialism permitted individualism to flourish, Edward Bellamy's 1888 *Looking Backward* made socialistic solutions seem less repugnant to some middle-class intellectuals. A group of young muckraking writers exposed the evils of the day in carefully researched articles published by the popular magazines. They focused attention on the ruthless methods used to build the trusts, harmful substances in foods and medicines, railroad exploitation of the farmer, gruesome working conditions in some industries, corrupt alliances of business, crime, and political bosses, and domination of the Senate by special interests. Thorstein Veblen's *Theory of the Leisure Class* depicted the wealthy as wasteful and parasitical. These ideas of the social gospel, social work, socialism, and muckrakers influenced many of the middle class to join the movement for reform.

The progressives pushed through reforms on all levels of government: local, state, and national. American cities were frequently controlled by bosses who maintained their political machines with funds exacted from businessmen in exchange for contracts, franchises and low tax assessments, and from criminals in exchange for permission to operate. To drive such corrupt machines from power required a revolution on the part of church and civic groups; but by 1901 reformers had triumphed in Chicago, Toledo, and Cleveland, and were on the attack in other cities. Once in power they adopted new government forms, such as the commission and city manager plans, designed to make it difficult for the boss to regain control. They then proceeded to clean out crime, to lower utility rates, to attack the slum problem, and to reapportion taxes.

Similar battles were waged against state machines and their big-business allies. Among outstanding progressive governors who rode the wave of reform into power were Robert M. La Follette of Wisconsin, Hiram Johnson of California, Charles Evans Hughes of New York, and Woodrow Wilson of New Jersey. Progressives adopted the direct primary, initiative, referendum, and recall to make state governments more responsive to the will of the common man. Woman suffrage laws brought women's votes to the support of reform movements. Corrupt practices laws restricted the power of wealth to control politics. Then progressives shifted some of the tax burden from the poor by enacting graduated income and inheritance taxes. They spent more for public health and education. They tightened state supervision of railroads. They restricted the employment of children, set maximum hours for women in industry, enacted workman's compensation laws, and provided pensions to widows with dependent children.

On the national level the accession of young Theodore Roosevelt in 1901 brought to the presidency a "new liberal" who believed that reforms were necessary in order to forestall more radical change. Also, as an intuitive politician, he sensed that the best road to popularity was to champion the rising Progressive Movement. Under Roosevelt's leadership, the liberals gained ascendancy in the Republican party, converting it into an instrument of social reform. His administration broke up some of the trusts, gave the Interstate Commerce Commission power to fix railroad rates, conserved national resources from private exploitation, established federal supervision over the manufacture of food and medicine, and sided with labor in a strike. Unable to outdo Roosevelt in progressivism, the Democrats switched sides with the Republicans and nominated conservative Judge Alton B. Parker in 1904. But so popular were Roosevelt's policies that he won an overwhelming endorsement at the polls.

The 1909-1913 administration of Roosevelt's chosen successor, William Howard Taft, carried forward his progressive policies.

Taft's administration stepped up the prosecution of trusts, imposed a corporation income tax, compelled publicity for campaign contributions, legalized conservation of coal and oil lands, established the Department of Labor, and ordered an eight-hour day on government contracts. Constitutional amendments authorizing a federal income tax, and requiring the direct election of senators were ratified during his administration.

But such was the strength of reform sentiment that the progressives in his party still considered Taft to be too conservative. Disappointed by Taft's failure to lower the tariff and his vacillation on conservation, insurgents led by La Follette and George W. Norris sought to displace him with a more progressive nominee for the presidency in 1912. Capitalizing on such sentiment, Theodore Roosevelt declared himself in favor of an advanced program of social legislation and campaigned for the nomination. Roosevelt was favored by the rank and file but Taft controlled party machinery and secured the nomination. With the cry of "naked theft," Roosevelt and his followers withdrew to form the Progressive party.

The election of 1912 was a high point of the Progressive Movement. The Democrats chose the most liberal of three contenders, the progressive governor of New Jersey, Woodrow Wilson. Thus none of three candidates was conservative, although Taft was the least progressive. All called for stronger antitrust laws and a federal corrupt practices law. While Wilson advocated more "trust busting" to preserve free enterprise, Roosevelt argued that consolidation was irreversible and called for stronger federal regulation. Despite such liberalism in the major parties, over 900,000 votes were cast for the Socialist candidate, Eugene Debs.

In the Wilson administration progressivism advanced to its high-water mark. He got the first real reduction in the tariff since the Civil War and enacted a graduated income tax which constituted a significant shift of the burden of federal taxes from the consumer to upper income groups. He continued to dissolve trusts and moved also toward more federal regulation. The Federal Reserve System brought banking under federal supervision. He established Federal farm loan banks to give farmers low-cost long-term loans. The Clayton Antitrust Act legalized strikes and boycotts, and exempted labor from the antitrust laws. The Adamson Act gave railroad workers an eight-hour day. Wilson increased federal spending for highways and public education.

World War I, which broke out in Europe in July, 1914, was not fully distracting, for the Progressive Movement carried well into the war years. In 1916 the Republicans nominated the independent and progressive Charles Evans Hughes as their presidential candidate. But, assuming a more progressive position than he had in 1912, Wilson attracted most of the former progressive Republican bolters to his support and won a narrow victory. When America entered the war in April, 1917, progressives pushed through steep raises in income and corporation taxes. Concern about the conduct of the young draftees away from home gave impetus to prohibition, and the democratic war slogans and war employment of women added pressure for a woman's suffrage amendment.

But the war also injected new elements of its own into American life, some of which were destructive of the measures and spirit of the Progressive Movement. To meet the demands of war the federal government assumed emergency powers that approached dictatorship. Congress restricted freedom of speech, assembly, and political activity. Popular outbursts of intolerance and hatred for anything associated with the enemy were aroused by war propaganda. Faith in the innate decency of human nature declined as belief in the necessity and efficacy of violence rose. This rising war spirit seemed to undermine the humanitarianism upon which much middle-class support of the Progressive Movement rested.

The war ended in November, 1918, but for a year or more after the armistice problems of demobilization, readjustment, and treaty-making so absorbed the energies of the country that it could not be clearly foreseen whether progressivism would be resumed. True, the prohibition amendment was ratified in 1919, and the woman suffrage amendment in early 1920. But the Wilson administration did not reassume its prewar liberal coloration. In the great 1919 wave of strikes Wilson sided against labor, and Attorney General A. Mitchell Palmer flagrantly violated civil liberties in a war on radicals. Meanwhile, Congress prepared emergency legislation to halt immigration. The outcome of the election of 1920 would have to be awaited for clearer indications whether the Progressive Movement had survived the war.

The World Peace Movement

In the decades before World War I the United States had assumed a growing role in world affairs. By 1894 America's industrial production had become the largest in the world. Awareness of America's new strength came slowly, for the relationship between industrial and national power was not then clearly understood, and America's large internal market minimized her impact on world trade. Exports, however, multiplied five times between 1869 and 1900 and the resultant increased interest in overseas markets stimulated American imperialism. By 1900 the United States had taken Puerto Rico, Hawaii, Samoa, Guam, and the Philippines and was deeply enmeshed in the politics of the Far East and of the European powers which dominated the area.

A vigorous international peace movement in America was one of the components of progressivism. Among members of the American Peace Society were William Jennings Bryan, Andrew Carnegie, and Woodrow Wilson. Delegates to a 1907 peace congress included nineteen congressmen, four supreme court justices, thirty labor leaders, forty bishops, sixty newspaper editors, and twenty-seven millionaires. Edwin Ginn and Andrew Carnegie endowed the World Peace Foundation and the Carnegie Endowment for International Peace respectively. America participated in the Hague Peace Conferences of 1899 and 1907, subscribed to their conventions, proposed an international court, and submitted the first case to the Permanent Court of Arbitration. Secretary of State Elihu Root negotiated twenty-three arbitration treaties, and William Jennings Bryan secured agreements with twenty nations to submit all disputes for study to commissions for at least a year before resorting to war. In 1915 leading Americans organized the League to Enforce Peace with William Howard Taft as president, which called for an international court of justice and the use of military force to secure acceptance of its decisions.

President Wilson fully subscribed to the ideals of the peace movement. Although he regarded the war as one of German conquest and favored the allies, he was shocked when he learned in early 1917 that the allies sought territory from the central powers. He called for "peace without victory" on the grounds that victory by either side would lead to unjust peace terms which would make a new war inevitable. A just peace, he said, must include freedom of the seas, disarmament and no annexations, except restoration of Alsace-Lorraine to France and free access to the Mediterranean for Russia. The idea of entry into the war became more acceptable to Wilson because that would give him a role at the peace conference. In his war message he insisted that America fought not for any selfish purpose but for democracy, and a "universal dominion of right by such a concert of free peoples as shall bring peace and safety to all nations and make the world itself at last free."

In January, 1918, Wilson set forth a masterly summary of the goals of the idealistic peace movement and proclaimed it to be America's war aim. We fought, he said, for open diplomacy, freedom of the seas, free trade, an impartial adjustment of colonial claims, self-determination for the peoples of Europe, and a league of nations. When Germany asked for peace on these terms, Wilson forced the unwilling allies to accept the Fourteen Points, with the exception of freedom of the seas, as the basis of German surrender. "It will now be our fortunate duty," announced Wilson on November 11, 1918, to assist "in the establishment of just democracy throughout the world." Arriving at the head of the American peace commission, he was hailed in Europe as a savior.

But during four years of war, powerful countertrends to the idealistic peace program had developed. Propaganda had convinced many that the Germans were barbarians guilty of launching an atrocious war in a mad scheme to destroy religion and civilization and enslave the world. To many "just peace" now meant retribution on Germany for her crimes and indemnification of her innocent victims. Shortly before the armistice Wilson asked the American people to demonstrate their support for his peace plan by electing Democratic congressmen. In answer, Theodore Roosevelt condemned Wilson's program as "soft" and demanded "unconditional surrender." The Democrats lost. Elections in England and in France also indicated that the Fourteen Points had scant appeal to voters. Gripped, apparently, by a war psychosis, the people of the victor nations righteously demanded vengeance.

At the Paris Peace Conference Wilson fought a losing battle to incorporate his peace program into the terms of the treaty. He moderated some of the demands of European leaders for dismemberment of the enemy, but the Versailles Treaty that emerged was a victor's peace that bore little resemblance to the Fourteen Points. His major success was to interweave his League of Nations so tightly with the treaty that no nation could obtain its spoils without joining the league. To Wilson the league was worth the price of the treaty's injustices and offered hope of remedying them.

But the league received a rude reception in America. Some progressives protested that it would perpetuate the illiberal terms of a victor's peace, but most of the opposition was of a less idealistic nature. German-Americans, Italian-Americans, and Irish-Americans were bitter at the treatment accorded their mother countries. Chauvinists feared that the league would vitiate America's sovereignty. Right-wing businessmen were suspicious of the league's International Labor Organization. Imperialists disliked the mandate system. Some critics were disgusted that Germany was not forced to accept a more Draconian peace.

Both political parties seemed to regard the question of American membership in the league as of less importance than the question of which party would win the election. After Wilson's 1918 appeal to the people to demonstrate support for his peace policy by electing Democrats, Republicans feared that he intended to make the league the vehicle for Democratic victory in 1920. Subsequently, he excluded Republicans from participation in the peacemaking to such an extent that the credit for creating the league attached to the Democratic party and to Wilson personally. Consequently, Republicans felt that they must either force Wilson to accept Republican amendments to give the league a bipartisan character or discredit and defeat it in the Senate.

As Senate leader Henry Cabot Lodge marshaled an attack on "Mr. Wilson's league"; Wilson launched a speaking tour to arouse popular support for it. His tour was interrupted by his physical collapse on September 2, 1919. On November 19 the treaty as Wilson negotiated it mustered only 38 votes to 53 in the Senate, and he refused to let it be ratified with the Lodge reservations. In January, he asked that the league be made the sole issue of the 1920 election. Pressure from his personal friends on the president, and from friends of the league on Lodge failed to produce a compromise. In March the league was again defeated and the issue passed into the politics of the presidential election.

The Situation in 1920

Although the election of 1920 would determine whether the two great crusades of progressivism and world peace would be carried forward, public opinion did not seem to be focusing on these issues. The headlines seethed with emotion-charged distractions. Four million workers engaged in strikes in 1919, including a general strike in Seattle and a police strike in Boston. A newly formed American Legion fought radicals in the streets; bombs were mailed to prominent opponents of radicalism; the Third International appeared in Moscow; and a Communist party was organized in America. Thirty-two states passed criminal syndicalist laws, the Senate Judiciary Committee launched an investigation of Bolshevism, and the New York legislature expelled five socialists. Attorney General Palmer arrested 6,000 suspected radicals on New Year's Day, 1920, and radical aliens were deported to Russia. In May, 1920, Sacco and Vanzetti were arrested for murder.

Revived during the war, the Ku Klux Klan began mushrooming in 1920 and enlisted millions in its crusade against Negroes, Catholics, Jews, and foreigners. Eighty-three lynchings and twenty-six race riots occurred in 1919. The homicide rate in 1919 was double the prewar rate. By November 300 murders had been recorded in Chicago; and young Al Capone was not to arrive there until 1920.

The cost of living soared 77 per cent above prewar levels in 1919, and 105 per cent in 1920. With profiteering "open, scandalous, and shameful," buyers went on strike and held blue denim parades. Radio stations multiplied, and the stream of automobiles rolling from assembly lines swelled to a flood. Eight players were indicted for throwing the 1919 world series; Man o' War made track history, and Jack Dempsey knocked out Jess Willard to become heavyweight champion of the world. Henry Ford sued the Chicago *Tribune* for calling him an anarchist. Mary Pickford married Douglas Fairbanks. Alcock and Brown flew nonstop across the Atlantic. Sir Oliver Lodge announced that there was enough atomic energy in an ounce of matter to lift the German navy to Scotland's mountaintops. Youth was in revolt with shorter skirts and more liberal views on drinking and extramarital sex. Most untimely, prohibition became the law of the land. "America's present need," Warren G. Harding told an applauding audience in May, 1920, "is not heroics, but healing; not nostrums, but normalcy; not revolution, but restoration . . . not surgery, but serenity."

When politics was discussed, most observers agreed that political tides ran against the Democrats. Wilson's victories in 1912 and 1916 owed much to the Republican schism. By 1920, most Progressive bolters had returned to the Republican fold, and victory in the congressional election of 1918 indicated that the voters were returning to the normal majority party. Furthermore, the coalition that elected Wilson in 1916 was seriously disrupted. Midwestern farmers were angered by the tight wartime ceiling on wheat prices. Postwar inflation rapidly canceled out labor's gains, and Attorney General Palmer further alienated labor. Feeling betrayed by entry into the war, German-Americans and Irish-Americans resented the peace terms of Versailles. Furthermore, the regimentation and privation incident to the war did violence to the American individualist tradition and raised suspicions of governmental bungling.

After Wilson's collapse, there was growing public unease concerning his ability to direct the government. Sparse and misleading medical bulletins from the White House gave scant reassurance. His peremptory dismissal of Secretary of State Robert Lansing for calling cabinet meetings during his illness revealed how far his hand had slipped from the helm of the government, and made it appear that his once inspiring leadership had degenerated into sickly petulance. Revulsion of feeling against Wilson was almost universal.

Republican optimism, however, was not unqualified. Memories of the 1912 split were still vivid and the resentments it engendered lingered beneath the surface. Furthermore, in the League of Nations, a disturbing foreign policy issue had arisen to pose a new threat to party unity, and might enable the Democrats again to frustrate the return of the Republicans to power.

In both parties the question of the 1920 presidential nominee was wide open. Theodore Roosevelt, the presumptive Republican standard-bearer, died in January, 1919. His death opened a scramble for the succession, with different aspects of his manifold personality represented by the fighting progressive, Senator Hiram Johnson of California, the military patriot, General Leonard

Wood, and the blue-blooded scholar-in-politics, Senator Henry Cabot Lodge of Massachusetts. Also highly receptive were such old guard decorations as Governor Frank O. Lowden of Illinois and Senator Warren G. Harding of Ohio.

Among Democrats, the dramatic leadership of Wilson had been so overshadowing that his administration had groomed no leader of outstanding national prominence except the chairman of the European Relief Council, Herbert C. Hoover, and no one knew his polictical affiliation. Thrice nominated William Jennings Bryan had been out of the limelight since his resignation as Secretary of State in 1915, and now seemed more a historical figure than a possible president. The able Secretary of the Treasury, William Gibbs McAdoo, and the red-hunting Attorney General Palmer were among "those mentioned," especially after Wilson's health failed, but the fact that the ill Wilson refused to deny rumors that he wanted to run again inhibited open campaigning by administration men.

On domestic policy the division between the parties was still vague, but the postwar outlines were beginning to emerge. In the era of Roosevelt, Republicans had assumed leadership of progressives to such a degree that it was difficult to say which was the conservative party, and during the war both parties had moved to the right. But Wilson had been the most recent progressive president. He had divested big-businessmen of political power, nurtured labor unions, lowered the tariff, tightened government control of business, and drastically raised taxes for the wealthy. Small wonder that conservatives hated him. Now, strengthened by the war, they had regained their former dominance in the councils of the Republican party and burned with determination to rid the government of Wilsonism. But first they had to beat off any challenge to their control by the former Progressives, returning to the party fold, in order to insure that the Republican party would be a reliable instrument of conservatism.

Chapter I

REPUBLICAN PRECONVENTION POLITICS

Roosevelt's Successor: General Leonard Wood

Before former-President Theodore Roosevelt's death in January, 1919, there had been little visible maneuvering for the 1920 Republican nomination because it was generally assumed that he would be nominated. His death left the party without a personality of dominating stature, but noteworthy campaigns for the nomination were soon launched by General Leonard Wood, Governor Frank O. Lowden, Senator Hiram Johnson, and Senator Warren G. Harding. Lowden and Harding adopted the traditional approach of wooing the leaders of existing Republican organizations, but Wood and Johnson sought to capture the nomination through the relatively new preferential primaries.

General Wood, the outstanding military figure in the country, was the natural choice for president after a victorious war. He had commanded Roosevelt's Roughriders during the Spanish-American War, efficiently governed Cuba after the war, and was a leading advocate of "preparedness" for entry into the World War. Like Roosevelt, he had been kept out of the fighting, which to many made him a military martyr for whom it would be a singular vindication to oust the Democratic administration. For months it appeared that his lead for the Republican nomination was unchallengeable. But Wood, who had exercised political power in his own right as governor of Cuba, was unwilling to accept the military hero's traditional role as facade for politicians, and blundered into a fight with party leaders which caused them to unite against him.

Two weeks before his death, Roosevelt told friends that if he was unable to run he hoped they would back Wood. Shortly after the funeral Roosevelt's family asked Wood to take over the leadership of the Roosevelt forces. "It would seem," wrote former-President William Howard Taft, "as if the funeral bake meats had furnished forth the feast for the heir." Seconding Roosevelt's attack on any league of nations which might impair America's freedom of action, Wood took Roosevelt's place as a regular contributor to the *Metropolitan Magazine,* and asked Roosevelt's manager, John T. King, to head his campaign.[1]

King, national committeeman from Connecticut, was a professional politician closely associated with the powerful Pennsylvania Senator Boise Penrose, titular Republican national boss. To those who were surprised that he had picked a man of this type to head his campaign, Roosevelt had said: "John supplies the efficiency and I supply the morals." King insisted that he be given sole direction of Wood's campaign, free from amateur interference. Advising Wood not to make an open campaign, King moved in the devious byways of politics, traveling and spending much money, presumably reaching understandings and making deals with organization leaders—a method of procedure that evidently met with success. Wood had more support than any other candidate, said Taft, and Kansas editor William Allen White wrote that politicians in the Middle West were hopping on the bandwagon. A poll of Republican congressmen in November, 1919, showed that an overwhelming majority believed that Wood would be the nominee.[2]

The general appealed mainly to eastern conservatives who did not share Roosevelt's economic and social liberalism. Elihu Root, former Secretary of State, was an early backer; and Henry Cabot Lodge, offered to nominate him. Peter Norbeck, Governor of South Dakota, Frank Knox, influential New Hampshire editor, and nearly all of President Taft's former cabinet supported him. In exposés, the New York *American* and the New York *World* charged that millionaires Dan R. Hanna, Ambrose Monell, Harry F. Sinclair, Henry M. Byllesby, William Boyce Thompson, Otto H. Kuhn, and Edward L. Doheny were his underwriters. J. Pierpont Morgan's son-in-law was Wood's chairman for New York City. A "terrific amount" of money was being spent by the "large interests" for Wood, wrote Harry Daugherty, because "they felt that he would use the military arm of the government to break up strikes and destroy the unions." Among his most devoted followers was the "Plattsburg group," made up of fervent nationalists who had agitated for the United States to enter the war. Educated and of adequate means, they were vigorous, patriotic young men, lawyers, writers, and businessmen, mostly veterans, and influential in groups such as the American Legion.[3]

Much of this large and enthusiastic following was not content to confine itself to raising funds for John King. Political amateurs, uninitiated in the mysteries of the processes by which delegates to national conventions were chosen, they attached exaggerated importance to publicity and assumed that popular support would automatically be translated into convention votes. Overly impressed with the presidential primary, they demanded an open campaign with visible results. Furthermore, they asked, was not King walking away with ther candidate, making covert personal deals, perhaps so committing Wood that their work in bringing him to power would be profitless?[4]

Forming a "Leonard Wood League" with branches in all the states and a membership upwards of sixty thousand, these amateurs established a national committee and, in October, asked Colonel William Cooper Procter of Cincinnati, a millionaire soap manufacturer, to assume the chairmanship. With his financial resources, advertising ability, and antipathy to Wilson dating from the Princeton graduate school fight, Procter seemed just the man to promote public sentiment for Wood. Conscious of his lack of political experience, Procter hesitated, then accepted on the condition that he be made head not only of the popular movement but of the entire Wood organization. This put the position of King in question.[5]

Wood now faced the most crucial decision of his campaign. Roosevelt had been the master in his partnership with King; but Wood had much less political experience. Roosevelt's daughter warned him that King would be difficult to control, and Elihu Root and Henry L. Stimson urged Wood to supplant him. It was charged that King had spent an excessive sum of money, had claimed that he personally would have control of all appointments below cabinet rank, and had already bargained away specific jobs. Calling King on the carpet, Wood told him that he intended to make his own decisions and appointments. Procter demanded that King give an accounting of his expenditures and deals, but King refused, maintaining that they were necessarily personal and confidential. When Wood backed Procter, King resigned in a huff, in what was for Wood, in effect, a break with the professional politicians of the regular organization. If the Wood movement was, as Taft said, "a rush of the Roosevelt element to get

somebody in the place of Roosevelt where the entourage would
have control," then control had indeed been retained, but at the
peril of a repetition of Roosevelt's 1912 unsuccessful assault on the
organization.[6]

Procter sought now to create a new nationwide Wood organization. "Being without political associations," he said, Wood had "to put his own organization into every state and go into every primary." At tremendous expense he formed Wood organizations of amateurs and a few insurgent politicians in 47 states, and menaced the regulars' control of state politics. He even challenged favorite sons Governor Frank O. Lowden of Illinois, and Senator Warren G. Harding of Ohio in their home states. Austere, intolerant, and autocratic, Procter was an "impossible political animal," whose ignorance of politics was "absolute and unqualified." Lacking talent for human relations and compromise, he had little respect for professional politicians, spoke with contempt of "bartering and manipulation," and declared for a "clean-cut fight in the open." To other candidates his tactics seemed ruthless, and they grew to detest Wood. To prevent him from amassing delegates, the old guard pushed Harding, Senator Miles Poindexter of Washington, and General John J. Pershing into the primaries, and welcomed the entry of progressive Hiram Johnson in order to split the Roosevelt vote. They even supported a damaging congressional investigation of Wood's campaign expenses.[7]

Wood made long speaking tours in 1919 and early 1920. Although no orator, his rugged sincerity usually made a good impression, and he could move those who were affected by sincere and passionate nationalism. He attacked "reds," insisted on "preparedness," and called for "Americanization" of the league. Of communism he said, "Kill it as you would a rattlesnake and smash those who follow it, speak for it, or support it," and quoted a minister who had said of alien reds, "Send them away in ships of stone, with sails of lead, with the wrath of God for a breeze and with hell for their first port." A military showman, he spoke in uniform and usually had numerous officers with him. Calling for a well-armed United States with universal compulsory military service, he said the idea that the league would prevent war was "idle twaddle and a dream of mollycoddles." He praised Hiram Johnson for preserving America's "independence of action," but declared in favor of ratification with the Lodge reservations or other reservations that would fully preserve American independence.[8]

On reds and preparedness, Wood exhibited strength of purpose, but became vague and platitudinous when he launched uncertainly into social and economic questions. Nonplused at demands from progressives for stands on such issues, he protested that views were many and confusing and it would be folly to go into detail on matters which could be settled only after months of consultation with the "best brains." People were not interested, he maintained, in a detailed statement on the tariff, "or anything of that kind," but whether a man was honest and courageous enough to protect life and property and maintain law and order in the face of the Bolshevik menace. However, he eventually came up with a program calling for repeal of the excess profits tax, private ownership of railroads, the protective tariff, a larger merchant marine, and government economy.[9]

As his movement took form, Wood's militarism began to cause concern in some quarters. When war fervor abated the antimilitarist component of American democratic theory began to reassert itself. William Allen White came to doubt the wisdom of nominating a man whose chief stock was militarism and antiradicalism. To nominate a man who had devoted his entire life to military affairs would be most unfortunate, said Senator William E. Borah of Idaho, for General Wood, all right in his place, was unfamiliar with civic and industrial problems. Alarmed by such opposition, his managers attempted to tone down the military aspects of his candidacy, and Root and others urged Wood to resign from the army.[10]

Although he posed as the bearer of Roosevelt's torch, much of Wood's program conflicted with the tenets of prewar progressivism, and many liberals began to consider him a menace. Organized labor opposed him. Wood had "no philosophy but the soldier's one of force and the rigid and violent upholding of authority," charged O. G. Villard of the *Nation*.[11] Walter Lippmann, in the *New Republic,* calling him a would-be dictator, described his followers in terms later used for fascism:

Their frayed nerves were easily infected with the fiercest phases of the war psychology, and they have boiled and fretted and fumed. The hatreds and

violence, which were jammed up without issue in action against the enemy, turned against all kinds of imaginary enemies—the enemy within, the enemy to the south, the enemy at Moscow, the Negro, the immigrant, the labor union—against anything that might be treated as a plausible object for unexpended feeling.
This sect has been called conservative. It is not that in any accurate sense of the term. The sect has been called reactionary. That also is inaccurate for the last thing this sect has in mind is a return to the easygoing, decentralized, unregimented America of the nineteenth century. It has been called capitalistic. It is not capitalistic, if that means that it is interested in the administration of capitalism. The sect is radical jingo with the prejudices of the junker rather than of the great industrialists. It is really incapable of distinguishing between the military government of an occupied country like Cuba and the civil government of the United States. It is a mystical sect of innovators who propose to exalt the federal government into a state of supreme and unquestionable authority. They are not finicky about law or principle. . . . They have the mood, if not the courage of the coup d'état. They have backed every attack on civil liberty.[12]

But Wood proved to be less formidable than had been feared. The general was out of his element in politics. The necessity for statements on complicated social and economic issues, the fierce play of rival ambitions among his followers, the uncertainties and dangers of hotly urged conflicting plans of attack, and the flow and ebb of his fortunes left him in a daze. Unable to distinguish experts from self-confident fakes, he often mistook social or economic prominence for political importance. Procter's financial contributions put him under ever increasing obligation. With a congressional investigation of his huge expenditures looming, Wood complained that his managers were going to "ruin" him. "Procter got me into this situation before I knew what he was doing, and now I can't get out."[13]

When, after two months of Procter's leadership, it became obvious to all that Wood needed an expert politician to handle the "political angle," he turned to Frank H. Hitchcock, Taft's former campaign manager and postmaster general. He was a specialist in tying up delegations on a contingent basis and joined the staff in February. But, fiercely determined to keep full control in his own hands, Procter refused to give Hitchcock money unless he would give a full accounting, and when the latter refused, Procter severed relations with the "political second story man," while

Hitchcock developed sources of income independent of the "soap bubble." When Procter appealed to Wood, the general assured him that he had "sole and entire authority" and instructed Hitchcock to keep Procter thoroughly informed. Nevertheless, on the eve of the convention Procter instructed Wood delegations to ignore Hitchcock and to take orders only from him. Under such circumstances deals with Hitchcock were of questionable value, and many politicians looked for more secure arrangements.[14]

Despite such bungling, the Wood camp contained some political acumen which, as the campaign progressed, influenced Procter and Wood. Some delegates were secured in nonprimary states, and Hitchcock's work in the South brought in such dividends as the majority of the Texas delegation. Ambitious Governor Henry Allen of Kansas was handled so carefully that he agreed to present Wood's name to the convention. Wood endorsed the party chairman, Will Hays, for campaign manager. A contingent agreement was made, so Wood noted in his diary, whereby Wood's sixteen Pennsylvania men would vote for Pennsylvania Governor William C. Sproul until Wood came within twenty votes, plus the Pennsylvania vote, of the nomination, whereupon Sproul would swing the entire 76 delegates to Wood.[15]

HIRAM JOHNSON

Wood's principal opponent in the primaries was Senator Hiram W. Johnson of California. A progressive whose daring battle had broken the grip of the Southern Pacific Railway on California state government, he was enomously popular in California and, through a noisy career as governor and as Progressive vice-presidential candidate in 1912, had become a national figure. Elected to the Senate in 1917, he was a bitter opponent of the League of Nations and was chosen by antileague forces to trail Wilson on his western tour, where he was greeted by large and enthusiastic audiences. The stocky, spectacled, stentorian Johnson was one of the best known men in public life, and the only presidential candidate irreconcilably opposed to the League of Nations.

Johnson was closely associated with Rooseveltian progressivism and his forces insisted that he, not Wood, was the real heir of Roosevelt. With Roosevelt dead, there was no one for whom he had such "political affection," wrote William Allen White, and such progressives as Senators William E. Borah of Idaho, William S. Kenyon of Iowa and the agrarian liberals of the Nonpartisan League declared for him. Receiving wide backing from labor, Johnson acquired much of the Roosevelt organization in Detroit. Some proleague liberals, such as Senator Charles L. McNary of Oregon, backed Johnson despite his league stand, while other liberal voices, like those of the *Nation* and *New Republic,* agreed with Johnson on the league because they believed that it was designed to perpetuate the injustices of the Treaty of Versailles.[16]

The most liberal of the prominent presidential contenders in 1920, Johnson condemned American military action in Russia, denounced violations of civil liberties in the red hunts, and championed free speech. He attacked big business for raising the cost of living by profiteering and for financing the campaigns of his opponents. On the other hand, he voted to return the railroads to private ownership, and his record as governor was satisfactory to the conservatives of California.[17]

Johnson's violent opposition to the league brought nonliberal elements into his camp. Irish-, German-, Italian-, and other hyphenated Americans, William Randolph Hearst, and Mayor William H. Thompson of Chicago supported him as the clearest way of expressing opposition to the league. On the other hand, his league stand alienated such liberals as William Allen White who was "heartbroken" that Johnson had "gone wrong." Consequently, as conservatives joined and progressives deserted, the Johnson movement became less a progressive campaign than a nationalistic concert for the preservation of "Americanism."[18]

Interrupted only by his return to Washington to vote against the league, Johnson campaigned from early January, 1920, until the opening of the convention. Like Wood, Johnson made his fight in the primaries; but, unlike Wood, he had no choice, for party regulars were hostile from the first to this progressive bolter who had bullied Lodge in the treaty fight and had fought Boise Penrose. Announcing that he did not intend to have his fate determined by "politicians in convention," he actively entered eleven of the twenty state primaries. Less bungling than Wood, he avoided an open fight in the home states of Lowden and Harding and, as it was no place for a Republican underdog, made practically no fight in the South. With but light support, small campaign contributions, and almost no organization, he was forced to bear almost the entire burden of his campaign himself. Johnson was an effective speaker, and often worked large crowds into a state of fervor by vigorous emotional oratory.[19]

Johnson did surprisingly well in the primaries but the old guard was able largely to nullify his victories. Because he lacked the resources to set up rival organizations in each state, the regulars, even in states where he won the popular preference vote, selected the personnel of the state delegations. Such Johnson delegations were frequently actually hostile to Johnson.[20]

Attempting to create an impression of overwhelming public support, Johnson arrived for the convention in Chicago with a brass band and parade. However, gradually realizing that despite his primary successes, the nomination would be made by the regulars who comprised a majority of the convention, he appeared anxious to make himself acceptable to them. Toning down his stand to a declaration against the league "as submitted," he even refused to condemn the mild reservationists, and showed a conciliatory willingness to "go along" with the platform that had been tentatively agreed upon. Significantly, however, the Wood managers tried to frighten the regulars with the prospect that Johnson might be nominated unless they accepted Wood.[21]

Frank O. Lowden

Wood's campaign effort was powerful and Johnson's primary showing was spectacular, but, of those who failed, the man who came closest to the Republican nomination in 1920 was Governor Frank O. Lowden of Illinois. Lowden was an able governor, a party man in good standing, and capable of eliciting much popular support through good publicity. A blacksmith's son, he had been born in a log cabin in Indian country, and as a boy had walked behind a prairie schooner westward to Iowa. He worked his way through college, graduated at the head of his law class, accumulated a fortune, and married a Pullman heiress. Entering politics, he served in Congress for five years, was a long-time member of the Republican national committee, and for the previous four years had been governor of Illinois.

Lowden's record as governor was distinguished. Installing a budget system, he reduced taxes while demonstrating rare ability to get along with the legislature and with politicians of both parties. James M. Cox called him "one of the most attractive and ablest men of his time"; and he was Nicholas M. Butler's choice for president after himself. "In mind, he was able; in temperament hearty and forceful; in personality agreeable," wrote Mark Sullivan. Even liberal Harold L. Ickes thought that he had been "fair and open minded," and had shown that "no man or interest controlled him."[22]

Many were anxious to campaign for so logical a candidate. As early as March, 1919, Illinois' Secretary of State Louis Emmerton announced that Lowden's name would be put before the national convention and, in November, Lowden filed for the South Dakota primary. He soon became Wood's most dangerous rival.[23]

Lowden's record was satisfactory to the conservatives of the party without being offensive to liberals. He symbolized efficient, economical administration, harmoniously conducted. He criticized the league for being "political" rather than "judicial," but then took a stand for ratification with reservations. Although he advocated deportation and imprisonment of reds regardless of constitutional guarantees, his "red hysteria" was not as great as Wood's; one theme of his attack on Wood was "the goose step vs. the forward step." Labor leaders who had bitterly opposed his election as governor found him an "exceedingly agreeable surprise" and preferred him to Wood. Big city Republicans were offended by his "dryness," and irreconcilables were displeased by his league sentiments, but opposition to Lowden was not fanatical in any quarter.[24]

Confining himself largely to the budget system and government of Illinois, the stocky, undramatic Lowden made many speeches without arousing popular enthusiasm. He might make a good president, said Walter Lippmann, but he was not a good candidate. However, he met the specifications of the party workers only less than Harding, and, backed by many influential leaders of the old line Republicans, garnered as many potential delegates as Wood.[25]

Lowden made little more than a token entry in the primaries. Capturing his own state by a good majority, he ran slightly behind Wood and Johnson in South Dakota, Michigan, Indiana, and Oregon, but polled more votes than Harding in Indiana—the only state in which they were opponents. Stating that he did not want to place himself under obligation, he financed nearly all of his $400,000 campaign fund personally. His major effort was in South Dakota where he and Wood spent large sums in an advertising battle. Lowden protested the personal vituperation of some of Wood's speakers, and the hostility between the two became bitter when the general made a major effort to defeat Lowden in his home state of Illinois.[26]

Outside of South Dakota, Lowden's primary campaign was "lackadaisical." Instead, he addressed himself to party workers, even co-operated with the old guard plan of choosing uninstructed delegates. Consequently, he antagonized none of the favorite sons, and Penrose relaxed his early hostility. He acquired support in nonprimary states, and oilman Jake Hamon, who controlled the Oklahoma delegation, declared for him. The consensus of Republican leaders was that it would be "Lowden or a dark horse," and the rank and file of the delegates thought that Lowden would be named.[27]

Not that Lowden was an ideal candidate from the old guard point of view. He was not really intimate with the inner circles of the party, and had shown a degree of independence as governor of Illinois that made politicians fear that he might not be as pliable as desired in the presidency. The Pullman Company, with which he had such close ties, was in great disfavor with organized labor. Polls indicated that he ranked below Wood, Johnson, and Herbert Hoover in popular support. Moreover, Illinois was considered safely within the Republican column so that the nomination of a man from Illinois would not particularly add to the party's chances of capturing the presidency.[28]

Under such circumstances the sensational revelation by a Senate investigating committee of a corrupt use of Lowden campaign money was a disaster. Lowden's total expenditure was less than one-third that of Wood's, but $5,000 had gone into the private bank accounts of two St. Louis men who afterward became Lowden delegates. Lowden denied any knowledge of the contribution, and repudiated the delegates, but his boom "lost all momentum" and fell into a state of "almost complete paralysis," "smashed" by "spectacular defections." The old guard now believed that it was "impossible for him to go out and get the votes." Wall Street betting odds against Lowden rose from three to one to ten to one.[29]

However, Lowden did not withdraw and, as the convention

assembled, some of his strength apparently returned. The rumor circulated, however, that the old guard, henceforth, would use Lowden only to stop Wood, and then discard him to nominate a dark horse.[30]

WARREN G. HARDING

The nomination of Warren G. Harding for president surprised most newspapermen and the public. However, Harding was not really a dark horse, but was one of the early leading contenders, and considered a strong possibility by professional politicians throughout the fight. Overestimating the importance of primaries, political writers gave him little space after his poor showing in the primaries of Ohio and Indiana, but Harding had other sources of strength.

Harding was an extremely valuable asset to his party. A strongly handsome man, genial and modest, he was a speaker of the impressive yet relaxing kind popular among those who wanted a good restatement of Republican principles undisturbed by new ideas. If McKinley was the party worker's ideal, Harding approached it—his kindliness, friendliness, and personal popularity were noted. He had nominated Taft in 1912, was "keynoter" of the convention of 1916, and had been the model of a Republican senator since 1914. A "benediction on the platform" who "looked like a President," Harding was a "regular," extremely amenable to the wishes of party leaders, and he represented the pivotal state of Ohio.

A small-town newspaperman, Harding was editor and publisher of the Marion, Ohio, *Star*. As a boy he made no strong impression on his associates and there are no stories of exceptional diligence, ambition, or intelligence. At Ohio Central College he was not outstanding for scholarship, but was popular, edited the school annual, and debated. After successive flings at school teaching, reading Blackstone, and selling insurance, Harding, at the age of nineteen, with two companions, bought a dying daily newspaper for three hundred dollars and made it a success. At the age of twenty-six he married Florence Kling, a divorcee of thirty-one and daughter of the town's richest man, despite her father's violent objection, which was presumably based on the rumor that Harding had Negro blood. Becoming manager of the *Star*, she furnished drive for the genial Harding, who, orthodox and inoffensive except toward anarchists and Mormons, a speaker of handsome presence, flowery phraseology, and pleasing intonation, soon became the leader of the Republican party in Marion County. In 1900 he was elected to the state senate.

In the Ohio senate he was "regular," popular, effective, stood well with party bosses, showed genuine talents for human relations, and held his Republicanism as a faith. Re-elected by an increased majority, he returned as floor leader. Although adhering to the Foraker faction he preserved good relations with others and was elected lieutenant governor where his talents as a harmonizer had full scope. In 1910, attempting to stem the march of progressivism, William Howard Taft's forces secured Harding's nomination for governor. Harding made a valiant effort to "harmonize" the progressives. "In deliberate and appreciative retrospection," he said, "the American who fails to see a progressive Republican party is blind to the irresistible onward movement and deaf to the triumphant shouts of the all-conquering American people." However, he was defeated by progressive Democrat Judson Harmon who made capital of Harding's association with the bosses.

In 1912, his first appearance on the national scene, Harding nominated Taft in the Republican convention. Taft, he insisted, was "the greatest progressive of the age," and opposition to him was "fostered in mendacity." Horrified at Theodore Roosevelt's bolt, Harding's Marion *Star* said Roosevelt was "utterly without conscience and regard for truth, the greatest fakir of all times." In 1914, Harding, leading his ticket, won election to the United States Senate by 75,000 votes. Because of his fame as a harmonizer and because he was less reactionary than others of the old guard, he was chosen keynoter and chairman of the 1916 Republican convention, a role he performed well and with dignified poise.[31]

As a senator Harding's record, of course, was eminently "regular." He opposed tariff reduction, government economic controls, aid to agriculture, income taxes, conservation, and grew most earnest on the menace of socialism. Faithfully following Lodge's leadership in the treaty fight, he voted for ratification with the Lodge reservations. With a much remarked sense of "fitness," however, he favored exempting religious objectors from military service, opposed censorship, and denounced the New York Assembly for expelling five Socialist members.[32]

Evidently, in the Senate Harding had reached the summit of his ambitions. Perhaps the most popular senator with his colleagues, he golfed and played poker, maintained friendships with members of all factions, and gained entry into Washington society; but he sponsored no major legislation and showed no ambition to excel. The senator from New York, James W. Wadsworth, who sat beside Harding in the Senate for six years, wrote that Harding, disliking the formality, lack of freedom, and social restraints, "did not want to be President."[33]

But Harding's manager, Harry M. Daugherty of Ohio, was more ambitious. A lawyer whose real career was politics, Daugherty served two terms in the Ohio legislature, but was unable to win higher office for himself although he ran for attorney general, governor, congressman and senator. Variously charged with unethical law practice, extorting money from corporations, and bribing legislators, he survived official investigations without winning public confidence. Nevertheless, being a legislative representative for large corporations, Daugherty was a decisive factor in Ohio intraparty fights. Attaching himself to Harding, who "looked like a President," Daugherty now sought power by the political management route. It was largely at Daugherty's urging that Harding ran for the Senate in 1914, and the ensuing successful campaign did much to put Harding, or Daugherty, in control of the Ohio Republican organization. But it took much prodding and a peculiar combination of circumstances to induce the Ohio senator to run for the presidency.[34]

In the summer of 1919 the Republican national boss, Senator Boise Penrose of Pennsylvania, summoned Harding to his office and asked him how he would like to be president. The surprised senator said he was having such trouble in Ohio that he would be glad if he could be re-elected to the Senate, and, besides, he had no money for campaigning. Penrose told Harding that he could conduct a front porch campaign like McKinley's, and that Penrose would take care of the rest. He then began "talking up" Harding. This, however, does not prove that Harding was Penrose's choice, despite the unique degree to which Harding represented the professional politician's ideal: for at that time Penrose was seeking a full field of candidates with which to prevent either Wood or Johnson from amassing delegates. Indeed, after listening to a Harding speech in Philadelphia, Penrose seemed to have concluded that Harding did not possess even the modest abilities he desired to see in the presidency.[35]

In 1920 enemies of Daugherty and Harding sought to seize control of the state organization by joining with Procter to secure a delegation pledged to General Wood. This would threaten Harding's chances of re-election to the Senate. Thus it seemed necessary for Harding to stand for the presidential nomination himself as a "favorite son" candidate in order to maintain control of the state organization. At Daugherty's urging, he made a preliminary series of speeches, striking the "America first" theme that was to be the keynote of his campaign, while Daugherty sounded out political leaders around the country. Daugherty reported to Harding that his chances were good, because Wood's militarism, Lowden's wealth, and Johnson's record as a bolter would prevent the nomination of any of these leaders. To Harding's protest that he was unfit, Daugherty replied that greatness in the presidential chair was "largely an illusion of the people," and that the truest greatness was in being kind.[36]

Reluctantly, Harding moved deeper into the contest. To a friend he wrote that he was reluctant "to get into the presidential game" but a man in public life could not always follow his own preferences. In November, when he formally announced his candidacy, he said he "could not assent to an enterprise designed merely to control Ohio's representation in the national convention," but, with "encouragement beyond the borders of the state," would work seriously for the nomination. If only to combat the charge that his campaign was insincere, Harding was forced to campaign in other states. Indiana, where he had the support of Senators James E. Watson and Harry S. New, was the only other primary that he entered, but Daugherty announced plans to fight for delegates in the nonprimary states of Kentucky and West Virginia. Harding also made a speaking tour of Texas, Missouri, Kansas, Colorado, Ohio, and Indiana.[37]

Newspaper reporters soon sensed that Harding was more than just another favorite son. Soon after Roosevelt's death Carter Field, of the New York *Tribune,* wrote that next to Wood, Harding was the most likely nominee because he was the member of the old guard most acceptable to Republican progressives. In March, 1919, David Lawrence reported that in Washington Harding was the most mentioned possibility; and the New York *Tribune* predicted that he would lead on the first ballot. A congressional poll in November placed only Wood and Lowden ahead of him, and Republican national chairman Will Hays said that Harding, strong in the Middle West and eminently satisfactory to Wall Street, was the most likely choice.[38]

Early in January, 1920, Colonel Procter offered not to fight Harding in Ohio if Harding would consent to the election of a delegation whose second choice was Wood. This, however, was exactly what Daugherty feared—a delegation which, nominally for Harding, would really be for Wood. Furthermore, Hiram Johnson threatened, if such a deal were made, to enter Ohio to contest with Wood for second choice. When Harding, declaring that he wanted more than "perfunctory support," renounced the plan, Procter launched an all-out campaign in Ohio.[39]

In 1919 the state organization, most county committees, and just about every Republican newspaper in Ohio had endorsed Harding. But after Wood entered the state, practically no large city newspaper gave enthusiastic support to the senator; and the Cleveland *News,* the *Columbus Dispatch,* and the *Ohio State Journal* were outspokenly for the general. Wood made an all-out campaign; Daugherty estimated that his expenditures in the state would reach two million dollars. On the other hand, the Harding campaign was not conspicuous—with no billboard advertising, almost no newspaper advertising, and, according to Daugherty, no paid organization.[40]

Nevertheless, Harding's unexpectedly poor showing in the Ohio and Indiana primaries came as a severe jolt. Wood captured nine of Ohio's forty-eight delegates, defeating Daugherty as a delegate-at-large. In Indiana, Harding, despite organization support, ran a poor fourth to Wood, Johnson and Lowden. "It looks like we're done for," Harding told Daugherty. But when friends advised him to concentrate on getting re-elected to the Senate, Mrs. Harding stiffened him: "Give up?" she said, "Not until the convention is over. Think of your friends in Ohio."[41]

This poor showing "practically eliminated" Harding and "practically destroyed" his chances as a compromise candidate, the newspapers agreed. In the five weeks remaining before the convention, the New York *Times* remarked only that his boom was not booming. The New York *American* took little notice of him, and the New York *World* and the New York *Tribune* almost completely ignored him.[42]

However, Daugherty never expected a strong popular demand for Harding. Instead, hoping that the nomination of the more prominent contenders would prove impossible, he counted on Harding's popularity among political leaders to cause them to turn to him as a compromise candidate. Emphasizing his willingness to take advice and to work harmoniously with Congress, Daugherty traveled widely to talk with influential politicians, a method that had some effect. Harding supplied "a want of the Republican regulars that Lowden had not satisfied," wrote William Howard Taft; and Henry L. Stimson wrote that Harding's candidacy was more dangerous to Wood than he had anticipated. "Curious elements," reported Mark Sullivan, gave Harding unseen strength.[43]

Daugherty worked exclusively with leaders of existing organizations. His approach to W. L. Cole, chairman of the Republican party in Missouri, illustrated his method. Assuring Cole that "all the work that we do at all we will do through the local organization," Daugherty questioned him regarding Harding sentiment in Missouri. Cole replied that Harding did not have a chance of getting the delegation. What about a Lowden delegation that would go to Harding on second choice? When Cole said that might be possible, Daugherty, despite Cole's protest that he was not committed to Harding, wrote him a check for $1,250 to "find out that sentiment." In February, Taft wrote that, to the surprise of everyone, a canvass of Missouri county executive committeemen had revealed that Harding was the choice of more than half.[44]

While not very active politically in 1920, Taft was a close observer and was friendly to Harding. Writing Taft for an appointment, Daugherty said he wanted some suggestions about the making of a president, "I mean in a campaign for the nomination, not a riot." "My natural affiliations," Taft wrote in January, "are with Harding of Ohio, who is also a good man and to whom I am indebted for very effective support in 1912."[45]

Daugherty was particularly proud of his success in wooing Jake Hamon, millionaire oilman of Oklahoma, who controlled Oklahoma and a "big block of delegates numbering over fifty" from the Southwest. With tactics that included forcing down three eggs for breakfast to impress him, Daugherty secured from Hamon a promise to support Harding for second choice. The Oklahoma oilman, Daugherty thought, "had more influence among the delegates than any other man in the convention."[46]

Daugherty contacted not only the leaders but also as many as possible of the rank and file of the delegates. Before the convention Harding workers saw personally three-fourth of the delegates and compiled the most complete poll of their preferences, from first to fourth, Daugherty believed, that had ever been made.

In February, 1920, in an interview with a *New York Times* reporter, Daugherty made his famous prediction that Harding would be nominated by a 2:00 A.M. conference of the leaders of the convention:

> I don't expect Senator Harding to be nominated on the first, second, or third ballots, but I think we can afford to take chances that about eleven minutes after two, Friday morning of the convention, when fifteen or twenty weary men are sitting around a table, someone will say, "Who will we nominate?" At that decisive time, the friends of Harding will suggest him and can well afford to abide by the result.[47]

Later this statement was to appear remarkably prescient, originating one of the legends of American politics. Daugherty's statement was widely condemned as an indiscretion, as Mark Sullivan noted, because the Republican nomination might be determined in just such a "smoke-filled room."[48]

HERBERT HOOVER

Second only to Wilson, the best known American in 1920 was Herbert Clark Hoover, the widely admired food administrator and director general of European Relief. Hoover's life was an American success story. Left an orphan, he had worked his way through Stanford and made a fortune in foreign mining ventures. His countenance was open, his administrative ability legendary, and his humanitarian activities lent him an aura of the finest in Americanism. He had extensive knowledge of foreign countries, and was believed to have a comprehensive understanding of economic questions. None of the unfavorable connotations of "politician" clung to his name. Thousands had turned to him as a sort of "savior of society," said the *Review of Reviews,* and he was the one man whose achievements and character marked him to meet that need. To the *New Republic* he clearly outclassed "any other conspicuous American citizen," and looked like "a Providential gift to the American people for the office of pilot during the treacherous navigation of the next few years."[49]

When Hoover returned to America from Europe in September, 1919, there was great uncertainty whether he was a Democrat or a Republican. He had supported the Progressive party in 1912, held high office in the Democratic administration, and had backed Wilson's 1918 plea for the election of a Democratic Congress. However, he was critical of "radicals" in the Democratic party, stood for private ownership of railroads, and advocated the open shop. He strongly supported the league, but, pointing out the impossibility of a referendum on the issue, urged Wilson to accept ratification with reservations. Hoover said that he had been a progressive Republican before the war, nonpartisan during the war, and was now an independent progressive.[50]

Hoover's boom was at first nonpartisan. Julius Barnes, former head of the Grain Corporation, and other associates worked for him regardless of party affiliation. The New York *Tribune* reported that his closest friends said that he would accept either the Republican or the Democratic nomination. But his association with the Wilson administration meant that only a "practically impossible popular demonstration" could induce Republicans to nominate him. Hoover had insulted the Republican party by his support for Wilson in 1918, said Penrose. Believing that they would win the election without difficulty, Republican leaders were disposed to nominate only a regular member of the lodge.[51]

Democrats, however, appeared interested. So strongly were political tides running against them that something drastic seemed necessary to give them a chance of success. Perhaps Hoover might insure them the progressive, proleague and woman vote. Such Wilsonian Democrats as Secretary of the Navy Josephus Daniels, Secretary of the Interior Franklin K. Lane, Senator Gilbert M. Hitchcock of Nebraska, Governor Thomas W. Bickett of North Carolina, and former national chairman Vance C. McCormick favored him. Assistant Secretary of the Navy Franklin D. Roosevelt exclaimed: "He is certainly a wonder and I wish we could make him President of the United States. There could not be a better one."[52]

At the Democrat's Jackson Day Dinner in January, 1920,

former ambassador James W. Gerard advocated Hoover's nomination; and a New York *World* editorial calling Hoover "best equipped and best qualified to succeed Wilson," created a sensation. National committeeman John S. Cohen, editor of the *Atlanta Journal,* offered to help organize the South for him, and other Democratic newspapers were favorable. In the *Literary Digest* poll Hoover apparently received more Democratic votes than the highest Democrat, William Gibbs McAdoo. Democratic delegates pledged to Hoover were elected in New Hampshire, and he received more Democratic votes in the Michigan primary than any of the Democratic contenders.[53]

Homer S. Cummings, chairman of the Democratic national committee, arranged a meeting with Hoover for February 10. Hoover appeared to be receptive. Cummings wrote:

> He gave me clearly to understand that he favored party regularity and discipline and I gathered from what he said that it was his view that a person who was elected President would regard the party organization as entitled to consideration and respect. He rather went out of his way, I thought, to impress me with his personal view.
> With regard to political principles, he was not at all reticent. I did not gather that there was anything in the Democratic attitude with regard to either foreign or domestic problems which was distasteful to him.[54]

Although neither made any commitment, Cummings told Hoover that he would sound out the political possibilities and meet with him again. Consulting Democratic leaders immediately, Cummings found that they were favorable to Hoover; but the announcement that Hoover was a Republican abruptly ended this move to make Hoover the Democratic nominee.[55]

An open avowal of party affiliation was required to enter the primary in California, Hoover's home state. Expressing the hope that he would not be further embarrassed by suggestions of nomination by another party, Hoover filed on April 2 as a candidate for the Republican nomination. His reason for formal candidacy, Hoover insisted, was to give progressive California Republicans an opportunity to vote for the league. The *Post* thought that Hoover's announcement was a mistake, for, if he had not made himself unavailable to Democrats, the Republicans, meeting first, might have nominated him out of fear that the Democrats might nominate him.[56]

By the time of the California primary a Hoover National Republican Club was organized with about 150 chapters in California under the direction of Warren Gregory. Friendly newspapers included the San Francisco *Bulletin,* the San Francisco *News,* the *Sacramento Union,* the *Los Angeles Times,* and the Los Angeles *Express.* Most of the financial contributions to Hoover's campaign came from his earlier associates. Those directing his movement, like those of Wood's, were political amateurs who put much faith in publicity and primaries. Hoover took little part in the campaign, not even visiting California.

Senator Hiram Johnson was tremendously popular in California and, on May 4, won a smashing victory, with 370,000 votes to 210,000 for Hoover. However, some political commentators thought that Hoover had made a good showing considering Johnson's personal popularity. To others the results seemed a significant expression against the league, and, because the convention could not reject Johnson for his defeated opponent in California, fatal to the Hoover candidacy.[57]

Moreover, with Hoover openly in the arena, severe criticism of him appeared. Some thought he was too internationalist and pro-British, and too favorable to big business. To farmers he was a very wealthy man who, as food administrator, had favored business rather than the farmer. He was a "natural aristocrat," said Gifford Pinchot, whose sympathy was with "big business and the middleman as against both the producer and the consumer."[58] David Lawrence wrote that he was not a good speaker or campaigner, disliked the political fainaiguing that produced delegates, and lacked the political sagacity to translate his administrative ability into effective leadership.

Calvin Coolidge

In September, 1919, at the height of the great "red scare," the police of Boston went on strike, and focused the country's fascinated attention on a dramatic night of crap shooting on the Boston Common and a few smashed store windows. Governor Calvin Coolidge sent in the National Guard and took a firm stand against reinstatement of the striking police. When President Samuel Gompers of the A. F. of L. protested, he replied curtly, "There is no right to strike against the public safety by anybody, anywhere, anytime." Overnight he became a hero, a pillar of common-sense Americanism, a symbol of orderly government and, in November, he received the largest vote ever cast in Massachusetts for a gubernatorial candidate. President Wilson wired congratulations upon his "victory for law and order," the stock market rose, and the Democratic New York *World* wished for forty-eight Coolidges in the state capitols.[59]

Soon after this triumphant re-election, an organized Coolidge boom appeared, led by Frank W. Stearns, wealthy Boston merchant. The state committee, former Senator W. Murray Crane, and Speaker of the House Frederick H. Gillette of Massachusetts endorsed him, and Senator Lodge offered to nominate him. Republican politicians reportedly believed that the most likely ticket was Harding-Coolidge or Lowden-Coolidge.[60]

In January, however, without consulting his manager, Coolidge announced that he was not a candidate. Condemning the universal grasping for power, he declared he would not allow the office of governor to be used in any contest for delegates or for manipulative purposes. Apparently Coolidge suspected that Lodge was using him for his own ambitions, or that he was being used as a cover for the selection of a Wood delegation. Lodge, now cooled on Coolidge, indicated his wish to escape his commitment to nominate the latter, and during convention week was heard to exclaim: "Nominate a man who lives in a two-family house! Never! Massachusetts is not for him!"[61]

The Massachusetts primary chose only six Wood delegates, while the unpledged 29 were supposedly for Coolidge. A campaign fund of nearly seventy thousand dollars was collected and copies of his speeches, *Have Faith in Massachusetts,* were mailed to delegates. On the eve of the convention Mark Sullivan considered Coolidge in the first rank of dark horses and gave him the best chance for the vice-presidency.[62]

Henry Cabot Lodge

Senator Henry Cabot Lodge of Massachusetts lacked neither self-esteem nor ambition. Every honor his party could give, except one, was his, and frequently he had been mentioned for the presidency. Roosevelt's death left two leading antagonists on the national scene, Wilson and Lodge. Against Wilson, Lodge won a masterful victory, defeating the treaty while preserving party unity; and he quickly took up Wilson's challenge to make the league the issue of the election. Of course, if the league were the issue, Lodge would be the logical candidate, and some of his close friends thought he drove himself so hard because he expected to be nominated. But there was no demand for a Republican Wilson, and everyone preferred to assume that he was too old or did not seek the nomination. Only the mocking Democratic New York *World* supported him. At Chicago, Lodge was applauded and honored with both temporary and permanent chairmanships, but not with votes.[63]

WILLIAM C. SPROUL

The able and popular governor of populous and Republican Pennsylvania, William C. Sproul was a logical nominee if the prospective deadlock among the leaders developed. His candidacy, however, was complicated by the struggle for control of the Republican party in Pennsylvania which was brought on by the failing health of Senator Boies Penrose. At the height of his power, Penrose was regarded as national Republican boss, successor to Hanna, Quay, and Aldrich. Huge, of dominating personality, Penrose was a rich bachelor with a Harvard background. His mental power was impressive, and he had an enormous capacity for detail. As chairman of the Senate Finance Committee, he dominated the directing committees of the party, and, despite his illness, he was still titular boss, with enormous prestige among the delegates. Most newspapers and candidates believed that his word would be decisive in the convention.[64]

Penrose was willing to accept Wood only if he gave guarantees that he would co-operate with the old guard. He encouraged Lowden, if only for the purpose of stopping Wood. Harding, also was among those whom Penrose encouraged, and the *New York Times* thought that Harding was his real candidate. However, the poor showing of Harding in the primaries forced Penrose to hedge by preparing to make the best bargain possible should the nomination of Wood or Lowden become unavoidable. For such purposes he must preserve full control of a maneuverable delegation. Probably for this reason Penrose endorsed Pennsylvania's distinguished but elderly Senator Philander C. Knox as the "best qualified international statesman to meet the requirements of the situation."[65]

Shortly before departing for Chicago, the Pennsylvania delegation elected Penrose chairman, but endorsed the candidacy of Sproul. By some this was interpreted as a sign that Penrose' control was slipping. The *New York Times* reported that his defeat by Sproul forces so angered him that, in defiance of doctor's orders, he was determined to go to the convention.[66]

In Chicago, General William W. Atterbury of the Pennsylvania Railroad took charge of Sproul's boom amid rumors of a Sproul-Wood alliance. But Penrose' public announcement amounted to condemnation by faint endorsement. He was "entirely friendly" to Sproul's "aspirations," he said, but he recognized the "weighty problems of a general character" that prevailed at the convention.[67]

Henry Allen

In Kansas there emerged a home-grown amateurish presidential boom which ultimately involved as devious political maneuvering as any Eastern boss could have devised. Editor William Allen White launched the boom chiefly as a compliment to his friend, Governor Henry Allen, but nothing is more contagious than the presidential fever. Soon Allen was seriously hoping that, if General Wood faded out, he would be the second choice of Wood enthusiasts and, as an original Progressive, second choice of Johnson's delegates.

Allen did not proclaim his candidacy, but was pledged to Wood, and had been chosen to present Wood's name to the convention. Nevertheless, the Wood leaders were uneasy about him, and Allen sensed their suspicions. During the convention he told a group of them that he was loyal to the general to the last ditch—with one reservation. If lightning struck in the neighborhood of Henry Allen, he was for Henry Allen. A general might well watch such captains when the fighting closed in.[68]

Butler, Hughes, Taft, and Pershing

President of Columbia University, Nicholas Murray Butler received a complimentary endorsement from the large New York delegation. Long active in Republican politics, he had run for vice-president on the 1912 ticket with Taft. According to Butler, he received a "stupendous" amount of endorsement, and the press in all parts of the country was "surprisingly friendly and commendatory," but Wilson had made college presidents and internationalism unpopular. Harding, Lowden, and Sproul all assured him, Butler wrote, that they thought he should be nominated, but they ran little risk in expressing such sentiments.[69]

There was no move to renominate Charles Evans Hughes, the 1916 standard-bearer. Never popular among machine politicians, he had added to his political enemies in the campaign of 1916, and the press ignored him. William Howard Taft also cherished no illusions. His fight for the league had so alienated the regulars, he wrote, that they would no more think of nominating him than a Democrat. Dismissing every suggestion of nomination, he withdrew his name from the Oregon primary, while his son, Robert, worked for Hoover. General John J. Pershing entered the Nebraska primary but his reception there did not justify effort elsewhere.[70]

As the convention drew near, it was clear that the Republican party had a profusion of developed talent, and that the more conservative of the dark horses had grounds for hope in the prospects of deadlock between Wood, Lowden, and Johnson. But this presupposed that the politicians would first pass over Warren G. Harding.

Republican Primaries

The presidential preferential primary was a highly touted reform by the progressives who hoped that it would deprive the professional politicians, who usually controlled national conventions, of the power to name the party's candidate and give it, instead, to the rank-and-file voters. By 1920 twenty states had passed primary laws, and the vigorous campaigns of Wood and Johnson, with important entries by Lowden and Harding, gave the presidential primary its most thorough test. The chief result was to dramatize its serious inadequacies as a practical route to the presidential nomination.

The state primary laws were by no means uniform and there was wide variation in the degree to which the primary results were binding on the state's delegates. In only a few states did the voters elect complete slates of delegates tightly bound to vote for a particular man. Frequently the personnel of the delegations was made up locally by organization men who might not personally agree with the outcome of the state primary, so that control of the delegates remained in the hands of state bosses, who could change the vote of the delegation after the first or second ballot. To achieve even such limited and uncertain results a primary candidate found it necessary to spend money on publicity and campaigning on such a huge scale as to expose him to charges of attempting to "buy the presidency."

The primaries were held between March and June, 1920. Wood, with the influential support of editor Frank Knox, easily picked up the eight votes of New Hampshire, his home state. As the only candidate entered, Hiram Johnson won the primary vote in North Dakota, but the delegation, nevertheless, was made up of Wood supporters.[71]

The first direct clash between Wood, Johnson, and Lowden occurred in South Dakota. Attaching much importance to this state of small farmers, Wood campaigned for two weeks, Johnson and Lowden for one week each, while Wood and Lowden waged an expensive advertising battle. A personal admirer, Governor Peter Norbeck, put the regular state organization behind Wood who built up an early lead with a vigorous campaign which included an attempt to get through a blizzard on a handcar. Complaining of the huge expenditures of his opponents, Johnson charged that he was forced to fight the wealth and power of organized big business. The light balloting on March 23 gave Wood 31,265 votes; Lowden 26,981; and Johnson 26,301—a Wood plurality smaller than the smallest prediction of his managers. The surprising strength shown by Johnson, without newspapers, organization, or paid publicity, amounted to a moral victory.[72]

In Michigan, Wood and Lowden were defeated outright by the upstart Johnson. Johnson had fought to bring a Michigan regiment home from Siberia; the recent Newberry scandal made his attack on Wood's finances particularly effective; he got the votes of the antileague Irish- and German-Americans; and much of the old Theodore Roosevelt organization in the labor areas supported him. He reaped Michigan's thirty delegates with 156,939 to 112,568 for Wood, and 62,418 for Lowden.[73]

Despite the advice of experienced politicians, Procter decided to invade Lowden's home state of Illinois. Wood campaigned throughout the state where his forces spent at least $330,000. Lowden refused to campaign, on the grounds that if he could not win his own state on his record he should not be a candidate. He won, 236,802 to 156,719. Although Johnson made no speeches in Illinois and his name was not on the ballot he got a surprising 64,201 write-in vote, which the Chicago *Tribune* called a "remarkable success."[74]

In Nebraska, General John J. Pershing entered the primary. This split the promilitary vote with Wood to give the state to Johnson, who, running particularly strong in German-American counties, received 63,161 to 42,385 for Wood, and 27,699 for Pershing. In Montana, where Johnson was supported by agrarian liberals of the Nonpartisan League, he won an even more decisive victory.[75]

On April 27 came the important New Jersey test—a straight-out fight between Wood and Johnson. Wood, who could not afford further setbacks and preserve his position as leading candidate, was favored because of the opinion that the progressive Johnson would not run well in the business East. But, with over one hundred thousand votes cast, Johnson ran less than 1,300 behind Wood, which enhanced Johnson's prestige more than any previous development.[76]

Invading Ohio, Wood campaigned vigorously and with large expenditures for the vote of Harding's home state. There Roosevelt's following backed him, while Taft Republicans supported Harding. Harding got 123,257 to 108,565 for Wood, but Wood captured nine of Ohio's 48 delegates, defeating Harding's manager, Harry M. Daugherty. This feat was considered sufficient to eliminate Harding as the "white hope" of the old guard. However, because it intensified the hostility of regulars everywhere against the general, it proved an extremely expensive victory.[77]

Massachusetts chose a largely uninstructed delegation which seemed to favor favorite son Coolidge, with Wood as a strong second choice. In Maryland, where Wood had organization backing and where Johnson's dry stand was a handicap, Wood won 16 delegates, by 15,900 to 8,059.[78]

The much heralded contest between Johnson and Hoover in California was decided on May 3. Hoover was generally regarded as progressive, although somewhat less so than Johnson, consequently the sharpest issue between them was the League of Nations, which Hoover championed. Although Hoover did not visit the state, much money was spent in his behalf and important California newspapers supported him. Johnson won an impressive victory, 369,853 to 209,009. Contrary to expectations Johnson carried the Democratic districts while the strong Republican districts went to Hoover.[79]

Only in Indiana did all four leading Republican aspirants meet. Regarding Wood as the chief menace, the old guard encouraged not only Lowden and Harding, but Johnson as well to enter against him. By election time, however, Johnson was running so strongly that the old guard reportedly asked Lowden and Harding to unite against the former. Wood won the primary vote with 85,708 to Johnson's 79,840, while Lowden got only 39,627 and Harding 30,782. As no candidate received a majority, the primary was not binding and Wood secured 22 and Johnson eight delegates.[80]

Johnson captured Oregon with 46,163 to 43,770 for Wood. West Virginia instructed its delegates for favorite son Senator Howard Sutherland, but most of the delegates favored Wood. Johnson carried North Carolina with 15,375 to 5,603 for Wood.[81]

With the primaries completed, Wood had captured 124 instructed delegates, Johnson, 112; Lowden, 72; and Harding, 39. In popular votes Johnson had won 965,651; Wood, 710,863; Lowden, 389,127; Hoover, 303,212; and Harding, 144,762. Wood's attempt to storm the convention had failed, for he was not within striking distance of the number of delegates necessary to nomination. Hiram Johnson, despite the greater resources of Wood and Lowden, had won almost as many delegates as Wood, and more popular votes.[82]

THE CAMPAIGN FUND INVESTIGATION

Of course, the primary battle required huge expenditures of money. Wood's campaign was the largest and, in early 1920, the New York *American* carried an "exposé" of the general's rich backers. The Democratic New York *World,* under a headline, "Millionaires Back Wood Boom," asserted that he had been underwritten to the amount of six million dollars. Johnson's chief supporter, Senator Borah, charged in the Senate that Wood's managers were trying to "control the Republican convention by the use of money."[83]

Without debate or opposition, the Senate adopted Borah's resolution for investigation, and a subcommittee for the purpose was appointed under the chairmanship of Senator Kenyon of Iowa. Before the convention met, the committee uncovered Wood expenditures of $1,500,000, nearly half of which had been advanced by Colonel Procter. The sum was large enough to lend color to Borah's charges. However, the general's expenditures were probably less "sinister" than they might have been. His headquarters were elaborate, his organization large, and his publicity profuse; but his money was spent not to corrupt but in an appeal to the people for "an open verdict openly arrived at."[84]

The investigation, unexpectedly, was more damaging to Lowden. He spent only $414,159, most of which he supplied himself, but the revelation that his money had been used to bribe two Missouri delegates was a crippling blow to him just before the convention—at a time when his chances seemed to be very good.[85]

Although he initiated it, the investigation probably hurt Johnson more that it helped him. Republicans were resentful because it had provided Democrats with ammunition for the coming campaign. The investigation's ultimate effect of discrediting Wood, Lowden, and Johnson, and widening the rift between them, was to help make a compromise nomination inevitable. The beneficiary was Harding.

The great primary campaigns of Wood and Johnson had dominated the news, and most political reporters considered Harding to be out of the race; but, if Wood had hurt Harding in Ohio and Johnson had outclassed him in Indiana, neither had amassed enough delegates to ensure control of the convention, and neither was acceptable to the politicians who did control the convention. Lowden of Illinois, who also failed in the primaries, had a better chance for the nomination until the revelation of improper use of his campaign money. Next to these three leaders stood Harding. Of course there were many dark horses, but none inspired such comfortable affection as the Ohio senator. And, with political trends so favorable, were not the party politicians safe in nominating a man after their own heart?

CHAPTER II

DEMOCRATIC PRECONVENTION POLITICS

WILSON, A THIRD TERM, AND THE "SOLEMN REFERENDUM"

Maintaining unquestioned leadership of his party, the second Democratic president since the Civil War was engaged in great enterprises as the election of 1920 approached. As early as January, 1918, political reporters began conjecturing that two presidents, Theodore Roosevelt and Wilson, would campaign against each other for a third term, that Wilson would run in order to assure United States participation in the League of Nations, and even that he would resist a compromise ratification of the Versailles Treaty in order to make the league the issue for a third-term bid. The consensus of the press and politicians, at least before Wilson's breakdown in September, 1919, was that he would run again.[1]

Wilson's friends did not believe that he wanted a third term, reported the administration newspaper, the New York *World;* but Democratic leaders hoped he would run and, unless he indicated otherwise, would assume that he would accept the nomination. Analyzing the causes of Democratic defeat in the 1918 congressional elections, Homer Cummings, vice-chairman and shortly to be chairman of the national committee, wrote that only with the support of Wilson's personal followers, and under his leadership, could the Democrats win in 1920. No one but Wilson could secure the nomination agreed national committeeman Norman E. Mack; and Attorney General A. Mitchell Palmer predicted that the president could be re-elected. If the league were defeated, said Cummings, "the pressure brought to bear on the President to run again would be very great."[2]

Wilson was known to be an admirer of the British parliamentary system in which executive tenure had no arbitrary limits. In February, 1919, the White House denied that he had renounced another race. Senator Lawrence Y. Sherman of Illinois charged that Wilson's September speaking tour in the West, where he behaved much like a candidate, making unprecedented efforts to mix with people, was the "threshold" of a third-term campaign. Four days before his breakdown, the New York *Tribune* reported that the president had convinced the politicians of both parties that he intended to run again.[3]

It was thus in an atmosphere surcharged with presidential politics that the Senate decision on the Treaty of Versailles was made. If Wilson's league were ratified unchanged, his prestige might become unbeatable at the polls. Furthermore, a belief that he would be needed to inaugurate league participation might prompt a "draft" for a third term. To prevent the league from becoming the vehicle of Democratic victory, Republicans, perforce, had either to so amend it as to give it a bipartisan character or to defeat it.

After Wilson's breakdown in September, 1919, great pressure was brought on him to accept a compromise ratification of the league and/or withdraw himself from consideration as a presidential candidate. When the South Dakota state convention endorsed a third term, a wave of adverse comment followed. Wilson's career must not end in a conflict over a third term, said the New York *World,* and reported that most party leaders wished he would withdraw. However no withdrawal statement was forthcoming. On the contrary, the White House again denied reports that he refused to run. After the Senate rejected the treaty he said: "All the more reason I must get well and try again to bring this country to a sense of its great opportunity and greater responsibility." When the former chairman of the War Industries Board, Bernard Baruch, urged him to accept the Lodge reservations, he replied, "Et tu Brute," and turned toward the wall.[4]

To counter the Lodge reservations, Wilson drew up a number of interpretations of the treaty which were submitted by his Senate leader as the Hitchcock Reservations. The chief difference between the Hitchcock and Lodge reservations concerned the amount of obligation that the United States assumed under Article X of the League Covenant, guaranteeing the political independence and territorial integrity of each member of the league. Wilson would accept the reservation that the military and naval forces could not be employed for such purposes unless, in each case, Congress should so provide. Lodge worded his reservation, however, so that the United States *assumed no obligation* unless in each case Congress should so decide. According to Wilson this would cut the heart out of the covenant.

Republican Senate leader Henry Cabot Lodge was willing to make the treaty the issue of the election. What he would like best, he wrote, was for Wilson to reject Lodge's reservations and then go before the people as a candidate, for he would be "the worst beaten man that ever lived." After Wilson rejected them Lodge called for a referendum on the differences between himself and the president. Only "shrinking modesty," said the *World,* prevented Lodge from mentioning the superavailable Republican candidate on such an issue. Protesting against handling the treaty as if it were a private political feud, the newspaper called upon rank-and-file senators to seek a compromise without consulting either Lodge or Wilson.[5]

Clarification of his position on a third term was expected from Wilson's letter for the Jackson Day Dinners of January 8, 1920. Other candidates for the party's nomination wanted him to offer to compromise on the treaty and to withdraw as a candidate, and thus to clear the way for their own booms. Believing that it was their only chance for victory, other Democrats, however, hoped that Wilson would make the league the issue and run for re-election. Tumulty advised Wilson to offer to compromise and so put the responsibility for defeating the treaty on Lodge, "and thus you would be in a position to go to the country in the way that you have in mind." In Wilson's papers there is a note in his handwriting which asked if the people wished to make use of his services as president for another four years. But Wilson stopped short of a direct request for a third term.[6]

Traditionally the Jackson Day Dinner featured Democratic candidates for the nomination, but this time Wilson's letter overshadowed all else. Restating his arguments for the league, he demanded that the election of 1920 be conducted on the single issue of United States membership in the league: "If there is any doubt as to what the people of the country think of this vital matter, the clear and single way out is to submit it for determination at the next election to the voters of the nation, to give the next election the form of a great and solemn referendum."[7]

Wilson's letter created a sensation. William Jennings Bryan immediately rose to protest carrying the league into the campaign.

Irreconcilables, however, were jubilant at Wilson's refusal to compromise. The letter amounted to an announcement of candidacy by Wilson, said Republican senators and newspapers. It lent color to charges that Wilson was obstinately ambitious, said the *New York Post*. It made compromise on the league "next to impossible," regretted the New York *World*.[8]

Despite the expressed desire of both Wilson and Lodge to carry the league issue into the campaign, there was strong public pressure for a compromise ratification. In January agreement seemed near on an Article X reservation drafted by Senator Simmons of North Carolina; but, at this juncture, the irreconcilables threatened to remove Lodge as Senate leader, and Wilson condemned the suggested reservation as "very unfortunate." When, in March, compromise again seemed near, the president wrote to wavering Democrats: "I hear of reservationists and mild reservationists, but I cannot understand the difference between a nullifier and a mild nullifier." Wilson held enough Democratic senators in line to prevent the treaty with reservations from securing a two-thirds, but not a simple, majority.[9]

After the final defeat of the treaty in the Senate, Wilson turned his attention to securing a strong platform plank. To the Kansas state convention he wrote that the issue involved "nothing less than the honor of the United States." To Oregon he telegraphed that we could not, in honor, whittle down the treaty. This telegram, said the new Senate Democratic leader Oscar Underwood, removed the issue from the capitol and carried it to the party conventions.[10]

Among prominent advocates of the league, Wilson was almost alone in his adamant stand against the Lodge reservations. House, Tumulty, Mrs. Wilson, and Baruch urged him to compromise. David Hunter Miller said that the changes made were of a wholly minor character, left the league's structure intact, and "would have interfered with its workings not at all." Similar views were expressed by such outstanding proleague figures as General Tasker H. Bliss, William Howard Taft, Herbert Hoover, diplomat Henry White, and President A. Lawrence Lowell of Harvard.[11]

Some contemporaries and historians have felt that Wilson's policies in late 1919 and 1920 were affected by the fact that he was a very sick man. In Paris, in April, 1919, Wilson was confined for a few days with what was said to be a cold. From this time, wrote "Ike" Hoover, the White House usher, he became a different man, increasingly suspicious, with "much of his poise and consideration for others . . . gone entirely." Calling at the White House in September, George Creel was shocked at the change in his appearance. "Wilson confessed to being far from well, but neither the pleas of friends nor the implorations" of presidential physician Dr. Cary T. Grayson could dissuade him from embarking on a western speaking tour in behalf of the league.[12]

On his tour, Wilson suffered severe headaches and indigestion. Apparently less able to control his emotions, he wept and showed considerable asperity. At Pueblo, he intemperately charged that organized resistance to the covenant arose only from hyphenated Americans. That night, exhausted and in discomfort, he was unable to sleep. Canceling the rest of the tour, Dr. Grayson ordered the train back to Washington. Wilson walked from the train unassisted, but two days later was found in a semiconscious condition on a White House bathroom floor.[13]

For a month Wilson was almost completely incapacitated, and for additional weeks transacted only that official business which Mrs. Wilson saw fit to bring to his attention. The terse official medical bulletins from the White House did not satisfy the public mind, and the resulting gap in knowledge was filled with rumors. The *World* called for the truth whether agreeable or disagreeable; and Joseph Wilson, the president's brother, urged his doctors to issue a more detailed statement to refute the numerous rumors afloat. In November the Senate sent a committee to interview him, ostensibly about Mexico, but actually to ascertain the condition of the president's mind. On entering his bedroom, Senator Fall said: "Well, Mr. President, we have all been praying for you." "Which way, Senator?" he replied. "If there is something wrong with his mind," Fall concluded, "I would like to get the same ailment." George Creel found Wilson quite ill, with less control over his emotions, but with his mind unaffected. In May, Homer Cummings found him looking better, but uncharacteristically talking very little. Not that his mind seemed befuddled, wrote Cummings, for though he spoke rarely it was with "wonderful clarity."[14]

Other reports were not so favorable. Carter Glass found his interview trying; he thought that Wilson had lost some of his quick perception and clear decision, and that many facets of his mind had begun to cloud. When, on April 13, the president resumed cabinet meetings, cabinet members were announced to him as they entered. One of his arms was useless and, when he tried to speak, his jaw seemed to drop to one side. Though he spent several minutes cracking jokes he did not take the initiative, and even seemed to have difficulty in fixing his mind on what they were discussing. Charles L. Swen, Wilson's stenographer, said that after his illness Wilson never dictated more than five minutes at a time and was not competent to hold office. According to Ike Hoover and Edmund W. Starling, a White House guard, he became irascible and unreasonable. David Lawrence wrote that it was to his physical condition, his lapses of memory, irritability, and excessive emotion that many of his acts after October, 1919, must be attributed.[15]

After the defeat of the treaty, Democrats increased their pressure on Wilson to announce his withdrawal. The general feeling was that he was too ill to be a candidate, and that his failure to withdraw was embarrassing the party and preventing the emergence of other candidates. In mid-March Tumulty wrote Mrs. Wilson that "a dignified statement of withdrawal" would "strengthen every move the President wishes to make during the remainder of his term." On March 25, Representative Benjamin C. Humphreys of Mississippi, in a long speech against a third term, said that he regretted that the president permitted his friends, including members of the cabinet, to advocate publicly his reelection to a third term and "by remaining silent has allowed the country to believe he was willing to break the ancient precedent." Amid prolonged applause from both sides of the House, Democratic leaders, including Champ Clark and Claude Kitchin of North Carolina, crowded around to shake Humphrey's hand. When these moves failed to elicit withdrawal, the *New York Post* reported "increasing demand" and the *Cleveland Plain Dealer* spoke of "deepseated sentiment bordering on resentment," among Democratic leaders.[16]

The Georgia state convention passed a resolution against a third term. Most state conventions, however, endorsed the administration and sent uninstructed delegates to the national convention. A vast *Literary Digest* poll, amounting to more than five million ballots, placed Wilson second only to his son-in-law McAdoo as the popular choice for the Democratic nomination.[17]

Wilson told Grayson that Tumulty had sent him a letter asking him to say that he would not run again, but he would not do it. It would only turn the leadership of the party over to Bryan. Besides it might become imperative that the league and the peace treaty be made the dominant issues. If the convention deadlocked on candidates there might be a practically universal feeling that Wilson was the only one to champion this cause. In such circumstances he would feel obliged to accept the nomination. When Wilson asked Grayson if he thought he could physically stand another presidential campaign, Grayson declined to answer for fear of depressing him.[18]

Strictly instructing Tumulty to avoid giving the impression that he favored any other candidate, Wilson steadfastly refused to withdraw, or even to imply that he so intended. In February, Vance McCormick told Mrs. Wilson that he was anxious to launch A. Mitchell Palmer's candidacy, but was greatly embarrassed because the president had not made his position clear. Mrs. Wilson replied that it might be necessary for him to run. Palmer could elicit from Wilson only a testy statement that he would not object to his trying to get delegates, but that the convention must be left free to choose whom it pleased. Wilson then appointed an enemy of Palmer to a judgeship in New York. McAdoo, much embarrassed, distressed, and still seeking information about Wilson's intentions, refused to enter the campaign for the nomination in apparent opposition to the president.[19]

As the convention drew near, Wilson took what appeared to be positive steps to promote his candidacy. In early March he asked a group of his closest political friends to meet at the Chevy Chase Club. Among them were Homer S. Cummings, Bernard Baruch, Bainbridge Colby, Tumulty, David F. Houston, Albert S. Burleson, Carter Glass, A. Mitchell Palmer, Vance McCormick, and Josephus Daniels. A card was shown them on which he had written the question: "What part should the writer play in politics in the immediate future?" Everyone except Burleson opposed his running again, and even Burleson agreed that it would be suicide to go before the country on the issue of the treaty without reservations. All thought that Wilson should accept the Lodge reservations, but no one would volunteer to carry that decision to the White House.[20]

Six days after the nomination of Harding and ten days before the Democratic convention Wilson gave an interview to Louis

Seibold of the New York *World* which caused a sensation. Expressing confidence that the party would endorse his stand on the league, he asserted that the Republican platform had accepted his call for a referendum. Of the candidates, he said he had not raised his hand "to aid in the promotion of any ambition" for the nomination and believed that the delegates would not "permit themselves to be led astray in order to gratify the vanity or promote the uncharitable or selfish impulses of any individual."

Emphasizing the degree of Wilson's recovery, Seibold reported that he transacted important official business with all his "old time decisiveness, method and keenness of intellectual appraisement." "Now that his complete restoration to health seems assured," he fought to bring America to its sense of duty, "with the fullest realization of his own duty to America." One of his greatest discomforts, said Wilson, was that he was unable to "make a personal call on the people directly. Perhaps that will come later on. I am eager that it shall."

This interview had been encouraged by Tumulty who wished to use it as a vehicle for platform ideas and for renunciation of a third term. But Wilson rejected most of Tumulty's ideas and concentrated on the "referendum" and his own good health. Opposite the item, "Personal plans?" Regarding Wilson's personal plans, Mrs. Wilson wrote Tumulty, there was to be nothing in the published interview but exaltation of Wilson. "The views set forth by the President were plainly designed to announce to the country that the President is in every way still fitted to be a leader of his party and Chief Executive," remarked the New York *World*.[21]

On the afternoon of the day this interview was published the news broke that McAdoo had announced his "unequivocal" decision not to allow his name to be presented to the convention. The New York *Tribune* headline, "McAdoo Refuses to Enter Race, Wilson May Seek Third Term," was typical of newspaper reaction to the two events. When the Illinois boss, George R. Brennan, told Charles F. Murphy and Al Smith of New York that McAdoo's withdrawal looked like "a certain indication that the President would like the nomination himself," neither contradicted him. Two days later carefully posed pictures showed Wilson, looking better than even his friends had expected, at work at his desk. Wall Street betting odds, which had been twenty to one against Wilson, made him the favorite at nine to five by June 30.[22]

Administration leaders who visited Wilson before going to San Francisco received a strong impression that Wilson wanted the nomination. Homer Cummings called at the White House on May 31. The president expressed objections to all the candidates mentioned. He told Cummings, who, in 1918, had said the party could win elections only with Wilson's personal following, that he could be his representative at the convention. With matters apparently covered, Cummings rose several times, shook hands with the president, and started to go. Each time Wilson started talking again, held him for lunch and movies, but the subject he evidently had in mind was not broached.[23]

When Carter Glass visited the White House on June 10, Grayson told him that the president seriously contemplated permitting himself to be nominated, and that this would kill him. Burleson also believed Wilson wanted a third term, and Tumulty was greatly concerned. Wilson did not favor any of the candidates that Glass mentioned. Glass wrote:

> President asked me what I thought of McAdoo's letter. I said: "He nowhere says he would not accept a nomination." Very quickly the President responded with emphasis: "No, he does not; as I read it." We briefly commented on some of the men talked of for nomination. Of Mitchell Palmer I said he would make a good President but a weak candidate having, in the performance of his duty, offended powerful groups of men. "Exactly," said the President, "hence his nomination would be futile." "As for Cox," I started, when the President broke in, saying, "Oh! you know Cox's nomination would be a joke," to which I fervently assented.

After the conference Tumulty and Grayson anxiously inquired whether Wilson had charged Glass with any mission regarding a third term. When Glass told them of his conversation, Grayson implored him to help prevent Wilson's nomination. "If anything comes up, save the life and fame of this man from the juggling of false friends."[24]

Bainbridge Colby was the last administration leader to confer with Wilson, on June 21, before the convention. We have no evidence as to the nature of the conference, but subsequent events indicated that Colby was convinced that Wilson wanted a third term. Wilson had arranged the reluctant Colby's selection as a delegate from D. C., and wanted him to be permanent chairman of the convention. Wilson also insisted that Burleson and Newton D. Baker attend the convention.[25]

The *New York Post* reported a rumor that Wilson would be pushed through at the psychological moment; and the Chicago *Tribune* reported that many believed that he was following the shrewdest possible course to the nomination. "Wilson Held Up as Specter of Convention," headlined the Washington *Star,* cartooning him as the Sphinx. But most of the delegates believed that Wilson was disabled, and a conference at Salt Lake City, reportedly representing 40 per cent of the delegates, announced that more than one third of the convention was implacably opposed to Wilson's nomination.[26]

But Wilson remained the Sphinx—a smiling Sphinx. On the day before the convention he and Mrs. Wilson took a tour of Washington—stopping for a quarter of an hour at a Potomac Park bathing beach where, "with quick, efficient use of both hands," he "returned salutes and lifted his hat several times in greeting." At no time since Paris had he appeared in better health, reported the New York *World*.[27]

WILLIAM GIBBS MCADOO

William Gibbs McAdoo probably could have won the Democratic nomination in 1920 if he had openly fought for it. As the best known and, by reputation, the ablest Democrat produced by the Wilson administration, he was the logical candidate of administration Democrats. Yet for months before the convention McAdoo, who prided himself as a man of action, remained in a state of tortured indecision, now encouraging, now forbidding his followers to work for his nomination. On the eve of the convention, he announced that he would not permit his name to be presented. Later private assurances, however, that he was receptive to a nomination kept his boom going for forty-four ballots at San Francisco. But he gave the boom no personal direction. "I never saw a man before take the position that he did. It was different from any politics I have ever seen," exclaimed one perplexed supporter. His strange role was the result of an adaptation to an extremely complex and delicate set of circumstances.[28]

McAdoo, born in 1863 of an East Tennessee family, had attended the University of Tennessee where his father was professor of history and English. He practiced law in Chattanooga and organized the company that electrified the street railways of Knoxville. After this venture failed, he moved to New York where he formed the company that built the Hudson tubes. Entering politics, he played a leading role in managing Wilson's 1912 campaign, and was appointed secretary of the Treasury, chairman of the Federal Reserve Board, chairman of the Federal Farm Loan Board, and director general of railroads.[29]

Constantly before the country during the war, McAdoo's name was associated with the politically valuable Federal Reserve Act, Federal Farm Loan Act, War Risk Insurance, and higher railroad wages. His wartime patronage gave him the nucleus of a political machine. Moreover, he carried to his associates the conviction that he had real presidential timber, capable of handling "the crucial problems that lay ahead"; although some suspected that this tall, lean, hawk-featured figure harbored a Machiavellian love of power. Organized labor favored him; he was endorsed by the Anti-Saloon League; and he received 102,719 votes to 76,588 for Wilson in the *Literary Digest* poll.[30]

When the Democratic national committee met at Atlantic City in September, 1919, it was reported that Baruch and Thomas L. Chadbourne of New York had offered to underwrite the campaign to the extent of ten million dollars if the "right" candidate were nominated. However, most of the committee at that time seemed inclined toward Attorney General A. Mitchell Palmer, and little headway was made in getting the committee behind McAdoo. But by October McAdoo clubs and a McAdoo committee were forming, and it became clear that Texas and a number of other state delegations would support him.

To letters offering support, McAdoo replied that he could make no decision until the situation was more clearly defined. He discouraged his friends from starting a campaign, but said that he would welcome their support if he did decide to seek office. In late December, 1919, after a visit to the White House, he announced that he would not speak at the Jackson Day Dinner, which, in an election year, traditionally is the occasion for displaying Democratic talent for the nomination. Newspapers attributed his refusal to uncertainty as to whether Wilson intended to run again.[31]

Of such tortuous complexity was his position that, although he was by nature an activist, McAdoo could not decide what to do. His finances had suffered during his years in the government and a return to private law practice would probably restore his fortune. Aware of the rising tide of resentment against the administration, he might well have felt that no Democrat could win in 1920. As Wilson's son-in-law, exposed to the derisive epithet, "Crown Prince," he would be the candidate least likely to escape the effects of Wilson's unpopularity. Probably he would have a better chance of election if he waited until 1924; but would his chance of securing the nomination in 1924 be better if he took the helm of the party now? If he did not fight for the nomination, would his strong army of supporters desert, perhaps irretrievably, to some other man? Overshadowing all was Wilson's apparently receptive attitude toward the nomination. McAdoo's wife, Wilson's daughter, thought he should not seek the nomination. He could not fight his chief, yet he knew the delegates would never nominate Wilson for a third term, while he, McAdoo, could win the nomination if he fought for it. Little wonder that such conflicting considerations reduced him to a state of anxious indecision.[32]

If Wilson sought renomination, McAdoo's task was convincingly to escape any blame for Wilson's inevitable failure, but, at the same time, to keep himself available for a "draft," after the impossibility of the nomination of Wilson had been clearly demonstrated. In late January and early February he wrote to supporters that he could not be put in the position of seeking the nomination, but that he would accept the nomination if the convention offered it to him. In the meantime, he said, he would not prevent his friends from doing whatever they felt they ought to do under the circumstances.[33]

In mid-February, however, the situation in Georgia demanded a more positive stand. If McAdoo did not enter the Georgia primary as the administration candidate, the red-hunting Attorney General A. Mitchell Palmer probably would. Friends there urged him to enter, and, after much hesitation, McAdoo confidentially telegraphed his permission. But the next day he wrote an agonized letter to Wilson's private physician, Cary T. Grayson, seeking further light on Wilson's intentions:

Of course, the President's silence makes it very awkward for me, even if I had an inclination to stand for the Presidency—which, as you know, I have not, but it is not possible to resist the demands of one's friends to state either that they may proceed or that they may not. In the latter case, I should have to say flat-footedly that in no circumstances would I permit my name to be considered at the convention. It hardly seems fair to do this now with so many uncertain elements in the situation. . . .

Any suggestions you may have to offer I shall appreciate. I am really very much perplexed.[34]

We do not know what answer McAdoo received from Grayson, but he withdrew permission to use his name in the Georgia primary. Reluctant to "do anything that would create the appearance of a candidacy," but believing that it was a time to fight for "principles and not for individuals," he would like the convention to be composed of delegates "bound to no particular candidate," his public letter stated. However, he would "regard it as the imperative duty of any man to accept a nomination if it should come to him unsolicited." Wilson's private secretary, Tumulty, told McAdoo it expressed the proper attitude. It placed him on the high plane where he belonged, wrote Mrs. Antionette Funk, and yet did nothing to prohibit his friends from taking an interest —"Hail to the Chief!"[35]

Consistently refusing to become an open candidate, McAdoo suggested that Ohio Democrats stand by their favorite son, James M. Cox, and refused to enter the California primary. When he learned that he could not legally withdraw from the Michigan primary, he released in advance any delegates who might be instructed for him. He requested the secretary of state of Pennsylvania not to allow his name to be filed. He even abstained from one of those speaking tours which so many politicians unaccountably embark upon in the spring of election years.[36]

But while his public actions emphasized "I am not a candidate," his private letters emphasized that he would accept the nomination if it came to him unsolicited. He would feel it to be the imperative duty of any man to accept a nomination if it came to him unsought, and he would make the fight if asked to do so by a free convention—these were among statements in letters of appreciation to his supporters.[37]

Although abstaining from a speaking tour, McAdoo did issue a number of statements on public issues. For farm journals he composed an article in praise of the farm loan system. Calling for a billion-dollar tax reduction, he advocated delaying payments on the war debt for two years so as not to paralyze initiative. In April he set forth a kind of liberal platform—expressing concern about the tendency to impair free speech, advocating more taxation on unearned incomes, and suggesting that govenment ownership of railroads be considered if private ownership proved unsatisfactory.[38]

Under cover, McAdoo combatted the boom of Palmer who had pushed into open candidacy despite his doubts as to Wilson's intentions. Where Palmer sought delegates, McAdoo would counter with a call for an uninstructed delegation, and he protested to the national committee against its partiality for the attorney general. In North Carolina and in Iowa, respectively, Simmons and Meredith, friends of McAdoo, by running as favorite son candidates, forestalled moves to instruct delegations for Palmer. When Palmer protested a write-in movement in Pennsylvania, McAdoo replied that he had gone to considerable trouble to stay out of Palmer's way, that Palmer had sent his manager into McAdoo's state of New York, and that his protest made anything but an agreeable impression. By the eve of the convention the rift between the two was bitter and deep.[39]

When it appeared, early in 1920, that administration and progressive Democrats might back wartime food administrator and postwar director of European Relief, Herbert Hoover, who was of unknown party affiliation, but who had supported Wilson's appeal for a Democratic Congress in 1918, McAdoo objected. The Democratic party was not so utterly and hopelessly gone, he said, that its only hope lay in accepting a "cast off Republican . . . especially a sexless one." Hoover's nomination would wreck the party, he said.[40]

In the meantime McAdoo's friends were active. A meeting in March, which included Mrs. Antionette Funk, Robert W. Woolley, and George Creel, agreed to prepare newspaper and magazine articles, to gather information about the delegates, and to create the nucleus of a convention organization. Every precaution, it was agreed, would be taken to avoid the appearance of organized activity. The able and popular Daniel C. Roper, recently-resigned as commissioner of internal revenue, worked closely with McAdoo throughout the fall and spring, and was planning to go to San Francisco as his convention manager.

Bernard Baruch, also, used his extensive influence to promote McAdoo's strength. McAdoo visited Texas in January and the West Coast in May and early June.[41]

These activities secured delegates. Supporters wrote that McAdoo's managers were acting with wisdom and judgment, and that his interests were so handled as to excite the admiration of both Democrats and Republicans. "Everybody in Washington" believed that McAdoo would be nominated on the first or second ballot, wrote Burleson in mid-May. Claude Kitchin congratulated him on his imminent nomination. Carter Glass predicted that he would win on the first ballot, and it was difficult to exaggerate his strength with the rank and file, reported the New York *Tribune.* The *New York Times* listed a formidable array of McAdoo delegates: Texas, Oregon, Florida, both the Carolinas, Mississippi, two thirds of Virginia, half of Alabama and Pennsylvania, and others in Illinois, Michigan, New York, Indiana, Washington, Idaho, Montana, California, Nevada, New Mexico, Arizona, and West Virginia.[42]

This rise of McAdoo's star alarmed big-city bosses who feared he might continue Wilson's hauteur toward them and, as a dry southerner, might handicap local tickets in predominantly wet northern cities. There were reports of an anti-McAdoo entente of Charles Murphy of Tammany, Thomas Taggart of Indiana, Edwin H. Moore of Ohio, and George R. Brennan of Illinois.[43]

Suggesting that such success could not be obtained without spending money, the New York *American* charged that numerous millionaires were underwriting McAdoo. A congressional campaign expenses investigating committee, however, failed to uncover any McAdoo expenditures, or even the workings of his nebulous boom. Mrs. Funk once wrote him that she was approaching the subject of finance through "our friend," but she refused to accept open contributions; and when Burris Jenkins, publisher of the Kansas City *Post,* was asked to nominate McAdoo, he was told that they would not pay his expenses because they wanted to be able to say that not a dollar had been spent to obtain McAdoo's nomination.[44]

Just when the McAdoo movement seemed about to become a band wagon, on June 18, only ten days before the national convention was scheduled to convene, he startled politicians by announcing his refusal to allow his name to be put before the convention. His decision, he said, was "irrevocable." Having resigned from the cabinet in order to rehabilitate his fortunes, he said, he could not afford to make the campaign.[45]

McAdoo's statement was released at 6:00 P.M., after the morning newspapers published Wilson's sensational interview with Seibold. Naturally, his withdrawal was attributed to Wilson's apparent desire for a third term, and it was widely believed that he had withdrawn in favor of his father-in-law. McAdoo's denial was not very sweeping, maintaining merely that he "knew nothing whatever of the President's interview" until he saw it in the papers, and that the president had no advance knowledge of his letter of withdrawal. Mark Sullivan reported, however, that McAdoo tried without success, five times in June to see Wilson, and withdrew for fear that he was embarrassing Wilson's plans.[46]

McAdoo wired national committeeman Thomas B. Love of Texas, his strongest field general, that he hoped that he would yield to his withdrawal and help keep him out of public life. When Love replied that his sense of duty required him to go ahead with his attempts to nominate him, McAdoo wired that it was impossible for him to run and that he hoped his friends would accede to his wishes. When Love sought clarification from Roper, Roper said that no nominating speeches should be made, and that Love should stop messages to Roper. McAdoo also wired Burris Jenkins to the effect that his name must not be presented to the convention. Bernard Baruch and Thomas L. Chadbourne, who had planned to establish McAdoo headquarters in San Francisco, canceled their hotel reservations, as did Roper.[47]

Leaders of the McAdoo movement took his withdrawal at face value. Such a statement had been feared for months, Mrs. Funk told the press. Wiring McAdoo that she knew that his reasons were sufficient, she asked if he would endorse another candidate. Shouse now called for the nomination of Glass. McAdoo's action was a national calamity, said Woolley. Telegraphing that he had thrown his support to Palmer, Ray S. Baker told McAdoo, "If your reason is the one I have in mind you have no other course, but such a thing would be disastrous."[48]

But some felt that McAdoo had not completely removed himself from the race. Wilson asked Senator Carter Glass what he though of McAdoo's letter. "He nowhere says he would not accept a nomination," Glass replied. "Very quickly the President responded with emphasis: 'No, he does not; as I read it!' " Three out of four politicians on the scene at San Francisco regarded McAdoo as still in the race, reported the New York *Tribune;* and the Chicago *Tribune* concluded: "Mr. McAdoo wishes us all distinctly to understand that if the San Francisco convention does not offer him the nomination he will not accept it."[49]

Probably McAdoo's indecision continued. The day before he issued his withdrawal statement, he showed it to Carter Glass. When Glass protested that it would leave McAdoo men "in the air," McAdoo replied that he intended to ask them to support Glass and insisted that Glass talk to Roper. Roper told Glass that he had persuaded McAdoo to refrain from saying that he would not accept if nominated, and that he thought the withdrawal statement would strengthen rather than eliminate McAdoo. Evidently, the plan was to hold McAdoo's forces together until the proper moment arrived to put him forward. But Glass, who took himself very seriously, felt that he was being trifled with and did not co-operate with the plan.[50]

By June 21 Mrs. Funk had received a telegram from Roper that led her to hope still and to advise Ray Baker to stand firm and not go to Palmer. On June 23, C. M. Brown of Southern California, after wiring to ask if McAdoo had changed his plans as described to him, told reporters that months earlier McAdoo had told him that he would make a statement asking that his name not be presented, but with the understanding that the request would be disregarded.[51]

When newspapers carried a report by David Lawrence, chief political reporter for the Washington *Star,* that McAdoo was suffering from tuberculosis of the throat, McAdoo was infuriated. It was an example of the "dirty work the Palmer bunch" was doing, he told Baruch, and immediately issued a vehement public denial: "It is amazing that any reputable newspaper or individual would be guilty of such wanton falsehood. . . . It would be impossible for me publicly to characterize such despicable methods." Roper, regretting that political tactics could have fallen so low, telegraphed that the net effect apparently was to strengthen sentiment for McAdoo's nomination.[52]

Mrs. Funk received a telegram from McAdoo stating that Roper would not go to San Francisco, and that he believed that she and others would work things out so that a progressive platform and progressive nominees would be forthcoming. All was adjusted, Mrs. Funk telegraphed him on June 25: there was a tidal wave of sentiment for him, and the people were with him and "no one else." "Read this to Eleanor [Mrs. Eleanor Wilson McAdoo]." At the same time she told the press that he would accept the nomination: "Don't press me as to how I know but you can take it as authoritative." Again Love announced that Texas's 40 votes would be cast for McAdoo. On the day the convention opened, McAdoo telegraphed warm thanks to the Texas delegation for their support and he assured the North Carolina delegation that he would make no more withdrawal statements. Advising supporters to consult with Love, he wrote that if he should be called back into public life he would welcome their support, and that apparently he might be drawn again into politics in spite of himself. Newspapermen agreed that McAdoo had the best chance to win, and Wall Street odds placed him second only to Wilson.[53]

A. Mitchell Palmer

Having engaged in dramatic "red hunts," which in turn brought public acclaim, Attorney General A. Mitchell Palmer was the most publicized member of the cabinet as 1920 opened. At forty-eight, he was of impressive appearance, and personally popular with party leaders. He had served three terms in Congress, had assisted in the framing of the Underwood Tariff, and had run unsuccessfully for the Senate against Penrose in 1914. In 1917 Wilson appointed him alien property custodian and, in 1919, attorney general. In this last position Palmer showed great energy in arresting and prosecuting radicals, particularly alien radicals, which activity culminated in the massive New Year's Day arrests that were much applauded by the press.

A favorite of the national committee, of which he was a member, he made a good impression at the candidates' debutante ball, the Jackson Day Dinner. His speech imparted a new concept of his ability and force, said one of his severest critics. Moving skillfully over the dangerous ground of his antiradical program, he declared for freedom, but drew the line at those who advocated violence. He did not present, however, a social or economic program.[54]

When Palmer entered the Georgia primary, on the grounds that Georgia Democrats should be given an opportunity to vote for the administration, he became the first avowed Democratic contender. Palmer had written Tumulty that he would be a candidate if the president had no objection, that he would resign from the cabinet if the announcement would cause the president any embarrassment, or would support any other man the president endorsed. Wilson replied that the convention must be left entirely free to act as it thought proper, but that he would not interfere with Palmer's efforts. To those who suggested that Wilson sought the nomination, Palmer replied: "If the President wanted a third term he would have stated so before this time."[55]

C. C. Carlin of Alexandria, Virginia, was chairman of Palmer's committee and Wilbur W. Marsh of Iowa, treasurer of the national committee, took charge of western headquarters. In the Michigan primary, Palmer was the only active candidate and had the support of the state organization. Herbert Hoover, however, who had not authorized the use of his name, won the Democratic primary, while William Jennings Bryan, Governor Edward I. Edwards of New Jersey, and McAdoo all got more votes than Palmer. In Georgia, Palmer received only 47,000 votes to former Populist Congressman Tom Watson's 54,000 and Senator Hoke Smith's 46,000; but he did capture a plurality of county units.[56]

Palmer's boom never really flourished. He predicted a great outbreak of radical violence on May Day, 1920. When nothing happened he appeared slightly ridiculous; this strengthened a growing feeling that his red raids had been based on a hysterical diagnosis of the situation. He had alienated organized labor. The death of boss Roger C. Sullivan of Illinois cost him the probable support of that state's fifty-eight votes. Wilson's appointment of an anti-Palmer federal judge confounded his pose as the administration candidate. Even his friends had little confidence he would win, reported the New York *World* in mid-May.[57]

In May, an open letter by twelve eminent lawyers, including Roscoe Pound and Felix Frankfurter, accused Palmer of malpractices including viciousness, disregard of constitutional rights, use of *agents provocateurs,* forgery, cruel and unusual punishment, and using government funds for propaganda. Others charged that he used alien property to enrich men who were now contributing to his campaign. Calling for impeachment, the *Nation* accused him of inquisition, destruction of property, torture, sadism, crime, and thuggery. In an editorial, "Palmer the Impossible," the New York *World* maintained that no other candidate was so variously disqualified.[58]

Nevertheless, Palmer entered the convention with more instructed delegates, Pennsylvania's 76 and Georgia's 28, than any other Democrat. His backers also claimed support in New England, Illinois, Minnesota, Oklahoma, Arizona, New Mexico, New York, North and South Carolina, Arkansas, and Indiana. However, Wall Street betting odds were nineteen to one against the attorney general, and his chief effect was to create a split in the already disorganized administration forces.[59]

JAMES M. COX

In the Middle West, far from the tortuous developments around the throne, and almost unnoticed by the metropolitan centers of the Eastern Seaboard, the presidential boom of James M. Cox slowly developed. With no share in the national administration, he had been off the central stage of the drama of war and peace, and was known only as the Democratic governor of Ohio who had a knack for carrying that frequently Republican state. He was a mild progressive who had been called "wet," and had behaved commendably during a flood. Some might know also that he was a successful newspaper publisher who was not a fanatic on the league.

Cox was self-made in the best Horatio Alger tradition. Born in 1870 on a farm in Ohio, youngest of a family of seven, he taught school at the age of seventeen and, at twenty-two, became a reporter for the *Cincinnati Enquirer*. After three years in Washington as the secretary to a millionaire Democratic congressman, Cox, at the age of twenty-eight, bought the *Dayton Evening News,* a paper of 2600 subscribers. By 1905 he had begun acquiring other newspapers.

In Congress, to which he was elected in 1908, Cox supported progressive measures and backed Wilson for his first nomination. In 1912 he stumped Ohio for a new constitution which would permit social reforms and more regulation of business, was nominated for the governorship by acclamation and, basing his campaign on a reform program, received more votes than Wilson. Cox's first administration enacted a pioneering workman's compensation law as well as mother's pension laws, consolidated and extended the school system, built roads, reformed the prison and fiscal systems, brought the liquor trade under closer supervision, and put through a privately financed plan for Miami River flood control.

After a defeat two years earlier by Frank B. Willis, Cox was re-elected in 1916, but his second term was not notable for reform. He opposed entrance into the war, but once the United States had become engaged in it, his patriotism burned intensely, and his efforts to keep war materials flowing included measures against wartime strikes. Standing on his rather nonpartisan record as war governor, he was the only Democrat elected on the state ticket in 1918. Features of his third term were an anti-German-language law and restraints on labor violence—though there was no refusal to give labor fair treatment in other respects.

Thus Cox's progressivism, increasingly "safe and sane," was sharply modified by war-aroused nationalism and antagonism to turbulent labor. A political agent who went into Ohio to study Cox reported that he was more genial than Wilson but more dominating than Harding, a tremendously hard worker, self-confident, and ambitious. While he had made about two million dollars, he had always stood for the downtrodden against the wealthy. However, one heard his business ability and political shrewdness emphasized more than his convictions and principles.[60]

After a speechmaking tour of Ohio and Kentucky, Cox announced his candidacy on February 1, but for months his inactivity was such that he scarcely seemed to be a serious rival to Palmer or McAdoo. There was no challenge to his control of the Ohio delegation, and his only open fight was in Kentucky, which did not have a primary, where he won 20 of the 26 delegates. No one forced the fighting in the primaries, and he felt that he was in as strategic a position as any of the candidates, if the nomination was to be decided by unpledged delegates and political deals. His organization was small, publicity moderate, and his reported expenditure only $22,000. Shortly before the convention Cox described his strategy: "My friends are urging me to open up a vigorous campaign. But I prefer to wait. If, when the convention opens, they finally turn to Ohio, all right. We either have an ace in the hole, or we haven't. If we have an ace concealed, we win: if we haven't, no amount of bluffing and advertising can do much good."[61]

Of all the candidates Cox was the farthest removed from the league fight. His speeches supported his party's position, but did so in a general way; and he did not endorse Wilson's demand for unconditional ratification. His manager said the treaty should have been ratified with reservations if necessary, and should not have been made the sport of partisan politics. In May, Cox proposed two reservations of his own: The co-operation of the United States would depend upon the league's adherence to its sole purpose of "maintaining peace and comity among the nations of the earth"; and the United States in its turn "must at all times act in strict harmony" with the Constitution. This attitude strengthened him with those who thought Wilson was too unyielding.[62]

The chief issue with which Cox was associated was prohibition. The Eighteenth Amendment had just been ratified, but the "wets" wanted the Volstead enforcement act liberalized to permit the sale of light wines and beer. Cox's sympathies were with the wets, and some of his supporters said that his nomination would make an embarrassing plank on prohibition unnecessary. Calling his candidacy a "disgrace," William Jennings Bryan charged that Cox had "fairly won the dishonor" of wet leadership. Fearing that Cox would become too clearly branded on this issue, a spokesman said that his record was of law enforcement and he did not consider prohibition a proper issue for the platform. While not placating the drys, this somewhat reassured moderates.[63]

Cox advocated some mildly progressive measures including a federal survey of farm and educational conditions, governmental inquiry into facts bearing on industrial disputes, and a federal budget system. But, contrary to the principles of prewar progressivism, he also advocated repeal of the excess profits tax, opposed the federal inheritance tax, proposed a gross sales tax, and urged a federal Americanization agency.[64]

Most of his supporters were not liberals—these, instead, backed McAdoo—but those who wanted a nonadministration and wet candidate. To the Democratic bosses of the big northern cities, who challenged Wilsonian Democrats for control of the party, it was apparent that the Democrats had little chance to win the presidency, and they were chiefly interested in carrying their home areas. Big cities were wet, and they needed a presidential nominee friendly to the exemption of light wines and beer from prohibition. Democratic leaders of Illinois, Indiana, New York, Ohio, New Jersey, Kentucky, and Pennsylvania met at French Lick Springs, Indiana, to plan their strategy.[65]

Thus, although Cox controlled few delegates, his position was strong. As governor of a pivotal state, he might escape the burden of anti-Wilson animosity, and would be freer to compromise on the league. Of course, if administration forces could unite on a single candidate, Cox's prospects would fade. Reportedly, he feared a move to nominate Wilson more than any other prospective development.[66]

To be sure Cox had certain handicaps. In appearance he was not impressive. His build had been called Napoleonic, and some had seen in his spectacled face some reminders of Theodore Roosevelt, but these comparisons only served to accentuate the fact that there was nothing commanding or striking about him. His Jackson Day speech in Washington was described as "ideally and most satisfactorily boresome" so that listening was not obligatory. He was well liked by his associates, and was an experienced and effective campaigner, but there was little that was large or warm in his public personality—the public did not automatically cotton to him, and he often had to overcome an initial poor impression.

However, as convention time neared, newspapers began giving Cox more space. His movement, said reports, had gradually become a full-fledged boom which ranked with the candidacies of McAdoo and Palmer. He was more generally favored than McAdoo, reported the *World*. The *Cleveland Plain Dealer* thought he was in the best position for the nomination, and the New York *Tribune* even headlined, "Cox Against the Field."[67]

WILLIAM JENNINGS BRYAN

It was no secret that William Jennings Bryan had aspired to be president and there are those who believe that this affliction, which strikes many politicians, is difficult to cure. He was still second only to Wilson as a power in the Democratic party, and perhaps did not yet consider himself out of the running. The impressive turnout for a Washington dinner given him by former Governor Joseph W. Folk of Missouri, in December, 1919, convinced many senators that Bryan would be a contender for the nomination.[68]

Bryan supported the League of Nations, but opposed making it the issue of the campaign. After its defeat in November, 1919, he said that the United States should enter the league as soon as possible on the best terms obtainable in the Senate. Rising in opposition to Wilson's call for a referendum at the Jackson Day Dinner, Bryan said making the league the issue of the election would mean further delay, and success for the league only if a two-thirds Democratic majority in the Senate were secured, which was practically impossible. The democratic course, he said, was to accept the reservations advocated by the majority. Outlining "proper" issues, he called for a fight against profiteers, and advocated prohibition, national highways, a national bulletin, and the initiative and referendum. Headlines the next morning proclaimed that Bryan had broken with Wilson, splitting the party.[69]

Maintaining that he "loved Democracy too well to let it run into the crime of making peace a campaign issue," Bryan visited Washington to urge Democratic senators to ratify the league with reservations. A campaign for "ratification without reservations would result in overwhelming defeat" and "would prevent the consideration of pressing domestic problems." Wilson, Bryan charged, had failed to receive information "essential to sound judgment and safe leadership."[70]

The *Literary Digest* poll put Bryan in fourth place, after McAdoo, Wilson, and Edwards, but ahead of Cox. He was not a candidate, Bryan said, but if his nomination was demanded he would consider accepting. To a friend he wrote that he would have been glad to "rest this year, but with the wets trying to reopen the liquor question, the reactionaries trying to capture the party, and the president seemingly bent on making the treaty a campaign issue, I felt that somebody had to make a fight to save the party from shipwreck." But the Republican New York *Tribune,* evidently regarding him as the easiest Democrat to beat, reluctantly concluded that few Democrats wanted him for the presidential nominee.[71]

Nevertheless, in his home state, in "one of the most notable personal triumphs of his long public career," Bryan defeated Wilson's Senate leader, Senator Gilbert Hitchcock, for control of the Nebraska delegation. "The shining dome of Old Doctor Bryan, his face beaming with renewed ambition and strengthened determination, appears once more above the Democratic horizon after a long period spent in the basement," conceded Hitchcock's

Omaha World-Herald. "May a kind Heaven have mercy on our beloved but distracted country!" Wets and administration men girded themselves against his expected onslaughts, and Tammany's slogan on the train to San Francisco was "Beat Bryan."[72]

Dark Horses

John W. Davis, Ambassador to Great Britain, was the "favorite son" of West Virginia. His state's executive committee endorsed him, and "Davis for President" clubs were formed throughout the state. The *New York Times,* advocating his nomination, called him a man of "distinguished ability," "critical and impartial judgment," a "great man." To succeed, however, he would need the support of a large body of independent Democrats, and Davis was too conservative to arouse enthusiasm among liberals, most of whom were backing McAdoo.[73]

Vice-President Thomas R. Marshall, who had immortalized himself with his prescription, "What this country needs is a good five cent cigar," was receptive to the nomination and he advocated liberalization of the Volstead Act to permit the sale of beer and wine, and a more compromising course on the league. He was endorsed by prominent politicians in Indiana and Illinois, and preferred by Murphy of Tammany to Wilson or McAdoo, but he was still too close to the administration for most of the bosses. Shortly before the convention he announced that he was not a candidate and did not contemplate that the honor would be thrust upon him.[74]

Governor Edward I. Edwards, a crusader against prohibition, was New Jersey's favorite son. Virginia endorsed Senator Carter Glass, and New York presented Governor Al Smith, but chiefly for the advertising. Champ Clark, although seventy, said "Barkis is willin'."

On the eve of the convention the candidates challenging administration control did not appear to be very formidable. Bryan's call for progressive and moral issues won little support; rather he seemed something of an anachronism, a kindly but old-fashioned uncle. Cox was relatively unknown and not strongly endowed with the elements of popular appeal. Moreover, Bryan and Cox could never combine. Administration control of the convention could not be shaken unless the Wilson forces disintegrated.

CHAPTER III

THE REPUBLICAN CONVENTION

THE LINES ARE DRAWN AT CHICAGO

Although the big party powwow was not to open until the eighth of June, Republicans began to gather in Chicago about the first. The 984 delegates and their alternates included most of the party leaders: senators, governors, and bosses. Of these, 161 had been delegates in 1916, and 83 in 1912. For the first time there were women delegates, but only 26.[1]

Before the convention opened the national committee met to consider the claims of contesting delegates, of which there were some 137, chiefly from the southern states. For the first time, these hearings were public; but when Wood's Southern delegates did not fare well, Senator Moses cried "steam roller"—a slap at party leadership which Wood deplored. Will Hays replied that all cases involving large numbers were settled unanimously. Of the contested delegates seated, 88 favored Lowden, 34 Wood, and 7 Johnson.[2]

A fight developed over the naming of the permanent chairman. Most prominently mentioned for this post was ex-Senator Albert J. Beveridge of Indiana, whose selection seemed so likely that he prepared his speech. However, Hiram Johnson wanted Borah; and further opposition developed on the grounds that Beveridge had been a Progressive bolter, and was too antileague. By a vote of 22 to 9 the committee on arrangements instead gave the position to Henry Cabot Lodge, who was already temporary chairman.[3]

The convention met Tuesday, June 8, in the heavily flag-draped Chicago Coliseum. In the keynote address, Lodge, "the scholar in politics," said that war had created a troubled state of mind:

Through long years of bitter conflict, moral restraints were loosened, and all the habits, all the conventions, all the customs of life, which more even than law hold society together were swept aside.[4]

Reading with little effort at oratorical flourish, for an hour and twenty minutes Lodge berated Wilson. Driving from all control over the government his autocratic and socialistic "dynasty, his heirs and assigns," transcended in importance every other question. Wilson should have guaranteed that Germany was not "able to again threaten the peace" and should have left other European problems for Europeans to settle. The League of Nations was an "alliance" which contributed nothing to international law, or to the adjustment of nonjusticiable questions, but rather threatened "the very existence of the United States as an independent power." Article X was a "breeder of war and an enemy of peace." Declaring that "we have stopped Mr. Wilson's treaty and the question goes to the people," Lodge sought to make Wilson and the league the issue of the campaign.

Meanwhile the resolutions committee, in session through two days and nights, constructed the platform. The sharpest fight concerned the league plank. A proleague plank, sponsored by W. Murray Crane, declared for ratification with reservations "which protect the liberty and independence of the people of the United States." But Lodge, whom Taft said lacked sufficient courage or interest in the league to fight for it, wanted to praise the action of the Senate in rejecting the league without clearly endorsing either the Lodge reservationists or the irreconcilables, and to make no promises for the future. The committee at first seemed to favor the Crane plank, but when Borah, McCormick, and Brandegee threatened to denounce the party if it were adopted, Watson and Smoot dropped their support. The deadlock was broken when a compromise plank, drawn up by Elihu Root, was adopted with only one dissenting vote. This plank condemned "Wilson's League" as un-American, certain to produce injustice, and offering "mere expediency and negotiation," but called for an "international association," based on "international justice," providing "instant and general international conference whenever peace shall be threatened."[5]

Both sides claimed victory. Taft thought the plank said "the things that would lead the party into the league." At least it did not "preclude ratification," insisted the New York *Tribune*. Most newspapers, however, interpreted it as an antileague victory. It made Johnson the logical candidate, said the *New York Times;* it was an "astounding surrender to League foes," proclaimed the Baltimore *Sun;* "Bitter-Enders Score Complete Victory," headlined the *Springfield* (Mass.) *Republican.*[6]

Among domestic issues, the one which aroused the most feeling was that of organized labor. In the context of the Bolshevik revolution and the great wave of strikes in 1919, Republican opinion overwhelmingly favored stiff curbs on labor unions. The plank adopted did not deny the right of "collective bargaining," but insisted that labor had no right to strike against the government, and maintained that "government initiative" against strikes was justified. This plank was greeted by great applause.

Liberals Borah, McCormick, and White won endorsement of federal highways, conservation, equal pay for women, and prevention of child labor; but the body of the platform was conservative with overtones of the accentuated nationalism and hostility to radicalism which characterized the postwar era. Praising the Republican Congress for returning railroads to private ownership, the platform endorsed "rigid economy," a "more businesslike" government, a high protective tariff, and exemption of American vessels from Panama Canal tolls. The national debt should be "promptly liquidated," but taxes should not "needlessly repress enterprise and thrift." The remedy for the high cost of living was sound fiscal policy, increased production, prevention of unreasonable profits, and revision of taxation. There must be "no persecution of honest business."

Education should awaken "a sense of patriotic duty." Condemning the Democrats for "unpreparedness" and a weak policy toward Mexico, the platform called for proper maintenance of military establishments and more physical education. Immigration from Europe should be restricted, all Asiatics should be excluded, and aliens should be registered, forbidden to agitate against American institutions, and barred from citizenship until they became "genuinely American." No one should be permitted to advocate "resistance to the law or violent overthrow of the government."

The convention adopted the platform with virtual unanimity. Republican newspapers, of course, called it constructive, while Democratic journals branded it reactionary. According to the A. F.

of L., it denied the right to strike, proposed "industrial enslavement," offered no remedy for profiteering or inflation, and threatened exploitation of Mexico.[7]

Not until the fourth day of the convention, Friday, June 11, did nomination speeches begin. Calmly announcing that Governor Henry Allen was to nominate Wood, Lodge destroyed his chance for building dramatic suspense. Allen presented Wood as a business man, governor of Cuba, a preparedness leader, and a citizen soldier who could preserve order in a time of social upheaval. His speech, though halting and platitudinous, was followed by a 42-minute demonstration, with blue and red feathers floating from the rafters, bands blaring, and delegates shouting, "It's Wood: let's go!" Seconding the nomination Mrs. Corinne Roosevelt Robinson, Theodore Roosevelt's sister, said Wood was of the same type as her brother.[8]

Next, Representative Rodenberg, a big man with a big voice, warmed Lowden supporters to repeated cheering. Lowden, he said, stood for "law and constitutional government," and "sound and practical business principles" in government. The ensuing demonstration was drawn out three minutes longer than Wood's, with at least equal volume.[9]

Charles Stetson Wheeler, presenting Hiram Johnson, denied that California was remote and inaccessible. Furthermore, Johnson, he said, was neither red nor radical. Calling on Southern "hand-picked delegates" and Northern "political slaves" to revolt and "scourge" the bosses from the party, he reopened old wounds and further alienated the convention from Johnson with what Irvin S. Cobb called "the worst speech that ever was." However, determined Johnson supporters prolonged their demonstration for 37 minutes until protest from the delegates made them heed the gavel.[10]

Judge Nathan L. Miller, soon to be governor of New York, ably described Herbert Hoover as "the man possessing the qualities, the equipment and the ability to deal with the problems which are confronting us." But the delegates interrupted his speech with shouts and jeers, and Smoot, who was presiding, insisted that the seconding speeches proceed long before the gallery applause for its favorite had died down.

To enthusiastic applause, the chair recognized Ohio's former Governor Frank B. Willis, an ornate, old-fashioned stump orator.

He described all the nominees as "great men," and leaned over the rail to say in an intimate tone, "Say boys—and girls, too," setting off a laughing friendly demonstration. Harding's record, he said, was the record of the party. "Ohio's second McKinley," the friend of both Roosevelt and Taft, Harding had battled for "national independence." This "great, stalwart, modest, patriotic American citizen" had carried Ohio in 1914 by 103,000 votes and "the whole Republican ticket, with me on it, right along to victory." "Safe and sane," he would co-operate well with Congress. Perhaps the most effective of the convention, Willis' speech set off a ten-minute demonstration of considerable volume.[11]

The names of Calvin Coolidge, William C. Sproul, Nicholas M. Butler, Senator Miles Poindexter of Washington, Judge Jeter C. Pritchard of North Carolina, and Senator Howard Sutherland of West Virginia were also presented. The speeches completed, the chairman announced, to applause, that voting would begin and, amid high tension, the secretary began to call the roll of the states.

The candidates had been in Chicago since before the convention, but there were no reports of major deals or shifts in strength. A Wood attempt at reconciliation with John King failed. The *New York Times* reported that anti-Wood forces, fearing a Wood bandwagon, planned an "inconsequential test of strength" on the first three or four ballots, "then a long recess, during which the 'elder statesmen' may repair to the secret council chamber and select a candidate." Conversely, seeking to muster their full strength and to secure the nomination on the first or second ballot, the Wood forces demanded that complimentary votes for favorite sons such as Coolidge and Butler be omitted, a course which was sure to create some ill will.[12]

Lowden came off well in the delegate contests, but the Chicago *Tribune* admitted that the campaign fund revelations so weakened him that his nomination was "extremely problematical." Within his own Illinois delegation, Mayor Thompson of Chicago fought him bitterly. A group of leaders, including Alvin T. Hert of Kentucky, Jake Hamon, Bascom Slemp, John F. Adams, and John King, were reported to be bolstering Lowden only for the purpose of stopping Wood.[13]

"Nobody is talking Harding," "not even considered as among the most promising dark horses," reporters wrote. Harding said he was going to quit politics and devote himself to his newspaper. Daugherty, however, was operating "the most complete political organization ever set up for the nomination of a President." His staff, which grew to 2,000 men and women, met every train, interviewed the delegates, and compiled "the most complete poll of the delegates' second to fourth choices ever made." "We gave out no claims, made no statements to the press, and carefully concealed every move from the reporters," Daugherty said later. Of course, he co-operated with those who sought to stop Wood. Meanwhile, the Columbus Glee Club visited other headquarters and serenaded them to create a "sweet" Harding atmosphere.[14]

Many favorite sons received votes on the first ballot and some delegates were held in reserve, concealing the real strength of the major candidates. Wood, as predicted, led:

Wood	287½
Lowden	211½
Johnson	133
Harding	65½

New York voted for Butler, and Pennsylvania for Sproul. When Wisconsin voted for Robert M. La Follette the convention booed.

On the second ballot Wood gained only 2 votes, while Lowden rose by 48, Johnson added 13, and Harding lost 6½ from the southern states which had given increases to Lowden. On the third ballot, Wood added 13½ to reach 303, while Lowden, drawing from New York and the South, rose by 23 to make a total 282½ votes. Seeing the convention moving in the direction of the two leaders, the Johnson forces, supported by New York and Pennsylvania, attempted a vote of adjournment. However they could muster less than a third of the delegates in the face of a general desire to "get on with it." Encouraged by his gains on Wood, Lowden preferred to continue balloting rather than trust to conferences.[15]

On the fourth ballot Wood outgained Lowden by 11½ to 6½. Some votes, such as the four from Missouri, had been loaned to Wood's forces by the old guard evidently in an attempt to force Lowden to agree to adjournment. Johnson slipped to 140½ and Harding stood four below his opening vote. Conferring during this ballot, Chairman Lodge, Reed Smoot, Medill McCormick, Tobe Hert, Charles B. Warren and Borah agreed on adjournment. When Lodge put the question there was only a scattering of ayes and a loud chorus of noes, but Lodge pronounced the convention adjourned and turned from the rostrum before the surprised Wood forces could demand a roll call. Asked why the old guard had forced adjournment, Smoot replied: "Oh, there's going to be a deadlock, and we'll have to work out some solution; and we wanted the night to think it over."[16]

Smoke-filled Rooms

After a trial of strength, adjournment had come, as predicted, to allow the leaders to confer. Everyone knew that a night of maneuvering and bargaining was ahead. The night saw a bitterly futile effort by Johnson to wrest the nomination from a hostile convention, an attempt by Wood to renew the power of his stalled steam roller, and a holding action by Lowden who hoped that he might yet be the choice of the party bosses. The uneasy equilibrium between these factions lent significance to the groupings and regroupings of politicians in the Blackstone Hotel, and gave those who could shift a few votes the power to name the next president.

Johnson moved quickly. Through the hotel lobbies went men with megaphones announcing a meeting to consider the danger of nominating a candidate who did not have a clean record. To a packed hall, Senator Borah declared that he would not support Wood or Lowden if they were nominated, and might even go before the convention to challenge them on their use of money. If either were chosen, he said, the issue would be "the corruption of the American people."[17]

Johnson could do little else. Most of his instructed delegates were party regulars who waited only an opportunity to desert him, and could not be controlled by him. Sensing the convention's hostility to progressivism, even his friends knew he had no chance. He might, however, tilt the balance among the others. Impressed by his popularity in the primaries, all other candidates sought him as their running mate. During the night he rejected vice-presidency offers from Wood, Lowden, and Harding. "Nineteen twelve was a Sunday school convention compared to this," he remarked.[18]

For Wood, Friday night was tragic. Allowing adjournment without a roll call, while there was still some possibility of forestalling a combination of his enemies, had been a serious mistake. He needed only 82 more votes to collect on Sproul's promise to bring Pennsylvania into his column. On the other hand, Henry Allen had told him that if he fell behind Lowden, the Kansas delegates would be allowed to desert him. Learning of old guard conferences, he aroused the sleeping men at his headquarters at 3:00 A.M. "They are combining against me," he told them. To show gains on the first ballot in the morning was crucial, but he had already thrown his full strength into the earlier ballots.[19]

Lowden would be nominated only if there were no other way of defeating Wood and Johnson. For a time, after Harding's failure in the primaries, it looked as if the old guard could not avoid nominating Lowden, but the fund exposé had made him as weak as Harding. About midnight Lowden's manager, Hert, told a reporter: "It will be either Lowden or a dark horse." Now that it appeared that Wood and Johnson had been stopped, the old guard preferred Harding.[20]

The state of uneasy equilibrium invited those with political power and special interests to seek favors in return for tipping the balance. Of course, leaders of business, industry, and finance had converged on the convention as naturally as the politicians. Samuel Vauclain of Baldwin Locomotives, oilmen Harry F. Sinclair and Edward L. Doheny, Ambrose Monell of metals, Henry M. Byllesby of public utilities, William Boyce Thompson of copper, Dan Hanna and Elbert M. Gary of steel, and Cornelius Vanderbilt were in town. In the Blackstone, closely associated with George Harvey, were four J. P. Morgan partners as well as munitioner T. Coleman Dupont. These were men of power, their money was the lifeblood of political campaigns, and their influences were pervasive and persuasive. Never had he seen a convention "so completely dominated by sinister predatory economic forces as was this," wrote William Allen White.[21]

The work of such men is necessarily conducted behind the scenes, but some amateurish newcomers blundered into the headlines. "Big Jake" Hamon, the wealthy and exuberant oilman from Oklahoma, knew that millions could be made if the government would adopt the "right" policy toward naval, Indian, and Mexican oil lands, and he wanted the "right" men as secretary of the interior and secretary of state. With a generous use of his financial resources he achieved control of the Oklahoma delegation and a group of delegates from other southwestern states. He had more influence among the delegates, said Harry Daugherty, than any other man.[22]

Hamon first explored the possibilities of a deal with Wood, with unsatisfactory results. Ostensibly shifting to Lowden, he continued his efforts to strike a bargain. Friday night, in a last approach to Wood, he offered to support him if the general would allow Hamon to name the secretary of the interior and the ambassador to Mexico. Purple with rage, Wood exclaimed: "I am an American soldier. I'll be damned if I betray my country. Get the ......out of here!" Later Friday evening Hamon told his friend, Al Jennings, that the nomination would go to Harding the next day, which nomination had cost Hamon a million dollars.[23]

Senator Boies Penrose was too ill to go to the convention, but his contact with Chicago was sufficiently dramatic to attract much comment. He had private telephone and special telegraph wires to the Congress Hotel where Senators McCormick, Brandegee, and Watson, and Harry M. Daugherty, among others, communicated with him. John T. King held his proxy. The strain was too much for the senator, however, and early Friday morning, before the balloting began, his physicians ordered him to take no further interest in proceedings. Leaders of the Pennsylvania delegation were unable to get directions from him.[24]

Nevertheless, about 10:00 P.M., Penrose telephoned Wood. The general would not talk to him, but authorized an aide to take the message. Penrose said, "You may say to General Wood, if he were nominated tomorrow, would he give us three cabinet members?" An adviser remarked, "Now, General, one word will make you President." But Wood's answer was, "Tell Senator Penrose that I have made no promises, and am making none." "I am sorry, but we intend to see that we are going to have a Republican President, and we want the privilege of naming three cabinet members," replied Penrose. Such deals seemed dishonorable to the straightforward soldier, new at this "wicked game" and inept at the devious arts of politics.[25]

The main old guard conference took place in a suite on the thirteenth floor of the Blackstone Hotel, the legendary "Smoke-filled Room," a parlor and two bedrooms, rented by Will Hays. One bedroom was occupied by the solemn, horn-rimmed George Harvey, editor of the *North American Review*, who, since Hays was elsewhere that evening, acted as host. Before 1912 Harvey, searching for a conservative candidate with which to break the hold of Bryan on the Democratic party, had been an original supporter of Wilson, but when Wilson discarded him to avoid charges of Wall Street backing, Harvey fought Wilson's "New Freedom" and helped organize the strategy which defeated the league. Harvey has been called the "mentor" of the senatorial group. According to Calvin Coolidge, he was a "great power" in selecting the candidate, and Harvey's biographer called his room at the Blackstone the "real center of the convention."[26]

Harvey dined with Senator Frank Brandegee of Connecticut, and after dinner Lodge joined them. Among others who were summoned or drifted in during the evening were Senators James E. Watson of Indiana, Reed Smoot of Utah, Medill McCormick of Illinois, James W. Wadsworth and William Calder of New York, Charles W. Curtis of Kansas, Lawrence C. Phipps of Colorado, Joseph S. Frelinghuysen of New Jersey, William E. Borah of Idaho, Selden P. Spencer of Missouri, Mr. Joseph R. Grundy of Pennsylvania, and former Senators W. Murray Crane and John W. Weeks of Massachusetts. "Here is the Senate in epitome, with a non-senator [George Harvey] in place of the Vice-President, in the chair!" remarked one.[27]

According to Grundy, Lodge, opening the conference, said the delegates could not be held in Chicago over the weekend; the fund revelations made it inexpedient to nominate Wood or Lowden; no Republican had been elected without the vote of Ohio; and that the Democrats were likely to nominate the governor of Ohio. "For these reasons he believed the availability of Senator Harding to be so outstanding as to justify the convention nominating him on the following day." So logical a solution to the deadlock did this seem, wrote Grundy, that "all present heartily joined in the movement to bring about the nomination of Harding." Calder agreed that "the leader and moving spirit" in bringing about the selection of Harding was Lodge, and Watson described a "standing vote" which decided that "it would be the wise course to nominate Harding just as soon as this could be brought about."[28]

Senator Wadsworth, on the contrary, described the "Smoke-filled Room" as an unorganized conference arriving at no definite decision. He was in and out of George Harvey's room probably three times Friday night and talked indecisively with an ever changing group, he said. "At no time was any decision reached by a conference in that room. All was confusion, puzzlement, and divided counsels." Much time was spent trying to find out what various state delegations would do on the first ballot the next morning. No one seemed to know of any impending change. When Wadsworth left at about 1:00 A.M. the number of politicians in attendance was dwindling. "The alleged influential senators were as futile as chickens with their heads cut off," he concluded. "If they came to any decision at all it was a decision to let the Harding suggestion go through, the fact being that they did not have anyone else to propose."[29]

Certainly, in the long hours between 8:00 P.M. and 2:00 A.M. the conference, probably informally, discussed many aspects of the "situation." The qualifications of all the "dark horses" were reviewed, but there were objections to all: Sproul was from solidly Republican Pennsylvania, Coolidge was from New England, Allen was associated with compulsory arbitration, Hughes was opposed by the New York organization, Knox had voted against the Eighteenth and Nineteenth Amendments, and Will Hays was known only as a politician. When someone mentioned Lodge, the Senator "shook his head, half ruefully, and said, 'Seventy, a month ago!' " Some were more convinced of the necessity of turning to Harding than others, and some wanted only to use him to stop Wood and Lowden. Any unanimity must have been reached by a reduced group after Senator Wadsworth left at 1:00 A.M. Senators Curtis, Brandegee, Lodge, Smoot, and McCormick seem to have been most active in arranging to have delegates vote for Harding.[30]

At about 1:00 A.M. George Harvey and two senators called in two newsmen of the *Kansas City* (Mo.) *Star*. Explaining the objections to other candidates, they told the newsmen that they had turned to Harding, who came from a strategic state, had ample political experience, made a favorable impression in the Senate, was of impressive appearance, and could work well with Congress. "This man Harding is no world beater," they confided, "but we think he is the best of the bunch." Besides, the country was tired of supermen who would not take advice. The nomination would be delayed, they said, until after about four ballots in order to "avoid an appearance of manipulation so abrupt that it might cause a stampede."[31]

Later that morning, breakfasting with Alice Roosevelt Longworth, Harvey told her of the countless "conferences of elimination" at which he, Lodge, Smoot, Crane, Watson, and Brandegee, with Borah "not offering ponderable objection," had decided on Harding. If they had such power, Mrs. Longworth sputtered, why did they not choose a man with higher qualifications? Harding would "go along," Harvey replied.[32]

From what we know of Harding's movements during this crucial conference he spent a busy night. In early evening, shortly after adjournment, a reporter found him a picture of mental distress, with discouragement hanging about him "like a cloud." Passing Harding headquarters at 11:00 P.M. the same reporter was amazed to find him jaunty and beaming. When asked if he would be a candidate for vice-president, Harding replied, "I am the most likely candidate for President tonight."[33]

Hearing that five of the Ohio delegates were going to switch their votes to Wood, Walter Brown called a caucus of the Ohio delegation at midnight. Addressing them, Harding was at his best, exerting to the full his charm and persuasive powers in an *argumentum ad hominem*. Would the men from his own state be the ones to rob him of his chance for the presidency? He left the meeting in high spirits, though only one of the wavering delegates had been reconverted.[34]

"To preserve party harmony and keep the Johnson strength intact," Harding called on Hiram Johnson at about 1:00 A.M. and, according to Johnson, "informing him that he [Harding] would be nominated on the tenth ballot that afternoon," offered him the vice-presidency. At 2:00 A.M. when Smoot emerged into the hotel lobby from the Smoke-filled Room in search of him, Harding had just gone up in an elevator.

The conference had almost dissolved when Harding entered. Informing him that he was likely to be nominated, George Harvey asked if he had any disability which might jeopardize the campaign or disqualify him as president. Harding asked for ten minutes alone. Perhaps the rumor that he had Negro blood or his illicit love affair with Nan Brittan came to Harding's mind, but he told Harvey that there was no impediment. He left the room at about 4:00 A.M. At dawn, a delegate saw the senator sitting in his room; he thought that Harding had not been to bed all night.[35]

When the Harding family breakfasted Saturday morning it was

uncertain whether his name had been filed as a candidate for the Senate before the midnight deadline, and Mrs. Harding strongly criticized him for even considering giving up his Senate seat. Harding's brother asked him if he really thought he had any chance. "Deac., it looks like I might get the nomination on the seventh or eighth ballot," Harding answered with assurance. The leaders had fought each other with such vigor that none could give his votes to the other. "You see it never pays to become bitter in political warfare."[36]

In its Saturday issue the New York *Tribune* called the Smoke-filled Room the center of maneuvering, but reported that anti-Wood men had not united on any one man. But the Associated Press said votes were to be thrown to Harding: "Harding of Ohio emerged this morning from all night conferences of Republican chieftains as the man with whom they hoped to break the imminent deadlock. Delicate relationships were involved . . . but most of the leaders . . . appeared agreeable to trying Harding first among the large field of dark horses."[37]

If a considerable number of these conferees concluded that Harding should be nominated, apparently they had the power to implement the decision. In March the Chicago *Tribune* had reported that secret conferences of leaders from many states had agreed to secure uninstructed delegates in order that the convention might be an "old fashioned" one in which the decisions would be made by politicians and not by the people in the primaries. At Chicago, the men mentioned as the marshals of about two hundred floating and maneuverable delegates were John T. King and Joseph B. Kealing, national committeemen from Connecticut and Indiana respectively. After the Smoke-filled Room had wearily settled on Harding, Kealing was told to get his delegates into line and, with the help of Hert of Kentucky and David W. Mulvane of Kansas, arrangements were made to feed the votes of Missouri, West Virginia, Indiana, Wyoming, and part of Kansas to Harding.[38]

Also, the reports of the Smoke-filled Room which circulated on Saturday morning had considerable psychological effect on the delegates. As Will Hays has said, it was known that the conference had taken place and the news was spread that an agreement had been made on Harding. Significantly, the Wall Street odds against Harding fell from ten to one to five to one.[39]

The Smoke Clears

Before the convention reassembled at 10:00 A.M. on Saturday, June 12, a number of participants in the Smoke-filled Room told morning meetings of their delegations that Wood and Lowden would be given four more ballots to demonstrate their deadlock, while Harding was gradually pushed into third place. "It had been decided to give Harding a play after trying for a ballot or two to name Wood," Senator Curtis told the Kansas delegation. On the first ballot of the morning, the fifth, Wood dropped 15½ votes to 299 while Lowden, as predicted, rising 14, passed him with 303. Harding gained 17½ to reach 78.[40]

Ohio had been voting 39 for Harding and 9 for Wood, but, on the sixth ballot, four of Harding's delegates deserted him for Wood. However, Daugherty had passed the word among the delegates: "watch now for the attempted betrayal." The deserters were hissed and booed, and the result of the defection was a reaction in favor of Harding. Thanks chiefly to Missouri, Harding rose by 11 votes to 89.[41]

Wood recovered on the sixth ballot to 311½, within two of his peak strength, but Lowden received exactly the same number. On the seventh ballot they remained unchanged. Some thought that this equality on the first three Saturday ballots was an old guard superstrategy designed to convince both that they could not win—while in the meantime arrangements were being completed to swing the anti-Wood vote to Harding.[42]

Only Harding's vote increased. On the seventh ballot, with 105, he passed Johnson to take third place. On the eighth, while Wood fell to 299, Lowden to 307, and Johnson to 87, Harding jumped to 133½. Missouri now tried to switch her entire vote to him, but was ruled out of order. An Ohio demonstration was joined by many delegates. Ullman telegraphed Taft: "It looks more like Harding. Connecticut will go to him on next ballot."[43]

But during the eighth ballot Lodge called Walter Brown to the platform and asked him if the Harding forces would object to a recess. They would, most emphatically, said Brown. Nevertheless, Lodge recognized Alvin T. Hert, Lowden's floor leader, who moved to adjourn, seconded by New York and California. Leaping on a chair, Frank B. Willis, who had nominated Harding, roared for a roll call. Organization leaders frantically beckoned Willis and Myron T. Herrick to the rostrum and told them that there was no plan to stop Harding, that Johnson should be consulted, and that Harding should not force his nomination. Persuaded, Herrick and Willis signaled to the Harding delegates and, at 1:40 P.M. Lodge pronounced the convention recessed until 4:00, despite angry protests from Daugherty who charged to the front of the rostrum shouting: "You cannot defeat this man this way. This motion was not carried. You cannot defeat this man!"[44]

Hoping for some combination to check Harding, supporters of all the other candidates desired recess. But Daugherty, who had ordered the full Harding strength to be shown on the next ballot, hoped for a quick surrender by the tired delegates. Trying to soothe him Lodge said: "We all want a harmonious finish with a solid enthusiastic party. They are going to offer Johnson the Vice-Presidency and swing his stubborn followers over to Harding."[45]

Wood and Lowden used the recess for desperate efforts to salvage their sinking fortunes. Calling Wood on the telephone, Lowden told him that the rumors of a senatorial cabal intriguing to nominate Harding had been confirmed, and asked Wood to meet him for a conference. Shortly after 1:00 P.M. Wood's car picked up Lowden at the Congress Hotel. To Wood, Lowden appeared unnerved and frightened. Delegates elected through his own financing were being used against him, Lowden told Wood. They agreed that a coalition was the only way to stop Harding. With the help of Johnson and favorite sons, they thought they could muster enough votes to arrest the Harding drive and force adjournment over the weekend. Dropping Lowden at his hotel, Wood visited Johnson and got his promise to support weekend recess.

But when Wood's manager, Procter, visited Lowden's headquarters to work out the "details" of a coalition, Lowden, doubting his ability to move his delegates to Wood, asked if Wood would accept second place. "No," said Procter, and although Procter offered to step aside and let Hert be the campaign manager, Lowden refused to accept the vice-presidency. When Procter was reporting the impasse to Wood, he heard that Lowden was preparing to withdraw. Hurrying back to Lowden, Procter demanded that Hays be called in to avert imminent "disaster to the party." When Hays arrived all again agreed to seek recess to Monday.

The plan was to have Lodge delay reopening the convention

as long as possible while support was enlisted, then to have Hert move for adjournment during or following the ninth ballot. As they left the room, Hert dropped behind and tried to get Procter to agree that "Wood and Lowden are out of it, and we will have a chance by Monday to make our arrangement," but Procter refused. Furthermore, a canvass revealed that delegates, regardless of allegiance, were reluctant to stay in Chicago over the weekend; the effort for adjournment strengthened their feeling that to nominate Harding was the only practical way out of the deadlock.[46]

Some of the senatorial leaders who had favored Harding in the Smoke-filled Room on Friday night worked against him during the Saturday afternoon recess. Another old guard conference was now held which, though subsequently hushed up, is of such significance as to recast the role of the Smoke-filled Room in nominating Harding. As Wood and Lowden had been checked by throwing support to Harding, so now old guard leaders attempted to stop Harding by supporting Will Hays. George Harvey had been for Hays from the beginning. Doubtlessly, he received support at this time from those who desired the nomination for themselves.

J. Henry Roraback, chairman of the Connecticut delegation, was summoned to Senator Brandegee's room and told to cast Connecticut's vote for Hays. Demurring, Roraback said that Connecticut had voted to go to Harding. That would be foolish, Brandegee and George Harvey told him, because Hays was going to be nominated. Six hundred votes had been tied up absolutely for him, they said, and in the adjoining room were the men, including Lodge, who had the votes to deliver. Through the haze Roraback saw Smoot and a man he thought was Lodge, and Lodge had refused to permit Massachusetts to vote for Harding on the next ballot. Nevertheless, Roraback resisted this pressure, and Connecticut, instead, led the swing to Harding.[47]

This eighth ballot recess, wrote William Howard Taft, was forced by "bitter-ender" senators in order to "spring" Hays on the convention in a serious effort to prevent Harding's nomination. Harvey's secretly planned coup to nominate someone other than Harding was foiled only by "the stubborn independence of the Connecticut delegation," said Nicholas Murray Butler. But Harvey, Lodge, Brandegee, and Smoot, who later claimed credit for dictating to the convention, proved powerless to control it during this afternoon recess.[48]

Leadership had now shifted to Harry Daugherty, who left the convention to go first to Pennsylvania headquarters. There he called Penrose to ask for support. Agreeing that Harding could not now be defeated, Penrose said that he had prepared for the press a statement in which he said that he had learned "with pleasure of Senator Harding's prospects for nomination." Daugherty insisted that Penrose let him release the statement at his discretion and so avoid the appearance of boss dictation. Penrose notified John King to give Pennsylvania's vote to Harding. Daugherty did not ask for Pennsylvania votes until after the ninth ballot, but got 60 of 76 on the tenth. We can find no evidence of Penrose throwing any votes to Harding before this Saturday recess.[49]

Daugherty next arranged a meeting between Harding and Lowden at the Lowden headquarters, but when they arrived Lowden had already left for the Coliseum to withdraw his name. The ninth ballot was beginning when Daugherty and Harding found Lowden, with Hert and Warren, in a little room off the auditorium. Telling them that he had released his delegates, Lowden congratulated Harding on his imminent nomination. His most substantial help, said Daugherty, came from Lowden, "who, with his friends and delegation, was with us in the wind-up." When the roll call approached Kentucky, Hert rushed out on the floor to throw that state to Harding. As he entered the convention hall, Procter grabbed him and anxiously asked about the adjournment. "It's off," said Hert. "You damned liar, are you not going through?" "No," said Hert. Hert later explained to Procter: "Why, you knew we were out to beat Wood."[50]

The roll call had already reached Kansas, whose Governor Allen had put Wood in nomination. Allen had told the delegation it could go to Harding if Wood fell below Lowden. If it voted solidly, Allen would be chosen for the vice-presidency, the delegation had been told. Now Senator Curtis said the time had come. Knowing "that Kansas was the pivotal key to the situation," Mrs. Harding remembered that she got her real thrill of victory when Kansas went solidly to Harding. The announcement set off a tumultuous demonstration. Kansas' defection was the "first body blow" for which the general did not forgive Allen.[51]

When Kentucky was announced for Harding the convention knew that Lowden had capitulated. With additional votes from Louisiana, New York, Oklahoma, and Texas, Harding rose on this ninth ballot to 374½, while Wood held at 249, Lowden, 121½, and Johnson, 83.

The tenth ballot was a bandwagon. When Pennsylvania voted for Harding at 5:05 P.M., the number necessary for nomination was reached. Nevertheless, Wood still held 156 votes, Johnson, 81, and La Follette, 24. Despite a "goodly chorus of noes," mostly from Wisconsin, the nomination was declared unanimous. In the longest balloting since 1884, Republicans had nominated their first senatorial candidate.[52]

As the votes piled up for him, Harding was in a small room off the auditorium with Lowden and Nicholas Murray Butler. A roar was heard from the hall, the door burst open and Charles B. Warren shouted: "Pennsylvania has voted for you, Harding, and you are nominated!" Taking Lowden's and Butler's hands, Harding, in a choking voice, said, "I shall need all the help that you two friends can give me." Daugherty hurried Harding away.[53]

REACTION

Swift changes had taken place in the dramatis personae on the national stage. Harding was transformed at once from a worried, neglected bystander to a lionized statesman, while his rivals dropped as suddenly into political limbo. Bursting into a terrific rage, Wood had to be forcibly restrained from storming into the convention to denounce the "theft." The convention, he wrote, had been upset by "a cabal of the Old Guard, plenty of money and a great shortage of scruples," and never had there been a more corrupt use of influence on the uncommitted portion of the delegates.[54]

Lowden was, as we have seen, the first to congratulate Harding. Real loyalty to the governor had been rare and he had been too readily written off as a result of the indiscretions of his henchmen. Many of his delegates had taken orders from others; and, perhaps, even his managers, Hert and Warren, had co-operated too closely with those who chose Harding. But he might, philosophically, attribute his failure to an untoward stroke of fate.

Johnson departed righteously prophesying the ultimate triumph of virtue: "It doesn't make any difference if a few politicians sitting in the Blackstone Hotel in Chicago said, 'The people be damned,' for the time is coming when the people will come into their own." Once the election was over, he said, he would devote himself to holding up to "public obloquy the men who have founded such a cynical and contemptuous disregard of the expressed will of the people."[55]

The fact that the convention chose neither of the three candidates who had won primaries and had been prominent in the public eye before the convention, but, instead, nominated Harding, whose chances had been regarded as negligible, set off immediate speculation as to the forces and men responsible. For years later, because of evidence that the scandals of the Harding administration originated in deals made at Chicago, the convention figured in congressional investigations and court trials. The nomination of Harding was variously attributed, sometimes overlappingly, to Boies Penrose, to George Harvey and the Senate cabal of the Smoke-filled Room, to oil interests, and to Harry Daugherty.

Questions of backstairs control and of causation in a national convention are of great complexity. Attention is often focused too exclusively on leaders and too little on the ordinary delegate and the influence he exerts on his leaders. Participants often exaggerate their personal roles. As two men stood watching a log float downstream, one of them said: "That is just like Washington. That log is covered with hundreds of ants and each one thinks he is steering!" Perhaps the analogy is even more appropriate to national conventions.

Contemporary press accounts overemphasized the power of Senator Boies Penrose. There is no evidence that he even communicated with the Smoke-filled Room. Apparently, he did not contribute to the decisive build-up of Harding strength on the early Saturday ballots. While he refrained from throwing his strength to any other candidate, he apparently did not actively join the Harding movement until the Saturday afternoon recess when success was imminent. Mark Sullivan, Wadsworth, Calder, New, and Nicholas Murray Butler have agreed that Penrose' illness had taken him out of effective control of events and that he played no vital role in the 1920 convention. However, Penrose, as the "incarnation and epitome of plutocratic power in a democracy," wrote William Allen White, was a "sort of time spirit of the occasion."[56]

After the convention the press stressed the importance of the Smoke-filled Room. On Sunday the *New York Times* said the nomination "was arranged in conferences in hotel rooms," fulfilling Daugherty's prediction "to the letter." At the conference "the elements opposing Wood and Lowden got into line for Harding," reported the Chicago *Tribune*. "That conference will go down in the history of politics as the final breakdown of the American primary system," wrote David Lawrence.[57]

This Smoke-filled Room became a symbol of the thwarting of popular will by backstairs political plotting. However, such an interpretation constitutes a considerable oversimplification, even distortion, of the role of this conference and it must be carefully qualified. It was quickly to be challenged. The *New York Post* called it "melodrama." George Harvey was not the boss of the Republican party, wrote David Lawrence, and Harding was convinced that he did not owe his nomination to any one man or group. Daugherty said he knew nothing of the meeting at the time and did not work with the senators, whom he considered an "undependable lot," all hoping to be nominated themselves. Walter Brown, who considered himself Harding's floor leader, said that the Smoke-filled Room story was all fiction.[58]

To insist that a small group of men in a room imposed a candidate on the convention *is* "melodrama." This assumes that the Smoke-filled Room stopped the convention from nominating a given candidate and maneuvered it into nominating Harding. The available evidence does not justify such an interpretation. The regular delegates naturally opposed Wood and Johnson; and neither could be nominated in the 1920 convention as it was composed. The fund revelation disabled Lowden. Consequently, the only real decision to be made was whether to pass over Harding and nominate another dark horse. During the Saturday afternoon recess at least some of the leaders of the Smoke-filled Room actually attempted to delay or block Harding's nomination.

Unquestionably, many forces contributed to the outcome of the convention, and the nomination of Harding does not require explanation in terms of conspiracy. Given the prevailing political atmosphere of 1920, and the situation in the party, the nomination of Harding was a logical result of the convention. Perhaps many

The Republican Convention 99

thought or pretended to think that they had nominated him. Harry Daugherty claimed the credit, although, in his subsequent accounts, he did not, or could not, give a satisfactory explanation of how the nomination was accomplished. George Harvey pretended that the Smoke-filled Room, really more diagnosing than impelling, was the decisive factor. Financial leaders claimed it was their money, state leaders their strategic shifts, and Penrose his telephone calls. If credit must be assigned to any one person it should go to Harry Daugherty who, a politician's politician and a legislative representative of corporations, had worked with restless energy and astuteness for years to make Harding president. So many pressures and intrigues, however, combined to produce the nomination that it must be considered, as William Allen White wrote, a "movement" rather than a "plot."[59]

Harding's nomination was greeted with apparent satisfaction by some Republican journals, and with courageous words concealing disappointment by others. The independent Republican press wavered, as if from shock, but then talked itself into support of the party's candidate. The Democratic press attacked as if presented with a target at which they might fire without compunction, and the independent press was confirmed in the generally Democratic position it had already assumed.

The New York *Sun and Herald* called Harding "the exemplification of the best type of Americanism," and the wisest nomination the Republicans could have made. The Washington *Star* said he had an excellent record in the Senate, broad views, and a sense of political proportion. His nomination was a step toward returning the country to its "normal balance," said the *Baltimore American*, and the Chicago *Tribune* said it reflected a deep desire for "sound conservatism." The New York *Tribune* wrote disgustedly that it had hoped for a man of courage, vision, and ability (Wood) but got instead "one of the Senate group that controlled the convention."

An indignant *New York Times* received with "astonishment and dismay" the news that a "senatorial cabal" characterized by "imbecility," and made up of "white livered and incompetent politicians," had nominated this "respectable Ohio politician of the second class." To the New York *World* he was a "puppet candidate"; to the *New York Post* his nomination was "an affront to the intelligence and the conscience of the American people."

The *New Republic* called him a "party hack," without "moral and intellectual qualities"; and the *Nation* regarded him as an "errand boy for the old guard politicians and the business interests they serve," "a dummy, an animated automaton," who would be controlled by those who wanted a tough foreign policy, compulsory military service, no labor nonsense, and "one hundred per cent Americanism." Agreement was general that his nomination was a defeat for progressivism, and a victory for big-business conservatives.

THE COOLIDGE STAMPEDE

After the Harding landslide began, attention quickly shifted to choosing a suitable running mate. Most prominently mentioned for this position was Governor Henry Allen of Kansas, who thought he had been promised the nomination in return for throwing Kansas to Harding. However, he had advocated compulsory arbitration in labor disputes, and was too conservative, some thought, to run with the conservative Harding. Seeking release from his promise to nominate him, Senator Watson told him that the move was meeting with difficulty because of labor opposition.[60]

Beckoning to each other during the tenth ballot, the leaders met in a little chamber beneath the stage. There Hert, McCormick, Borah, Weeks, and Daugherty agreed that Harding needed balancing by a liberal. McCormick proposed Senator Lenroot of Wisconsin who had supported Roosevelt in 1912, favored the league with reservations, and was acceptable to Johnson. Plans were improvised, and McCormick went to the stage to present Lenroot's name. Seconding speeches by Hert of Kentucky, Remmel of Arkansas, Calder of New York, and Herrick of Ohio made it clear to the convention that Lenroot was the choice of the leaders.[61]

However, eight conservative Oregon delegates, none of whom liked Lenroot, consulted together and suggested that Judge Wallace McCamant nominate Coolidge. Climbing on a chair, McCamant shouted for recognition. In the confusion Willis, who was presiding, probably thought that he wanted to second Lenroot's nomination. McCamant's resonant voice made itself heard above the clatter of departing delegates, and his speech was followed by "an outburst of applause of short duration but of great power." Immediately there was a series of seconding speeches during which, sensing a stampede, Remmel switched from Lenroot to Coolidge. Henry Allen and Governor Anderson of Virginia were also placed in nomination, but the first ballot gave Coolidge 674½ to Lenroot's 146½, and was followed by a tremendous demonstration.[62]

The most genuinely popular act of the convention, Coolidge's nomination was indicative of the temper of the delegates. They were in no mood for a liberal from Wisconsin. On the other hand, Coolidge was a symbol of "Americanism," "law and order," and firmness toward rebellious labor. McCamant had been impressed with "the conservative trend of his thought," and, of course, he was "all right" with Daugherty. Leaders might want a liberal to balance Harding, but the delegates stampeded for an additional champion against radicalism.[63]

Coolidge was with his wife in the Adams House when the news of the convention sweep to him began to come in. As they were about to go out to dinner the telephone rang. Coolidge listened and turned to his wife with the one word, "nominated."[64]

As the expression of a representative body of Republicans, the choice of Harding and Coolidge was indicative of the political and social climate of the day. They chose a party showpiece who would "take advice," a "second McKinley," favorite of the old guard. His nomination was a bid for "normalcy." To the delegates he represented the antithesis of Wilson: modest mediocrity rather than arrogant genius; party government rather than one-man government; consultation rather than dictation; warm humanity rather than austere intellectualism; genial realism rather than strenuous idealism. It was an expression of supreme confidence—power was coming of its own accord to the party and so the leaders chose the figurehead whom they could best manipulate. Exceeding the conservatism of their political bosses, the delegates sharply rejected Lenroot of Wisconsin for Calvin Coolidge, a solid Republican of the old school whose reputation was based on his promptness in calling out troops against unruly labor. That Harding and Coolidge well suited the postwar mood of the Republican party and the country as a whole was demonstrated in the ensuing election.

CHAPTER IV

THE DEMOCRATIC CONVENTION

THE DEMOCRATS ESPOUSE PRINCIPLES

The Democratic convention assembled at noon, Monday, June 28, in San Francisco's Civic Auditorium. Of the 1,092 delegates plus their alternates present, 756 were uninstructed and many others only formally instructed for favorite sons. Five members of the cabinet, Burleson, Colby, Meredith, Daniels, and Palmer headed a long list of administration officials present. Prominent also were Senator Carter Glass, custodian of Wilson's platform ideas, and Homer Cummings, chairman of the national committee. The most conspicious absentees were Wilson, McAdoo, Baruch, and Roper. For the first time women sat as delegates; there were about a hundred, and their chief impact on the convention was to restrain smoking and provide numerous occasions for singing, "Oh, You Beautiful Doll."

Apparently the administration was in control. Most of the delegates had been chosen by pro-administration organizations. Cummings told Wilson that there were only about 125 Bryan men in the convention, though Bryan might inflate that support by championing a popular issue or threatening to bolt. A more substantial menace, of course, were the northern bosses who had chosen delegates expertly and formed antiadministration blocs.[1]

Few seats were contested. The national committee, with technical correctness, accredited the pro-Palmer Georgia delegation, despite the fact that most Georgia Democrats were antiadministration. The Fifth Missouri District insisted upon sending irreconcilable Senator James F. Reed despite his rejection by the state convention, but the committee ruled that the state convention was the authority. The fight to seat Reed was led by Cox's manager, who was supported by an antiadministration line-up of New York, New Jersey, Indiana, and Kentucky.

Of all the conventions he had attended, wrote William Allen White, San Francisco was the most pleasant physically. The restaurants were good, the people hospitable, the auditorium beautiful, and the weather ruled out such clichés of convention reporting as "tired perspiring delegates in shirt sleeves." Enthusiasm could be displayed with little risk of collapse, and there was much singing of "There's a Long, Long, Trail A' Winding," "I'm Forever Blowing Bubbles," "Sidewalks of New York," and "How Dry I Am."[2]

Homer Cummings' keynote address, it was known, had been approved by Wilson. The professorlike Cummings did not seem to be the convention-orator type, but he more than adequately filled the requirements of the occasion. The Republican party, which persistently served special interests, he said, had adopted a "reactionary and provincial" platform which concealed a sword for Mexico, and held no hope for the average man. "Shameless in waste of time and money," the Republican Congress had been "without parallel for its incompetencies, failures and repudiations." The Democratic administration had enacted more "constructive and remedial legislation" than the Republicans had in a generation, and had conducted the war with "unexampled skill" carrying America to "greater heights of honor and power and glory than she had ever known before." Eighty Republican investigations proved only that it was conducted with less government corruption than any other war in history.

Wilson had sacrificed himself for the cause of peace, Cummings said, and even his sick chamber, where he lay close to death, was invaded by the malice of his enemies—all because he sought a reign of universal peace. His vision had given him a place of honor and immortality in history. The honor of the United States was pledged to the treaty, the one great asset that had come out of the war, and the Republican proposal for an "association of nations" was "fatuous futility." In rejecting the treaty the United States placed itself in isolation with "revolutionary Mexico, Bolshevist Russia, unspeakable Turkey." The choice was between "peace, disarmament, and world fraternity," or "provincialism, militarism and world chaos," and there was "no blacker crime against civilization" than the Republican defeat of the league.

Cummings' address, Mark Sullivan wrote, incomparably better than Lodge's, was "a lofty effort not easily equalled." It showed real conviction and emphasized real issues, said the *New York Post*. Soon a Cummings boom was underway with the slogan, "A Great Moment Has Produced a Great Man."[3]

Wilson suffered his first setback in the selection of the permanent chairman. His choice was Bainbridge Colby, but opposition developed to giving a cabinet member the post. Bryan proposed Senator Thomas J. Walsh of Montana, and others backed Vice-President Marshall. Cummings wired Wilson that it would be better to put Colby on the resolutions committee where he could meet the expected attack on the platform from the floor. Reluctantly Wilson conceded and Joseph T. Robinson of Arkansas was chosen as a compromise.[4] Attacking Republicans on profiteering, campaign expenditures, Armenia, and Mexico, Robinson did not emphasize the league issue to the same degree that Cummings did.

Wilson's choice for chairman of the important resolutions committee was Carter Glass, author of the Virginia platform which incorporated Wilson's views. Antiadministration organizations, Bryanites, and westerners supported Senator Thomas J. Walsh, who had voted for ratification with the Lodge reservations. The Wilsonians, however, safely installed Glass. The platform committee included many of the party's leading figures: Thomas Marshall, Bainbridge Colby, William Jennings Bryan, Vance C. McCormick, David I. Walsh, Pat Harrison, and Thomas J. Walsh.[5]

This committee began work on Monday, but so prolonged were the fights on the league and prohibition planks that the convention was forced to mark time until the fifth day, Friday, when the platform was ready. Bryan sought to commit the party to ratification of the league with whatever reservations were necessary to command a majority in the Senate; but administration leaders decisively defeated him. Then, however, Senator David I. Walsh of Massachusetts sought to add to the plank endorsing the league the words, "but do not oppose reservations which make more clear or specific our obligations to the associated nations." Wilson strongly opposed this concession; but Walsh, in a tempestuous all-night session, succeeded in getting his amendment adopted. "League Compromise Forced on Wilson," headlined the New York *American*.[6]

The administration was believed to favor silence on prohibition. Actually Wilson sent the draft of a plank advocating liberalization of the Volstead Act, but the dry Glass did not produce it at the committee meetings. Burleson urged that the party denounce the Volstead Act as absurd and unreasonable. Bryan, on the other hand, wanted a strong committment against any increase in the alcoholic content of beverages. None of the prohibition planks produced gained a majority, and Bryan announced that he would carry his fight with the wets, together with his ideas on the league, onto the convention floor.[7]

Frank P. Walsh's unsuccessful attempt to get an Irish independence plank brought some stimulating debate during which one shouting redheaded girl had to be carried from the room. When Bryan spoke of the callousness of those who, having sacrificed nothing, opposed a veterans bonus, Glass replied that he had given two sons and numerous relatives. Stung by this rebuke, Bryan retired to a corner and wept, returned to shake hands with Glass, and the two worked out a compromise. A firmly Wilsonian subcommittee used Glass's draft as the basis of the platform which, with thirty-eight planks and eight thousand words, was the longest in the party's history. It took the exhausted Glass over two hours to read it to the convention.[8]

The platform called the league the "surest, if not the only practicable means" of maintaining peace and lifting the burden of armaments. It was "America's war aim," to which our honor was pledged. "We advocate the immediate ratification of the Treaty without reservations which would impair its essential integrity; but do not oppose the acceptance of any reservations making clearer or more specific the obligations of the United States to the League associates." This plank received enormous applause.

Sympathy was expressed for the "aspirations of Ireland for self-government." Armenia should be aided to establish a government of its own. Territorial government was favored for Puerto Rico and Alaska, and independence for the Philippines.

The list of Democratic accomplishments emphasized the Federal Reserve System. The platform favored the repeal of wartime taxes, a tariff for revenue only, and a national budget system. It promised to expand farm credit and guarantee to farmers the right of collective bargaining.

Labor, said the platform, was not a commodity but human, and the Democratic party was its "firm friend." Both capital and labor had the right to organize and bargain collectively, but neither should jeopardize the public welfare. The platform rejected compulsory arbitration and endorsed woman suffrage, the abolition of child labor, the protection of women in industry, and federal aid to education.

The heroism of the war veterans constituted "a sacred heritage of posterity, the worth of which can never be recompensed from the Treasury, and the glory of which must not be diminished by any such expedients." However, the platform endorsed aid to disabled veterans, and vocational education and home-ownership aid for all veterans.

While defending the wartime administration of the railroads, it advocated private ownership without government subsidy. It endorsed federal aid for highways, inland waterways, the St. Lawrence Seaway, the merchant marine, reclamation, and flood control, and said that the livestock market and harbor fees should be supervised.

While, as a whole, the Democratic platform was progressive, it contained some items indicative of the intolerant wartime nationalism. More petroleum should be acquired; and Mexico must "realize the propriety of a policy that asserts the right of the United States to demand full protection for its citizens." Free speech did not imply "toleration of enemy propaganda or the advocacy of the overthrow of the government . . . by force or violence." Exclusion of Asiatics was "a true expression of the judgment of our people."

The delegates waited through the long reading in anticipation, for it was known that William Jennings Bryan would challenge the platform on the floor. When he rose, Bryan praised the platform and those who made it. He endorsed almost all of it, he said, but he would not be true to the party that he loved, which had honored him as much as a party could honor a man, if he did not state his convictions. He proposed new planks calling for a pledge against "any increase in the alcoholic content of permitted beverages"; a "national bulletin"; co-operatives; criminal liability for corporate officials; publicity for, or a legal limit on, profits; state trade commissions; and no "universal compulsory military training in time of peace." He also sought to amend the planks on the league and prohibition.

His league plank, Bryan said, would not detract from the glory the president earned "in giving to the world a great idea" and securing "a better treaty than anyone had any right to expect." It simply provided for early establishment of the league. He sought to commit the party to ratification "with such reservations as a majority of the senators may agree upon." Then delegates to the league should be popularly elected and instructed not to vote for war unless Congress so authorized.

The liquor traffic was dead, Bryan said, the only question was whether it should be decently buried. It was better to have the gratitude of the mothers than "the wild hurrahs" of "those who would make money by selling poison to their fellowmen." A national bulletin would get the political facts before the people and reduce the necessity for large campaign expenditures. His profiteering plank would insure that when profiteers were imprisoned they would "enter as Republicans and not as Democrats." America, moreover, must not "train every young man in the gentle art of taking human life."

Following Bryan, Bourke Cockran spoke for a wet plank. "All the mistaken legislation which has resulted in oppression, in tyranny, and in persecution," he said, "was conceived in the ill-digested hope of making people good by violence and coercion." To enforce the Volstead Law would require the exercise of powers ruinous to free government. Should the Constitution be destroyed to combat a fancied evil? The restoration of white supremacy in the South, said Cockran, was an example of how public sentiment transcended a constitutional amendment.

Bryan's second speech concentrated on the league and prohibition. He had made more speeches than anyone, Bryan said, for ratification without reservations, but that was impossible and would be more so after four months of partisan denunciation. The changes proposed by reservations were pitifully small when compared to the great provisions in the treaty:

You cannot call me an enemy of Woodrow Wilson; it was my treaty plan that he took to Paris; I have helped him to become immortal. If

I could secure ratification without reservations and give to Woodrow Wilson the honor of securing it, I would walk up to the scaffold today and die with a smile upon my face. But I cannot do it, my friends; nobody else can do it. . . . Some day I shall stand before His judgment bar; and when I appear there, there shall not be upon my hands the blood of people slaughtered while I talked politics.

He closed on prohibition:

Be not frightened; time and again in history the timid have been afraid. But they have always found that they underestimated the number of those who had not bowed the knee to Baal. . . . In just a few days another state will ratify the Suffrage Amendment, and then on the mountain tops you will see the women and the children of our allies in every righteous cause. We shall not fail.

The convention had not been disappointed. It was the same old Bryan, in the same old alpaca coat, the same voice, a little husky perhaps, and the same smile. Altogether kindly toward everyone, a few years older, a few pounds heavier, but recapturing for a time all of his old-time force, vigor, and eloquence, he made one of the best speeches of his life. To all he carried conviction of his moral courage and sincerity. With cleverness, keen retort, skill at springing dramatic climaxes, and the grand emotional fervor of real oratory, he had carried his audience along in a common high emotional experience.

When Bryan appeared for his second speech he had difficulty in quieting what one observer called the largest personal demonstration of the convention. When he closed "a great shout went surging up into the vaulted dome of the roof in an endless sea of sound." It was a "simply tremendous demonstration" given to him "with an utter abandon." Again and again he was forced to come to the edge of the platform to bow his acknowledgments while spotlights gleamed upon the tears that rolled down his face. Order was not restored for twenty-three minutes. At the center of the hall, however, a block of delegates sat unmoved.[9]

Some leaders feared that Bryan sought to repeat the stampede of 1896 and, amid the thunderous demonstration, that outcome did not seem too fantastic. For the first time, however, amplifiers enabled others to compete on more equal terms with the Great Commoner.

To counter Bryan the administration brought forth its best orator, Bainbridge Colby.

Colby was polished and witty. "It is a thankless task which now devolves upon me," he began, "to bring you down from the pleasurable heights where you have been disporting yourselves to the lower and somewhat humdrum levels of reason and judgment and duty." Praising Bryan's contributions to Democracy, he passed to pricking humor, calling the national bulletin a "somewhat hurriedly assembled" proposal, and referring to the "scientific and dispassionate temper" in which Bryan was wont to discuss prohibition. Bryan had changed, Colby charged, from sincere advocacy of the league to co-operation with those who would destroy it. America was going to enter, he said, and neither Bryan nor "the embattled egoists of the Senate" could stop it, for the question had passed from the stranded, futile Senate to the higher tribunal of the people in a "solemn referendum." Applause was slight, but the Chicago *Tribune* called Colby's speech the best of the convention.[10]

Supporting Colby, Glass spoke with less polish and more asperity. Prohibition must not be drawn into the campaign to obscure the issue of the peace. The real reason why the Republicans were attacking the league, he charged, was to transfer credit for it to Henry Cabot Lodge.

The convention cheered Bryan but it would not follow him. His prohibition plank got only 155½ votes and his other proposals were defeated by a voice vote. Bourke Cockran's plank to legalize light wines and beer got only 356 votes; but Bryan was heard to mutter to himself, "I never thought they would beat me so badly."[11]

The platform was well received. The *New York Times,* in the Democratic camp since the nomination of Harding, called it "strong and sound . . . intended to reassure and strengthen every legitimate commercial and financial enterprise in the country . . ." To the *New York Post* it was "an excellent pronouncement"; to the *Cleveland Plain Dealer,* progressive and liberal. The New York *World,* however, had reservations on prohibition and Palmer's activities, and the *New Republic* said it would not arouse "flaming enthusiasm among liberals which could alone have made a Democratic victory possible this year."[12]

The Democratic Nominations

While the resolutions committee was preparing the platform, the convention proceeded with the nomination of candidates. John H. Bigelow presented Attorney General Palmer as the man to save America from threatening revolutionary forces. When the "insidious evils of anarchy and her lawless litter arose" Palmer "deported and imprisoned the defamers of the nation— aye, even at the threat of the terrorists' bombs." He was a "new Navarra . . . panoplied in the armor of a Vulcan, striking with all the might and majesty of the nation, confusing the columns of sedition and scattering the serried ranks of reds." The ensuing demonstration, determinedly continued for thirty-six minutes, grew to include two to three hundred delegates.[13]

Governor James M. Cox was presented by James G. Johnson who praised his record as a practical statesman and emphasized his ability to carry Ohio. In an attempt to attenuate the image of Cox as a wet, Pat Harrison, of dry Mississippi, was enlisted for a seconding speech. In the ensuing demonstration standards were raised, the organ played, the crowd cheered, but the noise was not so general that the Ohio delegation could not be clearly distinguished. Friends of Cox were disappointed, but kept the demonstration going for thirty-two minutes.

Bourke Cockran of New York nominated Al Smith, whose life, he said, savored "of a page from romance," and was the most complete refutation of the pernicious doctrines of anarchists and socialists. New York offered him reluctantly, and only for the presidency. Cockran's masterly oratory sparked a complimentary demonstration that was one of the surprises of the convention. A band struck up "Sidewalks of New York," henceforth inseparably Smith's, and for fully a half an hour the convention tumultuously cheered, paraded, and sang. Among the seconders of Smith's nomination was Franklin D. Roosevelt.[14]

Burris Jenkins, originally scheduled to nominate McAdoo, rose to announce that he would not make a speech because of insistent requests from his candidate that no nominating speech be made. Nevertheless, Jenkins said, he was sure that the convention would draft him: "And, furthermore, we know that if so drafted he will accept the nomination. And any rumors of telegrams supposed to have been received by me or anybody else now or in the future denying that he will accept the nomination, are falsehoods perpetrated by the enemies of our party. I therefore place in nomination William Gibbs McAdoo." Jenkin's remarks were a signal for a forty-minute demonstration which was more convincing than those for Cox and Palmer. Most states joined in, but New York, Illinois, Ohio, Pennsylvania, Indiana, and New Jersey remained seated.[15]

In a festival of complimentary oratory ten other candidates were nominated, most of them with two seconding speeches. West Virginia's Governor John J. Cornwell said that John W. Davis had a perfect record, unchallenged ability, growing fame, and was the best equipped to lead a campaign for the league. Charles F. S. O'Brien frankly presented Governor Edwards of New Jersey as a wet; the convention's reception was not enthusiastic. Also named were Homer S. Commings, Gilbert M. Hitchcock, Carter Glass, F. M. Simmons, Robert L. Owens, James W. Gerard, Edwin T. Meredith, and Francis Burton Harrison.

The candidates had been busy during the five days of the convention that elapsed before the balloting began. William Jennings Bryan said he was interested only in principles: "If I can help this world to banish alcohol, and after that to banish war . . . no office, no Presidency, can offer the honors that will be mine." There would be no difficulty in finding a candidate, Bryan said, if the delegates would use common sense—he must be dry, for woman suffrage, and against Wall Street. Meeting Burleson in a hotel corridor, Bryan told him that he felt like Daniel entering the lion's den. "Yes, and you are trying to get hell bit out of you," responded Burleson. The overwhelming defeat of his platform planks proved that, no matter how much sentimental regard they might have for him, the delegates would not follow him. "When a country gets into a frame of mind where it smiles indulgently at such a man," wrote Bruce Bliven, "it is in a bad way, and the convention smiled indulgently at Mr. Bryan."[16]

The McAdoo boom continued to puzzle both friends and enemies. Organizing without his direction, his supporters in San Francisco selected Samuel B. Amidon as nominal leader, formed a steering committee, and rented hotel rooms for conferences. Postmaster General Burleson sought to join with the leadership, but found other McAdoo men cold to him. By endorsing beer and McAdoo simultaneously, Burleson felt he could make McAdoo acceptable to the predominantly wet delegates; but the dry McAdoo management did not welcome his interference. When Burleson announced: "McAdoo is going to be nominated. . . . This is a Wilson convention," Roper, in rebuke, wired Burleson that the press seized upon every statement of his to connect McAdoo disadvantageously with the administration.[17]

Shortly before the nominating speeches were made, Roper wired from Chicago that McAdoo would accept if nominated, and told the press that he was "confident that Mr. McAdoo would receive the necessary two-thirds vote after the first few ballots." When unfriendly San Francisco newspapers, nevertheless, implied that he would refuse the nomination, McAdoo leaders decided that Jenkins, without a formal speech, should announce to the convention that McAdoo would accept.

They agreed upon the strategy of showing the full McAdoo strength on early ballots in the hope of starting a band wagon which would break the unity of the Cox or Palmer forces. McAdoo's opponents need hold only one third of the delegates to block his nomination, but the anti-McAdoo coalition had weaknesses: Murphy of Tammany might accept him in exchange for a wet plank; while Thomas Taggart of Indiana refused to identify himself too closely with antiadministration forces, and thus might conceivably defect to McAdoo.[18]

Cox's managers continued to moderate their campaign. Developments were favorable. Harding's nomination strengthened Cox because of the necessity of carrying Ohio. Wilson's receptive attitude kept administration forces in semiparalysis while the split between Palmer and McAdoo deepened. The Ohio delegation was unusually strong, and included former Governors James E. Campbell and Judson Harmon, Senator Atlee W. Pomerene, W. A. Julian, and Congressman George White; it provided the Cox men with invaluable liaisons. Moore studied the preferences of the delegates from the various states, met as many as possible, avoided enmities, and worked for second- and third-choice votes.[19]

Balloting began on Friday night, but only two were taken before the convention adjourned. On the first, McAdoo led with 266, while Palmer received 256 votes, and Cox, 134. Al Smith, Edward I. Edwards, Thomas A. Marshall, Robert L. Owens, John W. Davis, Edwin T. Meredith, Carter Glass, and Homer Cummings led the field of twenty favorite sons. Votes for administration men far outnumbered those for antiadministration candidates. On the second ballot McAdoo rose by only 23 votes, Palmer, by 12, and Cox, by 25. McAdoo's strength was mostly in the South and West, the nucleus of Palmer's power was Pennsylvania and Georgia, and Cox's vote came from Ohio, the metropolitan states, and Mississippi.

Friday night was filled with conferences, but none that corresponded to the central Republican Smoke-filled Room. Because of the persistence of a full field of favorite sons, the strength of the leading candidates had not yet been tested. The dominant administration group was unable to agree; and a 2:00 A.M. conference between Palmer and Cox's manager produced only the agreement that the nomination of McAdoo was undesirable. He doubted if he could deliver his delegates to Cox if he tried, Palmer told Moore, because of the dry sentiment among them.[20]

The first ballots on Saturday morning brought but gradual change; and on the sixth ballot the vote was McAdoo 368½, Palmer 265½, and Cox 195. On the seventh ballot, however, New York and New Jersey, leaving their favorite sons, threw most of their votes to Cox, which increased his tally by 118½ votes to 295½ and put him in second place. When McAdoo slipped slightly, the big Cox drive began. Cox passed McAdoo on the twelfth ballot, and by the fifteenth, the vote stood at Cox 468½, McAdoo 344½, and Palmer 167. Cox had now gained the bulk of the votes of Illinois, Indiana, Kentucky, Iowa, Louisiana, Mississippi, and Tennessee, while McAdoo retained his southern and western support and minority votes from the metropolitan states.

Cox, however, was unable to drive through to the nomination and slipped back on the sixteenth ballot when Tennessee transferred twelve votes from him to John W. Davis. With McAdoo now down to 337, an administration delegate moved for recess. The Cox forces demanded a roll call; but they were outvoted and the convention recessed at 5:40 P.M.

During this Saturday-afternoon recess Jouett Shouse and other McAdoo leaders persuaded Palmer and his manager, Carlin, to join them in a neighboring hotel. But, because they lacked real authority to bargain in McAdoo's name, perhaps all they could do was to ask Palmer to withdraw and thus unite administration men behind McAdoo. Leaving in high dudgeon, Palmer announced: "If I am not nominated you can be assured that the nominee for President will be someone other than McAdoo or Cox."[21]

The brief recess brought no advantage to the leaders in the race, and the next six ballots produced little change. Finally, at 11:40 P.M., the convention adjourned for the week end, thoroughly deadlocked after twenty-two ballots, with the vote standing at Cox 430, McAdoo 372½, Palmer 166½, and, down the list, a new apparition on the ballot, Woodrow Wilson 2.

Sunday, July 4, was no sabbath in San Francisco. Probably the solution to the deadlock most advantageous to the party would be a McAdoo-Cox ticket. For a time in the spring such an outcome had seemed possible. McAdoo scrupulously refrained from interfering in Ohio; and at one time Cox's manager assured Mrs. Funk that party sentiment was for McAdoo, and intimated that Cox ultimately would be willing to take second place. But McAdoo's June 18 withdrawal statement encouraged Cox's ambition for the first place.[22]

On Sunday morning the McAdoo leadership, Amidon, Mullen, Love, and Mrs. Funk, met to consider what action they should take if the nomination of McAdoo proved impossible. They could support none of the dark horses, they agreed, although there was some sentiment for Colby. A survey of the McAdoo delegates had revealed that their second choice was Cox, and the leaders decided they would throw their support to Cox if McAdoo's cause proved hopeless. But, publicly, they expressed determination to stick to the last: "We've just begun to fight," announced Jenkins.[23]

Some of the anti-McAdoo forces also felt discouragement. One report was that they planned to throw their support to Bainbridge Colby who, although close to Wilson, was wet and exempt from the "crown prince" epithet. "When the break came," Josephus Daniels wrote later, New York and California were ready to vote for Colby, but the trend to Cox had set in too strongly. However, Mrs. Funk and Mullen met with Moore later on Sunday and agreed jointly to resist the promotion of any dark horse.[24]

The opening ballot on Monday the twenty-third, showed little change from the earlier ones. Cox got 425, McAdoo, 364½ and Palmer, 181½. Dark horses Cummings, Owens, Davis, Clark, and

Glass were joined by Irving S. Cobb and Ring Lardner. Grimly the ballots ground on through the morning, with the same deadly sameness. Pat Harrison tried to force the favorite sons out of the contest by moving that the name of the lowest candidate be dropped after each ballot, but the move commanded little support and the chairman said it could not be enforced if it passed.

On the twenty-ninth ballot, Indiana moved from Cox to McAdoo, and on the next ballot McAdoo regained the lead with 403½ to 400½. Repassing Cox gave McAdoo his best opportunity, and on the thirty-third ballot the vote was McAdoo 421 and Cox 380½. But the McAdoo drive faltered.

When both Cox and McAdoo had slipped back, the pleas of Palmer men for votes met more success. With substantial gains from Tennessee and Illinois, he advanced from 174 on the thirty-first ballot to 241 on the thirty-sixth, when his drive was halted by an adjournment, during which Tennessee and Illinois deserted. Then, at long, long last, came the hoped for announcement. Palmer "unconditionally" released his delegates. An understandable shout went up, to be quickly stilled to a busy humming as a thirty-minute recess was taken.[25]

However, Palmer's withdrawal did not immediately resolve the deadlock. Georgia went to McAdoo; but nineteen Indiana delegates left him for Cox, who also got Massachusetts and Virginia and thus repassed McAdoo with a vote of 468½ to 440. But on the next ballot Pennsylvania gave most of her votes to McAdoo, narrowing the gap. To leaders of both camps it appeared that the deadlock could not be broken that night.[26]

According to Cox, the loose-reined, flexible floor strategy followed by Moore had never been equaled. Convinced that neither Palmer nor McAdoo could ever get the necessary two-thirds vote, he did not raise strenuous objection when Cox delegates cast their votes for either of them. He believed that they would return bringing others with them. Some deals were made with the bosses, but the circumstance of a wide-open convention forced him to work largely among the delegates on the floor. His most important conference took place under the speaker's platform, where he won the support of Joseph Guffey and other Palmer leaders.[27]

On the forty-first ballot Alabama shifted fifteen votes from Davis to Cox, widening the gap. A McAdoo move to adjourn was defeated. On the next ballot Georgia swung from McAdoo to

Cox. On the forty-third ballot Cox gained in Louisiana, Minnesota, Nebraska, Pennsylvania, Wyoming, and Virginia to reach 568 votes, more than a majority. Again McAdoo forces failed to get an adjournment, and Pennsylvania shifted from McAdoo to Cox. With so many states switching to Cox at the end of the forty-fourth ballot, Amidon moved that the nomination be made unanimous. At 1:40 A.M., July 6, the eighth day of the convention and the fourth day of balloting, James M. Cox was declared the nominee of the Democratic party for the presidency.

Analyzing Cox's victory after the convention, E. H. Moore concluded: "Cox was the logical beneficiary of the unwillingness of the Democratic party, after full deliberation on all the circumstances, to nominate McAdoo." More properly, Cox was the beneficiary of the circumstances which made McAdoo unwilling or unable to wage an organized campaign for the nomination. McAdoo's supporters rallied surprisingly well from the shock of his June 18 ban on the presentation of his name; nevertheless, irreparable damage was done. Many delegates hastened to make arrangements with more likely prospects. The popular Pat Harrison of Mississippi, who had planned to support McAdoo, joined the Cox forces, made an effective seconding speech for Cox, and became Moore's chief lieutenant on the floor. If Harrison had fought for McAdoo, instead of for Cox, the outcome might have been different. Similarly, after McAdoo's withdrawal, the McAdoo men in the Tennessee delegation made a compact with the Cox men to vote the entire delegation, under the unit rule, for Davis.[28]

Moreover, if McAdoo had been an openly avowed candidate, the Palmer boom might never have developed. McAdoo could have forestalled the entry of Palmer into Georgia and defeated him in the primaries. Unchecked, the activity of the red-hunting attorney general created a split within administration ranks so bitter that, after Palmer's withdrawal, most of his delegates went to Cox. In a sense it had been the administration's activities against radicals that made Palmer a presidential contender and dislodged Wilsonian Democrats from control of the party.

Furthermore, McAdoo's June 18 withdrawal stirred other administration leaders, such as Carter Glass, Homer Cummings, Gilbert Hitchcock, and Bainbridge Colby, to hope that a deadlocked convention might turn to them. A large number of delegates, who were chiefly proadministration, were throughout the balloting tied to various favorite-son candidates who were doing little to further McAdoo's candidacy. Mrs. Funk found Glass in a bad humor all the time, almost impossible to speak to, and using his sardonic smile and two-edged tongue on everything and everybody. When she asked him to release his delegates, he flatly refused. However, he "raised the very devil" about the administration forces not "standing by."[29]

McAdoo supporters were also handicapped by the fact that his manager, Roper, was not at San Francisco. With no one on hand with authority to speak for McAdoo in making necessary political bargains, high level political strategy was impossible. McAdoo's undirected supporters worked with ardor, but at the most critical moments it was impossible to get things settled.

Such weaknesses gave opportunity to anti-Wilson forces. While McAdoo was Wilsonian, liberal, and dry; Cox was nonadministration, a politician's candidate who would listen, and a wet: naturally the bosses of big northern machines threw their skillful support to Cox. They were aided, in the end, by a shift of southern delegates who, overcoming both repugnance for a wet and predilection for a southerner, voted against McAdoo as a symbol of Wilsonism.

WILSON'S THIRD-TERM BID

Unknown to both delegates and the press, a great but stricken leader and his embarrassed disciples enacted a poignant drama behind the scenes during the long deadlock. Despite his disabling illness, Wilson made an active bid for a third nomination.

As the convention opened press speculation on such a move was intense. The *New York Post* reported that the president would accept the nomination when drafted by a deadlocked convention. The delegates believed that Wilson's attitude was receptive, if not inviting, reported the Chicago *Tribune*. All conceded that only his health stood in the way, wrote Mark Sullivan. Political leaders in Washington were reported to be talking of a plan whereby the cabinet would suddenly ask the convention to nominate Wilson. The demonstration for Wilson at the opening of the convention was reluctant, one reporter thought, because of fear of an effort to start a Wilson stampede.[30]

Some Wilsonians insisted that the reason that Wilson made no statement on candidates was that he was following a strict policy of noninterference in the convention. But Wilson gave full and detailed instructions on the platform and vice-presidential nomination: "The names that are at the front of my mind are Judson Harmon, Champ Clark, and Representative Cordell Hull of Tennessee." During the convention Wilson sat on the back veranda of the White House sending and receiving coded telegrams, but not even Tumulty saw the messages to and from San Francisco.[31]

Believing that Wilson wanted a third term, Postmaster General Burleson sounded out sentiment regarding it. He found that most of the delegates, although supporters of Wilson, believed that he was physically unfit. Finding it impossible to remove this impression, Burleson threw his support to McAdoo.[32]

Bainbridge Colby, however, attempted to stampede the convention for Wilson. The last of the leaders to see Wilson before the convention, he was convinced that Wilson wanted the nomination. He told the press that a move to suspend the rules and nominate Wilson by acclamation could be carried at any time. On Friday, July 2, without consulting administration leaders in San Francisco, but after a telephone call to the White House, Colby sent Wilson a dramatic telegram. The outstanding feature of the convention, he reported, was "unanimity and fervor of feeling" for the president. No candidate before the convention could be nominated, and Bryan was threatening. "I propose, unless otherwise definitely instructed, to take advantage of first opportune moment to move suspension of rules and place your name in nomination."[33]

Learning of the telegram, the shocked Cummings demanded that Wilson's friends be consulted. The enthusiastic Colby told him that his move would sweep the convention, dissolve the deadlock, and gratify Wilson. It would be signing his death warrant, answered Cummings. When Joseph T. Robinson, Josephus Daniels, Burleson, Cummings, and Glass met in Colby's room early Saturday morning, all forcefully opposed Colby's move. "I never saw more indignation and resentment in any small gathering," Daniels wrote. Some felt that the proposal was cruel and could result only in humiliation to the president. He would rather vote for Wilson's corpse than for any man living, Glass said, but a third nomination was utterly unthinkable. Much distressed, Colby said pathetically that they made him feel like a criminal.[34]

Saturday reports to Wilson seemed designed to let him down easily. A conference had canvassed "the whole situation in the light of the phone message to Colby," Burleson telegraphed, and, if an opportune moment arrived, would take action, but the convention was moving rapidly with indications pointing to the nomination of McAdoo. Cummings wired that a static deadlock had not been reached, Cox was very strong, and the delegates' attachment to candidates already entered was inflexible. "I am in touch with your loyal friends," he added. Evidently Burleson's suggestion of McAdoo's nomination must have been unwelcome, for Wilson wired Cummings that the postmaster general "should not be included in the more intimate counsels which you are from time to time holding."[35]

When Cox telephoned Tumulty on Saturday requesting a denial of Glass's statement that Cox was unacceptable to the administration, Wilson refused to break his silence, and Tumulty, without authorization, announced he was positive that Wilson had not "expressed an opinion to anyone with reference to a particular candidate." When he learned from San Francisco of Colby's move, Tumulty immediately sent Mrs. Wilson a series of notes against it. Nothing should be done until a complete deadlock developed, he said, and suggested that a word from Wilson could nominate McAdoo, Cox, Colby, or Cummings, while delay might benefit Davis or Bryan. He received no answer.[36]

Sunday, with consultations broadened to include Cordell Hull, Ray Baker, and Vance McCormick, Colby was forced to send a sad "no" to Wilson. After exhaustive consideration, he said, the unanimous belief was that the lines of existing candidacies were drawn so tightly that Wilson's name would not command votes sufficient to nominate, and might draw a disappointing response that would injure the party in the coming campaign. While really an expression against a third term, a vote against Wilson would be misrepresented by Republicans as the true stand of the party on the league. Therefore, the conference suggested that Wilson telegraph them instructions to pursue such a course as they agreed upon as "practicable and judicious."[37]

Wilson's reply to Cummings seemed to suggest another, more restricted, conference. He said that he hoped that such a course would be pursued "as may seem practicable and judicious to yourself, Colby, Robinson, Glass, Hull, and McCormick, including Baruch, if you can get hold of him." Baruch was not in San Francisco but it was the unanimous opinion of the others that nothing further should be done.[38]

After the convention Wilson was cool toward his cabinet members. He summoned Burleson and told him he wanted to know just what had taken place. Burleson replied that he had written a detailed letter to Roper and would send Wilson a copy. After several days Wilson returned the letter with a note stating that he did not desire to read it. Burleson later admitted that Wilson resented what had taken place at San Francisco. Only with difficulty was he restrained from demanding Burleson's resignation.[39]

The Selection of Franklin D. Roosevelt

Before the convention reassembled at noon on Tuesday, the word was passed around that the leaders had decided to nominate Franklin D. Roosevelt as Cox's running mate. A promising young member of a famous family, Roosevelt had won favorable notice as an anti-Tammany member of New York's legislature and assistant secretary of the Navy. At thirty-eight he was handsome, personable, aristocratically democratic, reasonably dynamic, and reputedly intelligent, although his public statements were not so acute as to antagonize the more moderately endowed.

Roosevelt was a star of the convention. When the New York chairman reluctantly gave his consent to join the opening Wilson demonstration, Roosevelt leaped for the standard and grabbed it with such vigor as to drag the powerfully built Jeremiah T. Mahoney off his seat. Mahoney had not gotten the word, and supporters of both joined in the ensuing scuffle until Roosevelt carried the standard off into the Wilson procession. San Francisco papers overdramatized the affair as a fist fight, and Roosevelt was the hero of the day. That evening Roosevelt led a successful fight against the New York unit rule, freeing an upstate proadministration minority from the control of the wet, antiadministration Tammany majority. Once he vaulted a row of chairs on the way to the platform, where he received a complimentary band number, "Rose of Washington Square." He seconded the nomination of Al Smith.[40]

Cox said he told Moore that Roosevelt was his choice because he was from New York, independent, and had a well-known name. Moore told Murphy of Tammany that if he objected to Roosevelt they would choose Meredith. Cagily attributing his acquiescence to appreciation for being consulted, Murphy promised a nomination on the first ballot. To Mrs. Funk, Moore said that Bainbridge Colby and Roosevelt had been mentioned. The name Roosevelt was potent, thought Mrs. Funk, and his popularity in the West would help offset the fact that Cox was wet. "All right," said Moore, and left for the platform. "If you'd said Colby," Pat Harrison exclaimed, "we'd have had the Hearst newspapers."[41]

Nominating him, Judge Timothy T. Ansberry said that Roosevelt, with a name "to conjure with in American politics," was "splendidly educated" and "a fine type of American manhood." Giving Tammany's endorsement, the popular Al Smith vigorously discussed the prospects of the Democratic party more than he did Roosevelt, but "heartily" seconded the nomination of "one of our best-known Democrats." When Cone Johnson of Texas added McAdoo's blessings, other candidates were withdrawn and Roosevelt nominated by acclamation.

Most of the press viewed the nominations of Cox and Roosevelt favorably. They were worthy of their "noble and compelling cause," said the *New York Times.* Cox had a clean record, ability, and high political attainment, said the Washington *Star.* The *Cleveland Plain Dealer* thought that he was progressive and his nomination put his party in the position to make the strongest possible bid for the presidency. Ohio papers, both friend and foe, treated Cox with respect.

Nearly all newspapers, however, regarded Cox's nomination as a resounding defeat for the administration. He was "as far away from Wilsonian as possible," said the New York *Tribune.* He was selected because he was a nullification of the administration positions on the league and prohibition, said the Chicago *Tribune.* His nomination, reported the *San Francisco Chronicle,* repudiated the Wilsonian platform.

The liberal press was disappointed. Cox's nomination, like

Harding's, was a triumph of the professional politician, wrote Howland of the *Independent*. He must prove his independence of Tammany, warned the *Springfield* (Mass.) *Republican*. The convention, wrote Bruce Bliven in the *New Republic,* belonged to an era which far antedated Woodrow Wilson—it had forgotten the social vision of 1912 and 1916.[42]

Almost everyone agreed that the Democratic party had undergone a reaction to the right. The nomination, Boies Penrose observed, meant the resumption of control by the old-line leaders of the party from Wilson's "amateurs and alleged idealists." Tammany and Edwards rejoiced. Mrs. Funk, in despair, said Cox's nomination was wet, antiadministration and reactionary. It meant the passing of liberalism and Wilsonism, wrote William Allen White, and the seizure of control by the bosses, the wets, and the bitter-enders. He concluded that the war had left the world morally and spiritually shell-shocked:

If a man happened to be a reactionary, he would laugh himself into hysterics whenever he thinks what happened to the rainbow chasers. If he should happen to be a reformer he should throw a fit.[43]

CHAPTER V

THE CAMPAIGN

The conventions had not altered the fundamental political "situation." Republicans had not harmed their advantageous standing, and a general apprehension of defeat persisted among Democrats. Wall Street betting odds on Harding were two to one and rising. Republicans were in a position which they needed only to maintain; the burden of the campaign rested on the Democrats.

The Republican Battle Plan

Will Hays had been so obviously successful as national chairman, and was so ingratiating to all factions, that he became the first party chairman to be continued in office after a national convention. His slim figure, triangular face, and attractive smile were well known to the public. A precinct chairman at twenty-one, he had worked his way up as a political manager and, as a resourceful state chairman, held Indiana for the Republicans in 1916 —this resulted in his selection as national chairman. So seriously did he regard this new dignity that he went about his duties in a well-tailored cutaway coat. "Elder Hays" also broke with precedents by opening a session of the national committee with prayer.[1]

Harding was formally notified of his nomination on July 22. All who had been candidates for the nomination were invited to the ceremonies in Marion to sit on the platform as guests of honor. Senator Lodge's erudite notification speech was characterized by waspy references to the unworthy persons who, for an unfortunate period, had seized the reins of power. On the other hand, delivering a speech he had laboriously composed himself, Harding sincerely, almost diffidently, seemed to want the people to understand his limitations. He would not be his natural self if he did not "utter consciousness" of his limited ability, but he prayed that he might be as worthy in service as he knew himself to be faithful in purpose. His vast responsibilities made him humble, he said, but confidence in the support of all true Americans made him unafraid. The usually briskly efficient Hays furtively wiped away a tear. It was "an exalted and moving ceremony," reported Mark Sullivan, with "an atmosphere usually associated with churches."[2]

Early it was decided to wage a front porch campaign, which befitted both Harding's concepts of "seemliness," and the opinions of others regarding his mental ability. Such a campaign, Harding explained, conformed to the dignity of the presidency, "assured correct public version of deliberate statements," and would conserve his health. Remodeled a few years earlier, his porch was remarkably suitable, and the flagpole that had stood on McKinley's lawn was transferred to Harding's. Numerous delegations from all over the country made the pilgrimage to Marion. His first speech, on enterprise, class consciousness, and the excess profits tax, was disappointing, but succeeding speeches approached the issues.[3]

But requests for Harding appearances poured in from local leaders who felt that it would aid the campaign in their districts. Moreover, the expenses of pilgrimages to Marion were heavy, for the railroads were not as liberal with passes as in McKinley's day. And, finally, when Penrose raised objections to the porch campaign, Daugherty told him that Harding would make several speeches around the country.[4]

Harding's first venture from his front porch was a rail trip to the Minneapolis State Fair on August 8. His observation platform appearances, soothing, human, and sincere, were "as good as any campaigner's in recent years." Such success, said Republicans, led Harding to embark upon campaign tours; but Democrats charged that Cox's effectiveness had forced Harding off his porch. Before November, Harding had campaigned throughout the Middle West and Border States and had made speeches in New York, Pennsylvania, and Maryland.[5]

Coolidge, whom Hays called a "trade mark of Americanism," performed his duties as governor, pitched hay, and drove the buggy on his father's farm—for photographers. His major effort was an eight-day southern tour in October on a special train with Lowden and Governor Edwin P. Morrow of Kentucky. Pungent, concise, with a common-sense Yankee air, his speeches were full of epigrams—or platitudes. Not the type to hold an audience at a state fair, he was effective in smaller gatherings, and more of a success than expected as an observation platform speaker. A favorite theme of his was to call on his southern friends to help stem the rising tide of radicalism. On October 28 he led the "largest night parade in New York's history" up Fifth Avenue.[6]

Practically all leading Republicans joined in the campaign. William Howard Taft, Lieutenant Colonel Theodore Roosevelt, Jr., Hiram Johnson, William E. Borah, Charles Evans Hughes, and Herbert Hoover led a field of thousands. Only General Wood abstained. Under the supervision of the head of a Chicago advertising agency, massive publicity spread the Republican message by means of billboards, posters, newspapers, magazines, and motion pictures.[7]

Planning the campaign was, of course, a group project. Colonel George Harvey visited Marion for several days during the composition of Harding's league speech of August 28, and Coolidge said his advice was "very influential in directing the publicity." Will Hays and Harry Daugherty played more important roles. Despite fear that two such ambitious managers might clash, they worked well together, although Daugherty afterward felt that credit went too exclusively to Hays. Both participated in all of the crucial conferences on strategy.[8]

Harding sought the advice of diverse party leaders, but in almost every respect his campaign conformed to his own ideas and personality. He regarded himself as a harmonizer, and considered it his duty to seek a position which all factions of the party could support. Soliciting the opinions of the most various groups, he tried to find a basis of agreement among them. The resulting statements were not models of explicitness or clarity, but they were Harding's. Carefully avoiding personalities, he always referred respectfully to Cox or Roosevelt, invited Bryan to lunch, and described Wilson as "one of the most intellectual figures of a century and a half." He apologized for the arrest of a heckler and for misquoting Roosevelt. Altogether kindly, courteous, and seeking to confine the discussion to the issues, he created a favorable impression on the public and those who traveled with him.[9]

With the outcome of the battle scarcely in doubt, Republicans had to guard against overconfidence. Ohio, Indiana, Kentucky, West Virginia, Missouri, and New Jersey were given particular attention, and more money was spent in Ohio than in any other state. Moving even into the South, Republicans fought hard to elect John J. Parker and Alf Taylor as governors of North Carolina and Tennessee. Considerable effort, also, was made in Virginia.

From throughout the country came favorable reports on the condition of Republican organization. With almost perfect morale it was running with "the smooth power of a high class business organization," and handling even congressional campaigns with thoroughness and minuteness which "hardly any standard of efficiency could excel." The techniques for telephone conferences, moving-picture and phonograph appeals, and for swaying hyphenated Americans on foreign policy were perfected. Commercial travelers were enlisted for a "conversational campaign." Election schools, parades, and motor corps to carry voters to the polls were organized. Two thousand women speakers, and Girl Scout baby sitters were enlisted.[10]

In early 1919 the Republican national ways and means committee proposed a plan of "decentralized giving," which called for party organizations in each county, complete with teams, group leaders, etc., to conduct like the Red Cross a money-raising drive. Such a campaign naturally attracted more attention than did the old-fashioned solicitation of the wealthy and, although it was a move in the direction of intraparty democracy, it exposed the Republicans to charges of raising a "gigantic slush fund." Overambitious quota sheets fell into Democratic hands and were used with effect. Actually, the public campaign, embarrassed by congressional investigations, was less than a success. Contributions were supposedly limited to one thousand dollars, but wealthy Republicans were permitted to contribute a thousand dollars to both the national and congressional committees, and some larger gifts were accepted. The deficit at the end of the campaign was treated as a separate matter and was paid by big oilmen, as subsequent congressional investigations and trials were to reveal.[11]

Battle Lines of the Democracy

Soon after the convention, Cox and Roosevelt made a formal call on President Wilson, despite "clamorous representations" by those who thought the nomination of Cox meant "cutting loose from the White House." Moore was "much displeased," and even some of the administration Democrats wished the party could shed the handicap Wilson presented in their appeal to the foreign-born vote. But Cox felt that he should visit Wilson as a sign of loyalty; but in addition, the call was an unavoidable political necessity. For, although he had been given the nomination by Wilson's enemies, Cox could not hope to win the presidency without the hearty support of Wilson's friends, and had to do his best to conciliate those who felt defeated.[12]

The visit to the White House lasted for about an hour. "He is a very sick man," whispered Cox at the first sight of Wilson, whose weakness was so startling that Roosevelt noticed tears in Cox's eyes. "Mr. President, we are going to be a million per cent with you," Cox pledged. On leaving, Cox told the press: "What he promised I shall, if elected, endeavor with all my strength to keep." "The interview was in every respect most satisfactory and gratifying," said Wilson, and he and Cox were "absolutely at one with regard to the great issue of the League of Nations."[13]

National Chairman Homer Cummings was popular, worked tirelessly, had made a great keynote address; there was thus much sentiment for keeping him on as chairman. Cummings thought that he was favored by Roosevelt, Burleson, and at least 95 per cent of the national committee. When Wilson urged Cummings to accept, he told Cox that he would serve if he were asked. Cox welcomed the offer, but others felt that Cummings had been ambitious for the presidential nomination, had worked too closely with his administration friends in the convention, and that his retention would give the impression that Wilson was dominating the party. When Moore and Marsh threatened to resign from the national committee, Cox had to abandon the attempt to rename Cummings to the chair. Wilson was much depressed by the outcome.[14]

Normally, the post would have gone to Cox's campaign manager, Edmond H. Moore of Ohio. Moore, however, had fought Wilson for years in the national committee, was a pronounced wet, opposed making the league the issue of the campaign, and was, therefore, unacceptable to the administration majority. As a compromise the committee settled on George White of Ohio, the second in command of the Cox forces: he was not unfriendly to Wilson, supported the league, and was dry. Because it was required that the national chairman be a member of the committee, Moore surrendered his seat to White.[15]

Tall, rangy, and forty-eight years old, White looked, said Mark Sullivan, like "a professor of mathematics in a country college." He had taken courses under Wilson at Princeton, joined the Klondike gold rush, won a seat in Congress from an overwhelmingly Republican district, and made a million dollars in oil. His tolerance, amiability, and camaraderie were undergirded by a puritan conscience which brought him a telegram of appreciation from Harding for running a clean campaign. His experience in political management, however, was limited.[16]

Democratic notification ceremonies were held in Dayton, Ohio, on August 7. A parade, headed by Cox and Roosevelt on foot, formed downtown and marched to the fairgrounds where a crowd of an estimated 100,000 people assembled. For various reasons McAdoo, Palmer, and Bryan were unable to attend. Cox's acceptance speech was more in the tradition of old-fashioned politics than was Harding's; the latter's Marion *Daily Star* called the speech undignified, but to the *New York Times*, it was a refreshing contrast, "straightforward, explicit, bold and clear."[17]

Only a strenuous campaign, the Democratic candidates felt, could bring the country back to "a true sense of its responsibilities." The extent of his campaign would be limited only by his physical ability, Cox announced, and he would visit every state which was not Democratic beyond the slightest doubt. He spent August in the Middle West and in Pennsylvania, Connecticut, and New York. On September 2 he launched his western tour, "the most strenuous ever undertaken by a nominee for the Presidency," which covered over 11,000 miles and nearly every state west of the Mississippi. Returning, he spent October touring the Middle West, Kentucky, Tennessee, New England and the East as far south as Maryland, and concluded his campaign in Ohio.[18]

Cox was arrested for speeding, was in a railway accident, was hustled, crowded, heckled, and plagued by fatigue, hoarseness, and dyspepsia. He spoke as many as twenty-six times a day; one day began with a speech at daybreak and ended on the Boston Common at eleven P.M. Visiting thirty-six states, all of them except Maine, Vermont, and the deep South, he traveled 22,000 miles, gave 394 scheduled speeches and innumerable brief talks, and addressed perhaps 2,000,000 people. He concentrated on the Middle West, New York, Montana, California, and Washington.[19]

The athletic Roosevelt was almost as active. Opening his campaign in Chicago, he proceeded to Washington and Oregon, south through California, and back through the Mountain States and the Middle West. By September he was campaigning "all over New England and New York." Near the end of September he went west again to Colorado, and returned to conclude the campaign in New York. He traveled 18,000 miles and averaged ten speeches a day. Mrs. Roosevelt accompanied him most of the way, speaking to women's groups. Charles H. McCarthy was in charge of Roosevelt's New York headquarters, Steve Early preceded the campaigner on his route, telegraphing suggestions for remarks on local issues, while Louis Howe accompanied him.[20]

Other Democrats were not so active. Wilson confined himself to a few statements on the league. Sulking in his tent, Bryan took no part in the campaign. Offended by some implicit criticism of the red hunts by Cox, Palmer held aloof. McAdoo, on the other hand, made a three-week tour to the West Coast, contributed a thousand dollars, and urged his followers to do their best for Cox. Homer Cummings, Josephus Daniels, Al Smith, Joseph Robinson, Oscar Underwood, Thomas R. Marshall, Bourke Cockran, Bainbridge Colby, Rabbi Stephen S. Wise, and Newton D. Baker led the list of 3,500 speakers under the direction of the national committee. Most of them, however, began their efforts late in the campaign and were restricted by a shortage of funds.[21]

When National Chairman White arrived in New York on July 28 to take charge of the elaborate headquarters in the Grand Central Palace, he said it might be necessary to find additional space, for the campaign was to be conducted on a large scale. Assisting him were the able Senator Pat Harrison as chairman of the speaker's bureau, Wilbur W. Marsh as treasurer, and James W. Gerard as chairman of the finance committee. However, very little of a campaign developed. Roosevelt protested that he was "frankly disappointed at the slowness in getting the business organization going." To Mrs. Funk it appeared that the campaign might never start at all. Headquarters functioned neither efficiently nor enthusiastically, wrote McAdoo, and Shouse said that White was not the man for such a job.[22]

Growing alarmed, Cox wired Moore asking him to assume full charge. White, Harrison, and other leaders were summoned to a conference at Cox's Ohio home, but no change in management was made. White had done wonderful work, it was now reported, but was unable to put his plans into effect because of a "startling lack of money."[23]

The elaborate soliciting organization, built up to erase the deficit of 1916, and which utilized ten printing presses, had been disbanded in January, 1920. To re-establish it would take time and money, and other demands for funds were urgent. The campaign fund, therefore, was dependent on the willingness of the few wealthy Democrats, mostly Wilsonians, to make generous contributions at a time when Democratic prospects for victory were small and congressional investigations gave large contributions unfavorable publicity. So bad were Democratic finances about the middle of September, reported Sullivan, that some of the party managers favored closing the national headquarters and quitting.[24]

Against them were arrayed men of boundless wealth who knew how to get what they wanted from a reactionary administration, White desperately complained, while impoverished Democrats were fighting for the moral conscience of the nation. Boards of three or four Democrats were established in eight thousand cities and towns to "visit the brethren and acquaint them with our needs." When Wilson contributed five hundred dollars, White established a "match the President" fund. By October 24, Democrats had received $695,000—one fourth as much as the Republicans. For the entire campaign Democrats spent $2,237,770, while the Republicans spent $8,100,739.[25]

Throughout the country Democratic organization was in poor condition. Senator David I. Walsh of Massachusetts developed an inability to speak—because of reluctance, some thought, to talk to the Irish in a campaign based on the league. Homer Cummings, despite Cox's urging, refused to enter a hopeless contest in Connecticut for the Senate. Wilson and McAdoo elements in the West were reported to be holding aloof or working without enthusiasm. Democrats were entirely demoralized, Hays said, had given up the presidential election, and were merely trying to save senators.[26]

With the burden of the campaign falling substantially on Cox, his effectiveness became central. In many ways he was an excellent campaigner. Having great energy, resourcefulness, knowledge of politics, and readiness for a fight, he fulfilled the basic requirements. Although not a natural orator, he had gone through many campaigns and acquired proficiency. His platform personality may not have been easy and compelling, but it was effective, and at his best he could be genuinely moving. At his acceptance ceremony he was "wholly without self-consciousness—a man of straightforward directness." His was a "very winning personality," and had a "most happy way of handling a crowd," remarked a hostile Hearst paper.[27]

Reports on his success in winning votes varied. Ullman wrote that he was not making any headway; and David Lawrence reported that he drew big crowds, but did not make much of an impression, and that his western trip was a failure. Frequently there were no crowds to line his path. Others reported that he conveyed even to Republicans the impression that he was a bigger man than they had previously thought. Politicians sent each other confidential reports that he was making a splendid impression, making friends, and changing votes. Everyone felt that he was making a gallant personal fight.[28]

Cox's speeches were less restrained and dignified than Harding's. Most of them were not written out beforehand; material often was hurriedly prepared; and some of his statements were not well considered. Some thought that his discussion of national issues did not reach as high a level as Harding's. The predominant note of his first month of campaigning was not the league, but his charge of a Republican "corruption fund." When he shifted to the league, much of his discussion consisted of attacks on Harding for "wobbling." Taft wrote that he left an impression of "littleness," by speeches that had the tone of a ward candidate. The Chicago *Tribune* charged him with distorted quoting and reckless statements, and Coolidge accused him of "coarser and coarser methods, wilder and wilder charges." To the Washington *Star* he was "audacious, entertaining and clever at handling hecklers, but not presidential," and Mark Sullivan thought that he "practiced an aggressiveness which did not move the country but merely jarred it," and made it lean farther toward Harding.[29]

Toward the end of his campaign Cox threw increasing emphasis on the league and, in the last month, something of a crusade seemed to be developing. Never discouraged, he increased in fervor and strength until the very end. Some of his later meetings in Baltimore, Chicago, and Madison Square Garden, were genuinely moving. "It cannot be denied that Governor Cox has put into the campaign the best that is in him; and his best is very good," concluded the *New York Times*. Tumulty thought he had ably interpreted "the spirit of the things for which Woodrow Wilson fought and suffered." In McAdoo's opinion Cox proved effective and powerful, and John S. Bassett said his "brilliant campaign" made Democrats "hope for victory, where victory at first seemed impossible."[30]

The Scandal of "Slush Funds"

Cox's acceptance speech dealt mostly with the league and progressivism, the dominant issues of the campaign. In August, however, his charge that Republicans were raising an excessive fund to "buy the presidency" captured the headlines. Copies of quotas and other material relating to Hays's extensive fund raising fell into his hands. On the basis of this material he charged that a powerful combination of interests was raising $15,000,000 in an attempt to buy control of the government by arousing racial discontent, breeding unrest, and befogging the public mind. When the Kenyon Committee asked him to share his information, Cox replied he would soon produce convincing evidence of a conspiracy to buy the presidency.[31]

At Pittsburgh, on August 26, Cox charged that Republicans were raising a campaign fund "so stupendous as to exceed the realm of legitimate expense," and to carry "imminent danger of an odious and corrupt campaign." He read from a quota sheet assessing the larger cities over $8,000,000, and quoted a secret bulletin to the effect that many places had oversubscribed. This, he charged, was a "business plot" by those who wanted "the bayonet at the factory door, profiteering at the gates of the farm, the burden of government on shoulders other than their own, and the Federal Reserve System an annex to big business." As Cox produced his evidence, thousands went into a "frenzy of enthusiasm" in a demonstration that resembled the cheering at an athletic contest.[32]

Encouraged by the effect produced, Cox repeated and elaborated his charges in subsequent speeches. Accusing Hays of lying when he said contributions were limited to one thousand dollars, he cited a bulletin which advised that larger contributions be solicited secretly. The whole program was a "shady piece of business," he said, and he raised his estimate of the "corruption fund" to $30,000,000.[33]

Worriedly responding, Harding called Cox's charges "ridiculous and wholly without foundation." Treasurer Upham maintained that Cox was attacking a "roseate estimate," and that the real budget called for only a little over $3,000,000. Furthermore, Republicans charged, Democrats were guilty of receiving money from the British and assessing federal office holders in violation of the corrupt practices act.[34]

The Pittsburgh speech was "highly effective," said the *New York Times;* other reports said that it "put heart into an otherwise drooping campaign," forced the Republicans to the defensive, and challenged for a time the tremendous ground swell against the Democratic party. Incidentally, by engendering unfavorable publicity and forcing prominent men to testify before a congressional investigating committee, the attack handicapped Republican money raising.[35]

Nevertheless, the attack caused uneasiness among the Democrats. Involving Cox in a wrangle with Will Hays rather than a debate with Harding, accompanied by many variations of the epithet "liar," Cox's charges were regarded as "mudslinging"— and this hurt his chances among independents. Administration Democrats were distressed that Cox did not concentrate on the league. Why should anyone be disturbed, asked Boies Penrose, for everyone knew how high the cost of living was. The only real effect of such debate was to weary the country, concluded the friendly *New York Times*. After September, Cox seldom mentioned the fund charges and his emphasis shifted to other issues.[36]

Cox's campaign had not begun auspiciously. If he was to convince the people that he was of presidential stature, his method thus far had been mistaken. Emphasis on Republican corruption did nothing to bring administration Democrats to his support and less to loosen the purse strings of wealthy Democrats. The serene, kindly, modest, weightily dignified Harding had created a more favorable image.

Harding Beclouds the League Issue

Because the league had been the major subject of partisan controversy since 1919, it was necessary for Cox to defend and Harding to criticize it. The blurred issue between the parties, however, and the wide range of opinion within each party, gave each candidate considerable latitude in choosing his specific position. The considerable difficulty each experienced in doing so contributed to the confusion of the public. The primary need of each candidate was to preserve party unity which meant that each searched first for a position which all factions of his party could accept, and only secondarily debated the issue with his opponent.

When Harding welcomed a referendum on foreign relations, Cox's reply, "the things that the Senator believes vital and pertinent from his isolated perspective will not, in all probability, be so regarded by me," seemed to suggest some reluctance to run in Wilson's shoes. His faction of the party was anxious not to make the league the leading issue. "Considerable elasticity" was possible in interpreting the committment of the Cox-Wilson conference, George White told the press, and the paramount issue would be "progressivism"—by which he meant appeals to labor and the farmer. But Cox rebuked White and soon fully committed himself to the defense of the league.[37]

Many politicians in the Republican camp also wished to tone down discussion of the league, for the possibility that the controversy over the league might split the party seemed the only threat to victory. The main campaign effort, Hays announced, would be a repudiation of the administration's record of "maladministration," "extravagance," and "perverted purposes." People were more interested, insisted Penrose, in the high cost of living than in the league.[38]

In the Senate the final division was between the league with the Hitchcock reservations vs. the league with the Lodge reservations—and on this indistinct issue party lines were not clearly drawn. In convention the Democrats offered to accept reservations which did not impair the league's "essential integrity," while the Republicans declared for an "international association." Cox suggested additional reservations, while Harding voted for ratification with the Lodge reservations. Taft claimed that the "association of nations" was only another name for the league, but Johnson said the party stood "firmly against the President's covenant." Senator Reed, an "irreconcilable" opponent of the league, supported Cox. It might well have been hoped that the candidates would clarify the issue.[39]

Harding's acceptance speech praised Republican senators for saving America from "an obscure and unequal place in the merged government of the world," and welcomed a referendum on the "preservation of America's national freedom." On the other hand he "spoke unreservedly" of the "Republican committal for an association of nations, cooperating in sublime accord, to attain and preserve peace through justice rather than force." With most other newspapers, the *New York Times* declared that he had "unconditionally surrendered to Johnson and Borah. The Boston *Post* said that if he were elected we would not enter the league. But the proleague Republican New York *Tribune* maintained that his statements did not preclude ratification with reservations.[40]

In ensuing days Harding elaborated his attack. Article X would empower a council of foreign powers to summon American boys to war. America's war aim was not to end war, he said, but to defend American rights. No one could hold aloof from international affairs, but America could render its greatest service to the world by preserving its freedom of action.[41]

In his acceptance speech, Cox clearly espoused the league and condemned Harding's "association" proposal as either "madness" or "international bossism." The league, he maintained, could not override the Constitution, which reserved to Congress the right to declare war. Senator Harding proposed "in plain words that we remain out of it. . . . I favor going in." Opposing only reservations that disturbed the vital principle of the league, he said he would accept any reservations which would reassure the American people. The press agreed that Cox had committed himself fully to the league, and administration leaders were pleased.[42]

With Cox apparently intent on making the league the leading issue, proleague Republicans brought increasing pressure on Harding. When he saw an advance copy of Harding's acceptance speech, Taft tried to get him to recall and change it. Crane and Elihu Root also protested, and Clarence H. Kelsey concluded that Harding was a "platitudinous old fool." Harding would lose the West and make supporting him impossible, Hoover protested. Could one, who believed that the league offered the one practical opportunity to prevent war, support Harding with confidence that he would have the United States join, asked New York County Chairman Herbert Parsons. William Allen White, John Weeks, Dewey Hilles, and even Harry M. Daugherty joined in the pressure for a proleague statement.[43]

Attempting to appease this powerful proleague group without alienating the irreconcilables, Harding, with the aid of George Harvey, carefully prepared a major foreign policy address for August 28. He had voted for the league with reservations "most reluctantly and with grave misgivings," he said, but "the original League, mistakenly conceived and unreasonably insisted upon," had now "passed beyond the possibility of restoration." Cox was in favor of joining "on the basis announced by the President. . . . I am not."

Harding then elaborated his proposal for an "association." The issue, he said, was "the disparity between a world court of justice supplemented by a world association for conference, on the one hand, and the council of the League on the other." He preferred a "judicial tribunal to be governed by fixed and definable principles of law" to an "association of diplomats and politicians," sure to be influenced by "expediency and national selfishness." The Hague Tribunal consititued the "framework"; let teeth be put in it even if they must be taken from the defunct league. He would "combine all that is good and exorcise all that is bad in both organizations," and if the league were inextricably intertwined with the peace settlement, the league might be amended or revised. He promised earnest and practically undivided attention to this question from the day of his election.[44]

Harding now had the air of a man who was "getting on toward the League," said the *New York Times*. William Allen White was pleased; Hoover declared that the league principle was now favored by both parties; and Taft, soothed by further private assurances from Harding, entered the campaign. But still dissatisfied, A. Lawrence Lowell wrote that it was impossible to believe that Harding would either support or reject the league, and the League to Enforce Peace objected that the only practical course was to adopt the existing league with reservations.[45]

In ensuing speeches, Harding maintained the essence of his August 28 position, coupling denunciation of "Wilson's league" with promises of a new "association" for world co-operation. He saw in the league covenant a threat to the Monroe Doctrine, and said that meddling abroad would bring the United States into entangling alliances and would divide the country; but there was much good in the covenant and he wanted "those who believe in a new association of nations to feel that the cause is by no means flung aside." If the Senate had not rejected Article X, America would have been at war. Under Article X America could be plunged into war by an appointee of the president—the question was "the Constitution or the Covenant." The league was a "stupendous fraud"; and he preferred an association of nations to "give utterance to the conscience of the world" instead of an "internationality of force to suppress the freedom of the world." He was "frank to say" that he did not know "precisely what sort of association of nations" he would negotiate, but he did know that he favored an international court and a "new world relationship."[46]

After Harding's August 28 speech, disaffection among the irreconcilables became more dangerous. Proleague leaders such as Taft, Hughes, and Root might pout or circulate petitions, but they were party regulars, and not prone to wreck the campaign. Johnson and Borah, on the other hand, might well renew the disastrous schism in the party. Complaining that parts of Harding's speeches fell "like a wet blanket," Johnson remained out of the campaign. Borah returned his expense money on September 26, and instructed headquarters to make no more engagements for him because he might find it impossible to continue to speak for Harding.[47]

In this atmosphere of incipient party disruption, Harding composed his Des Moines speech of October 7. In his strongest denunciation of the "particular League proposed by Wilson," Harding asserted: "I do not want to clarify these obligations; I want to turn my back on them. It is not interpretation, but rejection, that I am seeking. . . . The issue, therefore, is clear. . . . In simple words it is that he favors going into the Paris League and I favor staying out." On the other hand, Harding renewed his promise to work to create an international association which would safeguard American rights and have the support of the people.[48]

This Des Moines address "definitely scrapped the League," the New York *Post* concluded, and even the proleague Republican New York *Tribune* headlined: "League Flatly Repudiated by Harding." To Borah, this "great speech" meant that Harding would refuse to enter "any League that impairs the sovereignty of the United States." Praising Harding's "forthright stand," Hiram Johnson wired headquarters that he would now begin campaigning. When distressed later by Harding's "whirling dervish performance," irreconcilables comforted themselves with Harding's statement that he sought not interpretation but rejection.[49]

The Des Moines speech, which brought the irreconcilables into the campaign, presented a new crisis to proleague Republicans. Some bolted the party. Herbert Parsons announced that he would vote for Cox because Cox was in favor of "going in" and Harding was not. Proleague Republicans were being deceived, he said, by promises of a new "association," for Harding's real policy was only what he would be squeezed into doing by opposing pressures. A statement by one hundred and twenty-one Republican bolters, signed by clergymen of all the principal denominations, as well as the presidents of Oberlin, Vassar, Smith, Bryn Mawr, and Mount Holyoke, maintained that it was too late to talk of a new association and urged all Republicans and progressives to vote for Cox. A similar position was assumed by the executive committee of the League to Enforce Peace, Hamilton Holt, economist Roger Babson, former ambassador to Belgium Theodore Marburg, and banker Thomas W. Lamont.[50]

Most proleague Republicans, however, refused to leave the party, and, instead, tried to capture control of the campaign in the hope of compelling Harding to abide by their interpretation of his position. William Howard Taft, the president of the League to Enforce Peace and, next to Wilson, the foremost American advocate of the league, had already made up his mind to support Harding regardless of the course of the debate. He agreed with the Democratic arguments for the league, he wrote, but there was a better chance of forcing Harding into accepting the league with the Lodge reservations than of securing agreement between Cox and the Senate on Article X. Therefore, why should he, who believed that it was of high importance to oust the Democrats from power, "vote for Cox on a mere abstraction"? Harding was sure to be elected anyway, Ullman advised Taft, so it was foolish to get into a wrangle with him. Herbert Hoover insisted that the "sincerity" and "integrity" of the party was pledged to an association of nations, and that those supporting the party in the contrary belief were counting on "infidelity." There was no difference between the parties on the league, wrote William Allen White, for though Harding was playing to the irreconcilables in a way that marked the low tide of American politics, they were not powerful and would be given short shrift after the election.[51]

The greatest proleague windfall for Harding was the "Declaration by Thirty-One Proleague Republicans" which declared that Republicans would take the United States into the league. The only issue, it said, was whether we should join under the exact provisions negotiated by Wilson or "under an agreement that omits or modifies some of those provisions." Among the signers of this declaration were Nicholas Murray Butler, Herbert Hoover, Charles Evans Hughes, A. Lawrence Lowell, Elihu Root, Henry L. Stimson, William Allen White, and Harlan Stone. According to Hays, this declaration was designed to "counteract" the interpretation of Harding's remarks on the league made by the irreconcilables.[52]

Root, Hughes, and Butler actively campaigned for Harding. When pressure was put on Taft to campaign for antileague senators, he was at first "a good deal troubled," but then cooperated even to the extent of supporting the irreconcilable Brandegee. A *New York Times* cartoon showed a bad boy Harding stamping on a hat labeled "The League," while indulgent father Taft said, "The little darling, he doesn't mean it."[53]

After Des Moines, Harding emphasized antileague arguments. Article X, the "most dangerous proposition ever presented to the American people," would pledge us to preserve despots and might require us to protect Japan from a "justfully" wrathful China. Creating a military alliance of five great powers which had gained from the peace conference, and proposing to "maintain this situation for all time to come," the league was "the biggest threat of continued warfare ever proposed to mankind." America owed an immeasurable debt to irreconcilable Senator Reed. Nineteen battle fronts aflame already showed that the league had failed.[54]

Harding kept talking of an "association of nations," however. "There is no issue drawn between the President's League and no league or association." The "Declaration by Thirty-One Pro-league Republicans" emphasized the growing approval of the construction that he had put on the platform. Democrats, he said, had attempted to deceive the people by making them believe that Republicans were against "entering into a fraternity of nations to prevent war and to cooperate for peace." The issue was simply whether we should enter a Paris league that contained Article X. He would do his best if elected to unite America behind an association of nations "which America might join with safety, honor, and good conscience."[55]

Indignant at Cox's charges that he was "wobbling," Harding offered a reward if anyone could prove "any inconsistency or change" in his position. He considered it constructive to refrain from dictation, he said, and to consult and harmonize America. Asked if he stood with Taft or Johnson, he replied that he had brought them closer together than they had ever been before.[56]

Supporting speakers adjusted themselves as best they could to the line set by Harding. Coolidge personally favored entering the league, but was restricted to pointing out that the platform had given its approbation to the senators who had voted for the league with reservations. The question, Coolidge maintained, was which party could best be trusted to carry out the league idea. Personally, he said, he favored adoption with reservations, a course which the platform and candidate's statements permitted. Lodge announced that he preferred Harding's "plan" to that of the league ratified with his own reservations. F. H. Gillette, Speaker of the House, said that only a Republican victory could save any part of the league. The instructions given out by the speakers' committee at headquarters were to refer to the league as "Mr. Wilson's league," and particularly to emphasize the obligations of Article X, and Britain's six votes.[57]

The impression that Harding conveyed to both factions of the party was that his ideas on the league were not clear, much less were they solidified, and that, therefore, he could be forced to accept their interpretation of the mandate given him by his election. The burden of his speeches was against the league, which he condemned as unconstitutional, world government, a ruthless alliance of great powers, and a breeder of war. On the other hand, in every speech he coupled this denunciation with advocacy of "international association," while admitting that he did not know "precisely what sort of association of nations" he would negotiate. Privately, he gave satisfactory assurances to both factions, and publicly welcomed support by both. That he succeeded in keeping such diametrically opposed groups campaigning together is no mean tribute to his special talents.

Cox, Wilson, and a League Crusade

During the first month of the campaign, Cox emphasized his campaign fund charges and his progressivism, but he also conducted a running debate with Harding on the league. The league, the "outstanding question," he said, meant the expansion of progressivism to world affairs. No president could order American soldiers overseas without the consent of Congress. He would accept reservations designed to "reassure Americans and define the limits beyond which the United States could not constitutionally go"; and would oppose only reservations which would "nullify and destroy" the country's participation in the league.[58]

When Harding, on August 28, propounded his new "association of nations," Cox hastened to answer. The proposal to substitute for the league the old Hague Tribunal, which had been "a distinct failure," indicated "bats in the belfry," Cox said. Did Harding oppose all moral obligations in international relations, and did not putting teeth into the Hague Tribunal mean just such obligations? Charging Harding with eight "wobbles," he said that men of all shades of opinion had come away endorsing Harding's position as stated in conference. "All of this would be laughable if it were not so tragic." In blocking the league, Republican "conspirators of hate," led by a "narrow-minded bigot," were guilty of "the greatest instance of partisan obstruction of human progress in all of human history." The causes of war, said Cox, were lust for territory, secret treaties, sudden ultimatums, and competitive armament—the league offered a remedy for all of them, substituting law for war.[59]

Harding's address of August 28, however, by narrowing the difference between the candidates, made a campaign on the league more difficult. This accentuated the pressures on Cox against campaigning on this issue. Cox, also, had a divided party. Antiadministration factions wanted to jettison as much of its record as possible, and some Democrats opposed the league on principle. Senator James E. Reed withdrew his support from Cox, and announced he would campaign only for antileague senators, while General Nelson A. Miles, and the former ambassador to France, William G. Sharp, bolted the party. Furthermore, even some proleague Democrats reported that the people were tired by the long deadlock, and were interested only in questions which affected them personally.[60]

Primary elections during the summer had demonstrated that the league was an uncertain attracter of votes. The proleague Breckenridge Long defeated James E. Reed for the Missouri Democratic nomination for senator; and the administration defeated antileague Joseph W. Bailey's bid for the Texas gubernatorial nomination. In Georgia, however, the antileague Thomas Watson swept the senatorial primary, and the Republican New Hampshire primary gave an antileague candidate a two-to-one victory.[61]

The Democrats were overwhelmingly defeated in Maine, where the presidential election was held early—on September 17. Democrats Franklin D. Roosevelt, Homer Cummings, Josephus Daniels, and Bainbridge Colby campaigned in the state, while the Republicans sent in Colonel Roosevelt, Calvin Coolidge, and Henry Cabot Lodge. The league was the main topic of debate, but the Republicans succeeded in making it appear that the issue was between "the" league and "a" league. Democratic leaders felt that if they could limit the Republican's majority in normally Republican Maine to 20,000, it would be a moral victory. The New York *Tribune* predicted a majority of 30,000. The actual Republican lead was 66,000 votes, which the party hailed as a harbinger of a national landslide. So discouraging were the results, wrote McAdoo privately, that he doubted that the Democrats could overcome their disadvantages.[62]

Wilson played only a minor role in the campaign. His health

did not permit him to make speeches, which, because they feared Republican charges that Wilson was running the campaign, some Democrats considered a blessing in disguise. Cox's managers, however, asked Wilson to issue a weekly address to the people. In reponse, the president, on October 3, proclaimed the election to be a genuine national referendum on the question of vindicating the national honor by joining the League of Nations. Those opposing the treaty, said Wilson, had invented an "Americanism" of their own which meant the defiant segregation of Prussianism; but America's founding fathers wanted her "to lead the world in the assertion of the rights of peoples and the rights of free nations . . ."[63]

This statement, however, did not prove to be the first of a series. Tumulty had urged Wilson not to call the election a referendum because conditions did not permit the proper presentation of proleague arguments. After the address, Cummings advised Wilson against any action which might lead to the charge that he had taken the campaign out of Cox's hands and had made himself responsible for the result.[64]

However, Wilson vigorously refuted a charge by Senator Spencer of Missouri that he had promised to send American troops overseas to defend the boundaries of European countries, and sternly rebuked Harding for implying that he had been asked by spokesmen of France to lead the way to a new "world fraternity." He also made at the White House a personal address to fifteen proleague Republicans whom he told that America had entered the war in order to ensure that imperialistic aggression would not recur, and that Article X was "the specific redemption of the pledge which the free governments of the world gave to their people when they entered the war." Maintaining that the people were a good jury where moral issues were concerned, Wilson seemed to be fully confident that Cox would win.[65]

Cox never toned down the league issue, but the tendencies of progressivism and corruption fund charges to eclipse the league were accentuated after Harding's August 28 address had narrowed the difference between the candidates. During his western tour in September, Cox did not appear to be staking his campaign on the league; consequently, he came under increasing pressure to give it more emphasis.

Thomas J. Walsh urged more effort to put the "moribund" league issue into the campaign, and a September 23 cabinet meeting agreed that Cox was mistaken in discussing other topics. Wilson was much distressed that the campaign was not conducted exclusively as a league crusade. If the Democrats would switch to the discussion of the league, they might yet "wrest victory from defeat," said the *New York Post*. When party leaders in Washington, including Cummings, Palmer, and Tumulty, urged that the league be emphasized to the exclusion of other issues, Cox's advisers in Dayton finally concurred. A great emotional campaign was being prepared amid rising popular interest, reported the Washington *Star*.[66]

Harding's statement at Des Moines on October 7 that he sought not "interpretation, but rejection," sharpened the issue and marked a turning point in the campaign. For the three weeks that remained before the election, the league received such increased emphasis from both sides that it became the overshadowing subject of debate. Cox turned to it almost exclusively. The isolationism of the Senate, he said, was a "gospel of selfishness," and an "offense to the decency of America." Harding's claim that Wilson insisted on the league without changes was a lie: "I suppose it is too much to ask that mediocrity pay to greatness the grateful tribute of truth." Did not Taft's articles favoring Article X and Harding's rejection of the league "in any form," join the two in a "deliberate deception"? he asked. His opponents were a "deceitful band of political freebooters." Harding "wobbled about" in the "aimless hope that this group or that group of voters can be pleased," in the "most pitiable spectacle in the political history of America."[67]

Cox grew ever more impassioned. In championing the league, he declared, he stood "for the creed of Christ and not the creed of Cain." Calling Coleman Du Pont the "Krupp of America," he said no man who was an enemy of America would vote Democratic. In Boston he called Lodge the "archconspirator of the ages," and a "buccaneering politician." Harding had "stupidly though deliberately attempted to deceive," and his claim to have consulted "spokesmen of France" was "so reprehensible as not to be excused as a stupid blunder." As Taft said, a new association was "unthinkable" and it was "this league" or "no league." "This subject of the League of Nations, frankly," Cox exclaimed, "has possessed my very soul."[68]

At Madison Square Garden on October 23, before a cheering

crowd of 12,000, Cox's campaign reached its climax. Reviewing his arguments, he said the league was not just Wilson's league but the product of the co-operative effort of many of the world's greatest thinkers. Against it was formed "the basest conspiracy in all of the history of the world." The league offered a remedy for the causes of war. It was not unconstitutional. It would not interfere with the right of self-determination. The revival of prosperity and reduction of armaments waited upon ratification. He offered to accept any "good" reservation, including a reservation that "the United States assumes no obligation to use its military or naval forces to defend or assist any other member of the League unless approved and authorized by Congress in each case."[69]

The public did not generally realize how far Cox had departed from Wilson's uncompromising position. Almost desperately, Cox tried to dispel the widespread impression that his election would only prolong the deadlock between the Senate and the chief executive. Repeatedly, he demanded that Elihu Root retract his charge that Cox was insisting on the league just as Wilson negotiated it. By the end of the campaign he was willing to eliminate from Article X that "obligation" which had been the main cause of dispute between Lodge and Wilson, and promised to accept whatever reservations were necessary to achieve ratification. But one observer said that no Republican newspaper had reported his statements that he would accept reservations.[70]

Cox closed his campaign at Chicago and Akron on a note of high idealism. "The true patriot," he said, "wants his country to be first in service, not first in selfishness." Reading the Parable of the Good Samaritan, he called the league an American idea for the salvaging of broken and bleeding Europe. The issue, he insisted was clear: "I am in favor of going into the League, Senator Harding is in favor of staying out. I am concerned about clarification, he is concerned about rejection. These are the outstanding words of the campaign." His campaign, he said, had been based on a great moral issue: "whether the civilization of the world shall tie itself together into a concerted purpose to prevent the tragedies of war." But he added, "Every traitor in America will vote tomorrow for Warren G. Harding."[71]

Roosevelt ably, somewhat more intellectually, seconded Cox on this "single paramount issue." The league, "not antinational but antiwar," at last placed within the reach of humanity "the method and machinery by which the opinion of civilization may become effective against those who seek war," and extended the operation of law to international relations. Democratic victory would be a mandate for ratification that the Senate could not ignore. Germany looked to the league for justice, Roosevelt warned, but if the United States did not join, the league would become merely an alliance for the preservation of the *status quo.* "Every sane man knows," said Roosevelt, "that in case of another world war America would be drawn in anyway, whether we were in the League or not."[72]

McAdoo, campaigning strenuously for the league, was greeted by enthusiastic audiences. Secretary of State Colby spoke widely, attacking isolation and defending Article X. Josephus Daniels charged that the Republican motto was "We stand at Armageddon and we straddle for the Lord." Vice-President Marshall said that Article X was the teeth Harding wanted in the Hague Tribunal, and government by statesmen was better than government by judges. There were greater risks in staying out of the league than in going in, said John W. Davis, because in the postwar world "age-long fears and hatreds have gone out of their slimy caverns to disturb the councils and the purposes of men." Organizing a "Cox and Roosevelt Independent League," Professor Irving Fisher of Yale toured the country in a special railroad car, accompanied by Herbert Parsons and Newton Baker.[73]

To the Democrats their league crusade of the last month of the campaign seemed to be a success. After Harding's Des Moines "rejection" speech, Democratic morale turned distinctly upward. Roosevelt wrote on October 11 that they were gaining every day and if the campaign had another month to run, success would be assured. Although the statement by "Thirty-One Proleague Republicans" brought a considerable chill to Democratic hopes, McAdoo found enthusiasm still strong, and Roosevelt thought the tide still continued toward the Democrats. Cox seemed to believe to the end that victory was possible.[74]

Progressivism

In their campaign the Democrats emphasized that complex of social, economic, and political issues known as progressivism, and did so second only to the league. At the beginning of the campaign McAdoo foresaw the greatest fight in American political history "between the forces of reaction and the forces of Democracy and progress." Progressivism was familiar ground for Cox and, after Harding's August 28 proleague speech, it appeared that he might give progressivism the heaviest emphasis. The Des Moines speech swung the debate back to the league, but progressivism remained a strong secondary theme.[75]

On economic matters Cox was scarcely radical. He advocated a budget system, and a reduction in armament spending. He proposed to replace the excess profits tax with a one per cent gross sales tax. Business, he said, was the foundation of civilization, and government should keep out of it except when supervision would be essential to the public welfare. However, he attacked profiteers, praised the leading progressive accomplishments of the Wilson administration, declared for the St. Lawrence Seaway, and implied that the question of governmental ownership of the railroads was still open. Calling farmers the foundation of the country, Cox endorsed scientific aid to agriculture, equalized agricultural profits, better rural schools, fewer middlemen, less tenant farming, more home ownership, more co-operatives, and promised to appoint a real "dirt" farmer as the secretary of agriculture. Cox favored collective bargaining for organized labor, and opposed child labor and abuse of the injunction. Continually he charged that big-businessmen were contributing huge sums to the Republicans in order to secure a government which would use the bayonet in labor disputes.[76]

Although rather weak in specific progressive proposals, Cox made much of the danger of reaction. Harding was the leader of the forces which sought to check progress, he said, and "normalcy" meant "the bayonet at the factory door, profiteering at the gates of the farm," and business' annexation of the Federal Reserve System. Did the people want "a change" to taxes that favored big business, high tariffs, reactionary politicians, banker control of the economy, and reactionary supreme court judges? Harding, in "bondage" to big business throughout his career, had voted for capital against labor on every issue, "for private greed against the public welfare," and his nomination was a "reactionary plot."[77]

The suppression of progress by reactionaries, he said, was the "manufacturing plant" of radicalism. The cure of radicalism was justice on the part of the government which would leave radical leaders without the power to arouse a following. Conditions in Russia were due less to the "crowd that is in control now" than to "the centuries of oppression that they have had," and Russia should be allowed to work out her own destiny, and then be admitted to the league. He advocated repeal of all laws that infringed upon free speech.[78]

Supporting Cox, Roosevelt maintained that education, rural communications, woman and child labor, working conditions, conservation, and increased government salaries were objects of Democratic concern. Higher tariffs, he said, would mean further concentration of wealth and a higher cost of living. The campaign was a "deepseated struggle between the progressively minded and the reactionists."[79]

A few Republican liberals were drawn into the Democratic camp. Harold Ickes, former Progressive national committeeman who had a considerable following in the Middle West, regarded Harding's nomination as "nothing short of a deliberate insult to every progressively minded man and woman" by a party that was "more deliberately and cold-bloodedly reactionary" than it was in 1912. Harding, he said, was a "platitudinous jellyfish" whose election would be "distinctly detrimental to the best interests of the country." Although opposed to the league, Ickes announced he would vote for Cox because of his "distinctly progressive record." A number of other leaders, including Matthew Hale and John M. Parker, joined in an appeal to former Progressives to back Cox.[80]

Most Republican progressives, however, stayed with their party. Johnson and Borah backed Harding because of their opposition to the league. Others felt that Cox was not sufficiently progressive to warrant a switch. Robert M. La Follette said that both conventions were controlled by special interests, and the election of either candidate meant a dictatorship of plutocracy. The great task of the moment was to rescue the country from "southern reactionaries," said Gifford Pinchot, and the only way to repudiate Wilson was to vote against Cox. Though Harding represented "all he had opposed for many years," proleague William Allen White felt that the nomination of Cox by wets, reactionaries, and the South served to sugar-coat the bitter pill. But, he was supporting Harding with all the enthusiasm of "an usher at his best girl's wedding." [81]

Of course, Harding sought to soften impact of his nomination and thus to appease the progressives with a broad, though vague, social and humanitarian program of his own. For farmers he advocated co-operatives and easier credit. Of labor he said he would try to reach an "understanding essential to industrial tranquility." It was not possible to give labor all it wanted, he said, but he endorsed collective bargaining and regulation of the employment of women and children, and opposed compulsory arbitration. Labor and capital, he maintained, were not in conflict. Thrift, economy, and the prevention of unreasonable profits would diminish the high cost of living. Expressing fear that he would be called an extremist, Harding declared for a federal department of public welfare, and said that the government should aid in solving the housing problem. Summing his program up at Buffalo, he said that he wanted "an America to continue where childhood had a right to happiness, motherhood to health, everyone to education, and all Americans the right to our equal opportunity," which would serve to the world as an "example of a government always responsive, always understanding, always humane." [82]

To businessmen Harding was of more specific comfort. He repeatedly denounced the excess profits tax (as a burden on the consumer), promised reduction of the income tax, and endorsed the protective tariff. Labor, he said, must not be permitted to dominate business or government; no one had a right to strike against the government; and only if the wage earner gave "full return for the wage received," could higher wages "abide." Advocating "more business in government and less government in business," he promised no more "pulling and hauling" of business by "weird economic and social theories." The government, he said, should be a partner of business and devote itself less to idealistic projects, and concentrate on such practical questions as securing foreign petroleum reserves and extending markets. He promised to develop the merchant marine, and to protect American businessmen abroad. Use, rather than storage, of natural resources must be emphasized, and private enterprise could do this job best. [83]

Before the menace of "the great Red conflagration" it was America's duty to "sober the world." Anyone, said Harding, who threatened the destruction of the government by force or who "flaunted his contempt for lawful authority" forfeited his right to the freedom of the Republic. The government had the right to "crush sedition" and "stifle a menacing contempt for law."[84]

Perhaps the most striking feature of the campaign was the degree to which the same progressive themes that had aroused such popular enthusiasm in 1912 and even in 1916, failed to evoke popular response in 1920. Progressives had gone back to the Republican party and progressivism was dormant, reported Sullivan. Cox's discussion of progressivism aroused as much hostility as support, wrote David Lawrence, for there was only one cry: "let's get back to normal whether we do it by a reactionary or anybody else." The progressive spirit was dormant and reactionaries were in control, said Bryan, and Hiram Johnson agreed: "Perhaps it is not unnatural that the war, and those things that go with war, have made more easy this control. Reaction is on. Whether the old spirit of progressivism can again be aroused, in either of the parties, during our generation, seems to me doubtful."[85]

WILSONISM

Wilson's popularity had sunk low by 1920. The press reported that the public mood was one of exasperated anti-Wilsonism, and it was "difficult to exaggerate the bitterness" against him. Steve Early wrote that bitter anti-Wilsonism was "evident everywhere and deeply rooted." As unpopular as he was once popular, wrote Franklin K. Lane, Wilson was bearing his party down to defeat.[86]

In the spring of 1920 most Republican county chairmen wanted to make the "autocracy" and extravagance" of the Wilson administration the leading issue. They would base their campaign on an appeal for party government, instead of personal government, announced Harding and Coolidge. Charging that Wilson would be the real force in a Cox administration, Harding called for the "restoration of constitutional government," and for "party government as distinguished from personal government, individual, dictatorial, autocratic, or what not." The quickest responses by his audiences, Harding said, came when he referred to "one-man government."[87]

The attempt to disassociate Cox from Wilson became a major concern of Democratic campaign management. Insisting on his independence, Cox said, if elected, he would be president in his own right, and denounced the Republican use of the term "Wilson's league." When, nevertheless, reports indicated the people believed that Wilson controlled him, Cox was exasperated into exclaiming: "Wilson isn't running for president this year. Cox is running for president."[88]

The "Liquor Issue"

The Eighteenth Amendment was ratified in January, 1919, and the Volstead Enforcement Act, outlawing the sale or consumption of beverages containing more than 0.5 per cent alcohol was passed over Wilson's veto in October, 1919. Though prohibition was much in the public consciousness, neither candidate sought to introduce it as an issue in the campaign. Harding was not an ideal champion for drys. He had voted for the Eighteenth Amendment and the Volstead Act, but had opposed the Antisaloon League and was known to be wet in his personal habits. However, liquor trade journals regarded him as dry in comparison with Cox. In his acceptance speech Harding had declared for law enforcement, and later said that he opposed re-establishment of traffic in intoxicating liquors.[89]

Cox maintained that prohibition was not an issue in the campaign and that he would enforce all laws, a position with which Senator Sheppard of Texas, author of the prohibition amendment, expressed satisfaction. Nevertheless, Cox was generally considered to be "wet." Northern bosses urged him to advocate liberalization of the Volstead Act, arguing that the South would vote Democratic anyway and he could thus win votes in the urban and alcohol-producing states. But the McAdoo wing of the party, which included most of the wealthy Democrats, was dry. When Cox proposed to advocate 2.75 per cent beer, McAdoo protested that such a course would ruin the campaign, and Baruch, Cleveland Dodge, Chadbourne, and Taggart telegraphed Cox urging him to declare that he would veto any attempt to change the Volstead Act. In the end Cox denied that his campaign was financed by wets and even compared Harding's record on prohibition unfavorably with his own. However, it was reported that Cox's reputation as a wet had dampened the enthusiasm of pro-league westerners, and had caused losses among the woman vote, which would nullify any gains he might make in the whiskey states.⁹⁰

THE WOMAN VOTE

By February, 1920, the Nineteenth Amendment had been ratified by thirty-one states, and efforts were redoubled to put the amendment into effect in time for women to vote in the election. The League of Women Voters' pressure on both parties became more effective as the prospect that women would get the vote improved. Harding urged a special session of the Vermont legislature; Cox called on Louisiana to ratify, and both urged ratification upon Tennessee, which state put the amendment into effect in August. Political observers speculated on the extent to which their supposed opposition to war would lead women to support the league, and how much wartime irritations would influence their vote. By all accounts they were more favorably impressed with Harding than with Cox; in addition Republican organizational efforts among women—as they were in all other phases of the campaign—were much more extensive than the Democratic.⁹¹

RACE

As usual, the Republican position on racial questions was more favorable to the Negro than their opponents'. In Oklahoma, Harding declared himself in favor of full rights for all citizens, although he said he did not mean that they must be made to enjoy these rights in each other's company. On the other hand, Cox, discussing oriental exclusion, said that God meant America to be a white man's country, and charged that Republicans were promising Negroes social equality which could not be delivered. When an Ohio Republican handbill featured a picture of Harding surrounded by six Negro candidates, Ohio Democrats countered with a circular entitled, "A Timely Warning to the White Men and White Women of Ohio," which posed for consideration the danger of Negro domination. Energetically organizing Negro voters, Republicans made considerable efforts to get Negro women registered in the border states, and capitalized on the increased voting potential brought by the wartime influx of Negroes to the North.⁹²

Rumors that Harding had Negro blood had been loudly whispered everytime he had run for office. Shortly after his nomination, Harding telephoned Robert Scripps of the Scripps-Howard newspaper chain and secured his promise not to print these charges. But, about mid-October, reports of a new whispering campaign against Harding began to appear. A genealogy compiled by Professor William Estabrook Chancellor, supported by affidavits from early neighbors of the Hardings, became the basis for cheaply printed circulars, one of which asserted that Harding was not a white man and prayed, "May God save America from international shame and from domestic ruin." Two hundred and fifty thousand of these circulars were discovered in the mails in California; and distribution of them on Chicago suburban trains produced a small riot. Wilson and Cox rejected their use, and White denied that they were distributed from Cox's campaign train. Somewhat less than tactfully the Republicans denounced this campaign as "detestable propaganda and malicious lies."[93]

This whispering campaign put newspapers in a quandary. Some suppressed the story, while others reported the whispering campaign without revealing its content. But New York newspapers reported that "everybody" was talking about the rumors. Ohio papers printed pictures of Harding's parents and genealogies tracing his ancestry to colonial times, which Harding resented because, while these efforts were designed to save votes, they also kept the story alive.[94]

Hyphenated Americans

Of America's 105,700,000 population, 14,000,000 were foreign born. Congregated mostly in the larger northern cities, their votes were vital to Democratic victory. Nearly all were disgruntled in 1920. Irish-Americans were angry because Wilson had not fought for Irish independence; furthermore, they feared that Britain's six votes in the league and Article X's guarantees of territorial integrity might be used to suppress Irish revolts.

Insisting that the league would not discourage the kind of emotions that had stirred America to fight for independence, Cox asserted that he favored self-determination in Ireland just as he did everywhere else. He would bring the Irish question before the league as soon as he was elected, he promised, and when Ireland had secured its independence the league would be obligated to defend it. The league, said the White House, provided a forum for the settlement of such problems.[95]

To his credit, Harding eschewed demagoguery on this question. He felt "very sympathetic" toward the Irish independence movement, he said, but Americans must limit themselves to private expressions of sympathy, because governmental action would constitute undue interference in the domestic affairs of the British Empire. He would no more tell England what to do in Ireland, he said, than he would allow England to tell America what to do in the Philippines.[96]

Despite this rather cold comfort, the Irish seemed irretrievably alienated from the Democrats. George White found them "offish," and Pat Harrison could not get Irish leaders to speak for the ticket. Instead of conciliating them, Cox's promise to submit Irish independence to the league, in which Britain had six votes, alienated them further. Unless the Irish could be won back, said Moore, the election was lost.[97]

German-Americans, also, were bitterly opposed to the Democrats. Many had voted for Wilson in 1916 because of his slogan, "He Kept Us Out of War," and subsequently felt betrayed. They resented Wilson's equation of "Prussianism" with evil. Hopes for a just peace raised by the Fourteen Points were bitterly disappointed by Versailles, and as an instrument for perpetuating the terms of that treaty, the league held no charm for them. Furthermore, fulminating against Germans, Governor Cox had outlawed the teaching of the German language in Ohio schools. Now, regarding the German-American vote as hopelessly lost, Cox charged that pro-German enemies of America supported the Republicans, and called George Sylvester Viereck the "junker of America."[98]

Harding's position was more acceptable to German-Americans. His insistence that America fought for its rights rather than to save civilization from Germany was less insulting. Implying that German "greatness" was spoiled only by "one-man government," Harding called for immediate peace and no meddling abroad.[99]

The Germans, said Viereck, were not so much for Harding as they were against Wilson and, since Cox supported Wilson's policies, the Germans were determined to defeat him. Representatives from twenty-two states formed a German-American

Citizen's League which Viereck said would influence five or six million people to vote for Harding. Traditionally Democratic Bismark, Nebraska, would exactly reverse its previous vote and would poll 100 to 2 in favor of the Republicans.[100]

Italian-Americans were almost as disaffected with the Democrats as were the others because of Wilson's stand against Italian expansion on the Adriatic. Italian-Americans had voted for Wilson in 1916, said the editor of Chicago's *L'Italia,* but they would now vote Republican because Wilson was an implacable enemy of Italy. A "National Italian-American Republican League" claimed a membership of 500,000.[101]

Labor

Samuel Gompers, the president of the American Federation of Labor, abandoning his nonpartisan policy, fully endorsed the Democrats. The elements of reaction, he said, had never been so "brutal and bigoted"; opponents of the league were traitors to the Republic; and the issue of the election was between reaction and evolution. Penrose thought that labor was more active for Cox than ever before, and Sullivan predicted they would deliver more union votes for him than for any previous candidate.[102]

However, in its last two years the Wilson administration had alienated much of labor. Presidents of the longshoremen's association and the carpenters' union declared for Harding, and a statement by thirty-nine labor leaders denounced Wilson and praised Harding's labor relations. Labor in the West, reported Lawrence, felt that Burleson's suppression of radical publications and Palmer's "red raids" must be punished even if that meant putting in another set of reactionaries.[103]

The Press

Democrats were much exercised by what they considered unfair treatment by the press throughout the campaign. Their extensive speaking tours were necessary, said Roosevelt, because most of the newspapers were Republican. "They decline to have the case tried before the jury," said Cox, charging that nine-tenths of the California papers were not printing the news of the campaign, that local papers were following Hays's instructions to slant the news against him, and that in some western states not a single newspaper of any size was presenting his point of view. Western newspapers were giving Cox little space, and that in an obviously unfriendly spirit, observed the *New York Post*. No Republican newspaper had reported Cox's statements that he would accept reservations to the league, said one observer, and Tumulty told Wilson that less than ten per cent of the newspapers were presenting the case for the league.[104]

THE RECESSION

However hotly political debates may be waged, they probably never penetrate the awareness of the common man as much as does the state of his economic well-being. In 1920 the common man was much vexed by the high cost of living. The war had brought prosperity, raising average individual income (in 1913 dollars) from $356 in 1914 to a high of $413 in 1917, and, with exports remaining high, the business boom continued after the war until the middle of 1920. However, inflation, more than nullifying the rise in monetary income, sharply reduced real individual income to $354 in 1920, which was lower than before the war. Public opinion took the higher dollar income for granted and focused its resentment on the higher prices. Buyers' strikes, blue denim parades, and demands for action against "profiteers" were high lights of the popular protest, and many, of course, attributed the distressing economic conditions to some kind of governmental bungling.[105]

Then, the postwar boom suddenly subsided in June, 1920, while the national conventions were meeting, and industries suddenly cut production back and laid workers off. By November some steel plants in Pennsylvania and Ohio were operating at 50 per cent of their capacities, the American Woolen Company was running its mills only four days a week, and the building trades were almost completely inactive. Prices fell rapidly. Particularly hard hit were the farmers, whose income dropped more rapidly than their costs. Unemployment figures jumped to nearly four million and, by the date of the election, economic distress was widespread.[106]

Angry administration officials suspected that big business was attempting to injure the Democrats and affect the coming election, and many Democrats believed that this sudden drop in business activity during the campaign was a political conspiracy. Everywhere the Republican high tariff program acquired friends. Mounting unemployment increased labor's discontent, and weakened the unions, while the recession alienated farmers in the West from the Democrats.[107]

The Demand for Change

The popular dissatisfactions, disapprovals, exasperations, and disappointments, the opposition of nationalists, drys, anti-southerners, liberals, reactionaries, hyphenated Americans, Wilson-haters, and business interests to the Democrats all added up to a vast determination to have a change. The Democrats were as depressed as the Republicans were filled with confidence by the great popular discontent with the Wilson administration—it was obvious, inescapable, and apparently immutable. Cox made his speeches against an oncoming tidal wave.

Politicians usually say the things they do for effect, but occasionally they may speak professionally as craftsmen in their field. The election would turn on the "desire for a change," said Coolidge, for the country sought relief from agitation and visionary ideals. The underlying desire for a change of administration would decide the election, said Daugherty. Such a desire was sufficient to bring victory regardless of other issues, said Penrose. The people were restless and susceptible to any influence promising a change, said W. L. Hill, they were ready to "swap horses," hoping for "reforms of some kind," but not caring much one way or the other.[108]

Political reporters agreed that the demand for change was decisive. People were so irritated over the "whole after-the-war mess," said Lawrence, they said "matters can't be any worse . . . and perhaps they will get better. That's about as far as the big mass of the voters have gone in analyzing the issues." Three hundred managing editors found no one issue working on the public mind except "that crystallized in the form of a demand for change of the control of the federal government." "According to all observers," deplored the *New York Times,* "dissatisfaction with the Wilson administration and desire for a change of party control at Washington," would prove the decisive factor.[109]

That Harding fully sensed this popular feeling was proved by his famous phrases: "What America needs is not heroics but healing, not surgery but serenity, not nostrums but normalcy." The world needed, he said, to steady down "once more to regularity." It was time for a change.[110]

Desperately Cox said that he knew that people were restive and inconvenienced, but asked them to stop and think what reactionary policies would mean. "Republicans, when they were honest, have acknowledged what is patent to everyone, that no one really wants Senator Harding for President," said Cox, "and yet they tell me that as partisans many expected to vote for him because they had been taught to believe that they 'wanted a change.'" But his attempts to paint the horrors of prospective Republican rule, and his attempts to inject stirring issues into the campaign, did not succeed in shaking the popular determination which had been long building. To many the popular attitude seemed to be one of apathy, but this might have meant that minds were already made up and that further discussion was useless.[111]

PREDICTIONS

Republican forecasts of victory were not only more sweeping than usual, but carried an air of conviction. By October Hays, predicting a landslide similar to Roosevelt's in 1904, was claiming every state outside of the South for the Republican column, and calling even Kentucky, Tennessee, and North Carolina doubtful. He had never seen such conditions, Coolidge wrote privately, the prospects were for "something more than a landslide." "If it were a prize fight the police would interfere on the ground of brutality," said Hiram Johnson. "Never within my recollection of politics has a Republican victory been so assured," said Taft. On election eve Hays claimed 368 "sure" electoral votes and said Harding's total might be more than 400.[112]

To political correspondents the situation appeared to be as the Republicans described it. Democrats were "justly apprehensive," the *New York Times* admitted. David Lawrence, the New York *Tribune,* and the Chicago *Tribune* all predicted a Harding landslide. Cox was going to fail to a degree "almost unique in recent elections," wrote Mark Sullivan. Well might Harding "await

THE CAMPAIGN   159

the results with complacency" after receiving such "delightful reports."[113]

Democratic contradiction of these predictions was weak. Cox seemed to have hypnotized himself into believing to the end that he had a chance, and Wilson was stubbornly confident that Cox would receive his mandate, but to Democrats like Houston, Tumulty, and Roosevelt defeat seemed certain. Burleson was confident in mid-campaign, but later predicted the worst defeat in years.[114]

The giant Rexall Drug Store poll gave Harding 684,701 votes to Cox's 456,351, with 382 electoral votes to 149. Betting odds, which stood at two to one for Harding in July, steadily climbed. By mid-October they were up to seven to one, the highest odds on a presidential election on record; and by November they had risen to ten to one.[115]

THE RETURNS

Although the one-sidedness of the contest was obvious, the magnitude of Republican victory exceeded all expectations. Harding received 16,181,289 votes to Cox's 8,141,750, giving him 404 electoral votes to 127. Only eleven states went into the Democratic column, and of these only Kentucky was outside of the South. Harding captured Tennessee, breaking the "Solid South" for the first time since Reconstruction. Boston went Republican for the second time in its history, and New York gave the Republicans an unheard of plurality of over a million and swept even the popular Al Smith out of office.

Achieving the largest shift of votes from one party to another between presidential elections since the Civil War, Harding won the largest popular majority, 60 per cent, in recent American history. The Republicans carried the House of Representatives by 303 to 131 seats, a majority of 172 that was the largest in the party's history. They also retained every seat they held in the Senate, gained 10 at the expense of the Democrats, achieving a majority of 22.

The shift of the progressives and the hyphenated Americans to the Republicans was particularly striking. The states which had given Wilson the largest increase in votes in 1916 over 1912, now shifted the largest percentage of votes back to the Republicans, which seemed to indicate that the Republican progressives who had voted for Wilson in 1916 had returned to the Republican fold. Equally striking was the correlation between Republican gains and the percentage of German-Americans, Austrian-Americans, Irish-Americans and Italian-Americans in that state.

Contrary to the popular impression, woman suffrage did not seem to aid Harding significantly. In the states where adoption of the Nineteenth Amendment greatly increased the vote, Republican gains were less than the national average. It is also difficult to find evidence that prohibition figured prominently in the result.[116]

INTERPRETATIONS

In post-mortems, the extent to which the election had been Wilson's "solemn referendum" received the most consideration. It was "the triumph of nationalism and the death of the League," said Borah. Hearst's New York *American,* the New York *Herald,* the Chicago *Tribune,* the Washington *Star,* the *Kansas City* (Mo.) *Star,* and the *New Yorker Staats-Zeitung* agreed that repudiation of the league had been "unmistakable," "complete," and "overwhelming."

But the Republican Washington *Herald* insisted that the returns showed that "an overwhelming majority" favored participation in international organization. Millions supported Harding in the belief, said the *Cleveland Plain Dealer,* that he would keep his pledge for an association of nations. To the New York *Tribune,* the "prospects of entering some kind of league" were "greatly improved." Other newspapers thought that only Wilson's league, not the idea of international organization, had been rejected.[117]

That the vote was really a repudiation of "Wilsonism," chiefly the domestic record of his administration, received general agreement. "The colossal protest was against Woodrow Wilson and everything that from every conceivable angle might be attached to his name," said the *New York Post.* "The country was weary of Wilsonism in all its manifestations," said the New York *Tribune.* The voters visited upon the Democrats "stored up resentment for anything and everything they have found to complain of in the last eight years," regretted the New York *World.*[118]

Politicians agreed. It was not a verdict against the league,

McAdoo told Wilson, but the people "simply determined on a change because of the prevailing discontent." "The war and its aftermath had brought so many resentments that there was no chance for victory," said Cox. Taft attributed the result to "the impatience and tired feeling among the people at the arbitrary nature of Mr. Wilson's rule." William Jennings Bryan blamed Wilson's dictatorial attitude toward the Senate. Roosevelt attributed it to "a kind of tidal flow of discontent and destructive criticism," as a result of the war. The basic factor, Hays thought, was that the people were determined to have a change.[119]

The "great and solemn referendum" had failed. The idea that a presidential election could be conducted as a national referendum on a single foreign policy issue had proven to be alien to American politics. The league was merely the chief argument used by Democrats in an attempt to shake the voters from the determination at which they had already arrived on other grounds. Business and industrial interests, hostile to prewar tendencies toward socialism and terrified by the specter of Bolshevism, wrenched frantically toward conservative government. Hyphenated Americans were determined to punish the Democrats, no matter what other issue might be involved. They found allies in a silent army of voters that had been convinced by the Republican press that the dislocations incident to war were produced by Democratic incompetence. Furthermore, Harding had whittled the league issue so fine that many were unable to see any real difference between the two parties. Harding had held the irreconcilables in his camp and had also won the support of proleague leaders who insisted that the country's chances of entering the league would be better with a Republican victory. This torpedoed any possibility of a referendum.

The Defeat of Progressivism

The most striking feature of the campaign of 1920 was the absence of the progressivism that had characterized the elections of 1912 and 1916. It is difficult to find evidence of continuation of the powerful prewar Progressive Movement. On all sides it was evident that the political climate had changed. To men like William Allen White, Newton D. Baker, William Jennings Bryan, and William E. Borah, the campaign and the election signified the exhaustion of the progressive impulse and a consequent movement into reaction. They were to see their interpretations justified with the adoption of governmental policies during the next decade which seemed designed to facilitate, instead of preventing the exploitation of the common man.[120]

The Progressive Movement which had been dominant before the war was most complex. Farmers were protesting against a government dominated by business, and labor was fighting to achieve a larger share of the national product. They were joined by the "new liberals" of the middle class who had abandoned the *laissez faire* idea, and were seeking to use the government to curb the "robber barons" and to remedy the social injustice that they regarded as the "cause of the rise of radicalism." Within progressivism, also, were contained the strains of older ideologies —rationalism, democracy, humanitarianism, and the social gospel —which attracted intellectuals and idealists regardless of class membership, and gave *élan* and spirit to its ranks. Many observers attributed to progressivism a considerable measure of altruism.[121] The cumulative energy of such forces was to overcome both personal rivalries and bitter schisms to achieve victory after victory for progressivism.

Although some aspects of progressivism were to carry on through the war, countertrends developed soon after America's entry into the hostilities. As war's necessities began changing the character of public policy, progressivism lost its force. Shocked liberal observers wrote that they saw the pulpit degenerate into a timeserver, obsequious to the state, the schools turned into propaganda centers, the Espionage Act used against social agitators, free speech and assembly denied, mob violence condoned, and the military develop the reckless ruthlessness of the Prussians. No war in history, wrote Harold Stearns, had seen more degradation of public life and public men. It was "the most noxious complex of all the evils that afflict man," said Randolph Bourne.[122]

As the hatred engendered by casualties and war propaganda grew, idealistic peace aims became increasingly unpopular, and a demand arose for "unconditional surrender." The Versailles Treaty was harsh, but the campaign against it in America was waged primarily on the grounds that it was too "soft," and committed America too heavily to internationalism.

Some liberals had feared that American entry into the war would undermine progressivism. "The war will degrade us . . .

make sheer brutes out of us," predicted Franklin K. Lane. Robert M. La Follette and Jane Addams feared that it would "set progress back a generation." In April, 1917, Wilson told Frank Cobb that the war would brutalize America:

We couldn't fight Germany and maintain the ideals of government that all thinking men share. I shall try it but it will be too much for us. Once lead this people into war and they'll forget there ever was such a thing as tolerance. To fight you must be brutal . . . and the spirit of ruthless brutality will enter into the very fiber of our national life, infecting Congress, the courts, the policeman on the beat, the man in the street.[123]

Wilson's wartime suppression of dissident opinion, the conquest of Haiti, and steady veering to the right was shocking to liberals. After the war, sponsorship of the red hunt, antilabor injunctions, censorship, and militarism gave his administration an atmosphere far different from the "New Freedom" of 1912-1917. Other men who had fought progressivism's battles before the war were now also errant or scattered. In Theodore Roosevelt's complex character the militaristic patriot had subordinated the progressive, and the political realist the liberal; he turned from the hosts of Armageddon to consort with conservatives and machine politicians like John King. The center of gravity in both parties shifted to the right as the old guard consolidated its supremacy over chastened Republican progressives, and Democrats turned from Wilson and Bryan to big city bosses for leadership. Bryan and La Follette found the postwar populace so out of sympathy with them that they were unable to get into a position from which to fight. Some progressives met to plan a progressive program, but so futile were their discussions that Harold Ickes, discouraged by the "wave of deep reaction," ceased to call the meetings together. Most Republican progressives, like the tired proleague William Allen White, fell in behind Harding.[124]

The postwar years furnished many contrasts to prewar progressivism. In addition to political reaction, the historian of the period must write of excessive nationalism, "red hunts," racial violence, a crime wave, cynicism, and materialism—all in all a general moral and cultural relapse.

The idea that force was the most effective means of resolving difficulties seemed to have gained general acceptance as indexes of violence climbed.

The 1919 strikes were characterized by ruthless violence on both sides. Branding the Seattle general strike a "rebellion," Mayor Hanson announced that any man who attempted to take over municipal functions would be shot on sight. Wilson warned labor that "there must be no threats," and ordered federal troops under General Wood to police the steel strike area.

Social tensions found violent expression. The homes of the governor of California and Attorney General Palmer were blasted, and thirty-six bombs were mailed to prominent opponents of labor or radicalism. Censorship of the press and mails continued into the postwar period, an I.W.W. sympathizer was lynched, armed clashes occurred, and 249 radical aliens were shipped in the direction of Russia. Twenty-eight states outlawed the display of a red flag. Arresting suspects wholesale, Attorney General Palmer used *agents provocateurs,* and sanctioned the torturing of suspects to extort confessions—all this amid newspaper rejoicing.[125]

The New York legislature passed the Lusk Laws barring the members of all "subversive" organizations from the ballot, which the New York *World* called the "most revolutionary blow ever dealt to representative government in the United States." Socialist Victor Berger was refused admittance to Congress when elected. Colleges as well as public schools discharged teachers who criticized the war or who were tinged with socialism, and many states required loyalty oaths of teachers.[126]

The revived Ku Klux Klan was antiforeign, anti-Semitic, anti-Catholic, and anti-Negro. It spread into North and West, dominating several state governments. Lynchings rose to 83 in 1919, as compared with 52 in 1913 and 1914. Twenty-six race riots occurred in 1919, including one in Chicago which left thirty-eight dead. Life insurance companies announced a new riot and civil commotion policy. Anti-Semitism surged, and antiorientalism won the total exclusion of the Japanese.[127]

A rising crime rate reached the proportions of a crime wave. Major offenses, particularly frauds and embezzlements, rose 70 per cent between 1913 and 1924, while homicides increased 240 per cent. Juvenile delinquency rose, and school attendance declined. Harshness in the punishment of criminals, which had gradually decreased before 1915, rose as both courts and legislatures prescribed more rigorous penalties. Widespread governmental corruption was dramatized by such scandals as Teapot Dome.[128]

Morals, as defined in the prewar code, were lower in the postwar period. As it was presented in popular periodicals, the general consensus seemed more favorable to sexual freedom. The divorce rate jumped from .9 in 1913 to 1.6 in 1920. In literature the old moral standards were defied in a "new cult of sex freedom and indulgence."[129]

Interest in reform had sharply declined. Discussion in periodicals of "movements to correct economic and social abuses and injustices" fell 45 per cent below the prewar level. In religion the revival of fundamentalism meant a turning from the social gospel to a preoccupation with personal salvation as opposed to social reform. The amount of money spent on foreign missions dropped markedly.[130]

Intellectually the postwar period was characterized by bitter cynicism. Henry L. Mencken, in the *American Mercury,* ridiculed ideals and the democratic faith in the ability of the common man to govern himself. His generation of writers, said Malcolm Cowley, believed that "patriotism, decency, and paternal sympathy" were "masks behind which existed cheap and nasty emotions." "To be a modern man and to have learned the lesson of war and peace meant you reduced everything to the meanest motives and applied to every human emotion the ugliest possible name." Realism before the war had been an agent of social protest, but after the war there was a note of hopelessness—society was not just criticized but ridiculed and rejected, and the intellectuals deserted the cause of reform.[131]

Creativity in science and industry also suffered. Research in the pure sciences decreased, and the number of patents issued declined. The publication of books dropped sharply to the lowest point in fifteen years in 1921 and did not recover until after 1929.[132]

Obviously, with the war had arisen a spirit antithetical to the progressive humanitarianism of the prewar years. Among writings on the postwar period one encounters such phrases as "spiritually and intellectually abnormal," "ancient moral concepts shattered," "slump in idealism," "far swing of the pendulum to reaction," "barometer of idealism visibly falling," "tired of issues, sick at heart of ideals, and weary of being noble." A war won in the name of ideals had set in motion forces which undermined progressivism.

Most writers on the post-World War I period make some attempt to interpret the causes of the reaction. Some point to surface events such as the death or defection of prominent leaders, or divisions within progressive ranks. Some say the war had overtaxed America's emotions and brought a desire to relax—to get back to "normalcy." Others emphasize the disillusionment the great gap between promise and accomplishment produced.

Many contemporaries, however, felt that the plight of progressivism was a result of the war. "War and those things that go with war" had extinguished the spirit of progressivism, said Hiram Johnson. It had left the world in "a state of disorganization and demoralization," wrote Ray Stannard Baker, "never did the crust of civilization seem so thin." "War, the Devil's answer to human progress," wrote William Allen White, had left the world "morally and spiritually . . . shell shocked," with "pessimism rampant, faith quiescent, murder met with indifference, the lower standard of civilization faced with universal complaisance."[133]

Analyzing progressivism's failure, Lincoln Steffens said that liberals made both the war and the peace, and if liberalism was fading out it was because of defects in the ideas of the liberals themselves. "Our ideal was clear and steadfast," said Samuel Gompers, "but our knowledge of the technology of accomplishing our purpose was inadequate." The "technique of liberal failure," said John Chamberlain, was progressivism's unwillingness "to continue analysis [of the war] once the process of analysis became uncomfortable. ". . . It took its eyes from the heritage of all past wars of history, and looked weakly to the New Jerusalem in the clouds. This war, liberalism said, would be different. And so it idealized the drift of events calling the drift decision. With what results, we know." According to Richard Hofstadter, war, always "the nemesis of the liberal tradition in America," "put an end to the Progressive movement," destroying "the popular impulse that had sustained Progressive politics for well over a decade before 1914."[134]

Of course, the postwar period was not one of unrelieved retrogression. By stimulating the economy, the war raised income of governmental units and made possible larger appropriations for social services which more than compensated for the decline in charitable contributions. Rising incomes also enabled a growing number of middle-class families to send their children to college. The reaction against the old order was not so severe in America as in Europe; and America was spared the tumult, nationalistic excesses, and Caesarism that afflicted Russia, Italy, and Germany.

Furthermore, the reaction was only temporary, and five to ten years after the end of the war signs of restoration appeared. Lynchings subsided to the prewar rate by 1923. The crime wave abated, and humane treatment of criminals increased after 1925. Popular literature became more conservative regarding sex, and more laudatory of family life. The number of newly issued patents returned to prewar levels by 1924, and the publication of books rose gradually. The Ku Klux Klan and the red scare passed their peak of influence, indignation at governmental corruption found its expression, and a progressive minority in Congress passed from defense to offense. In most areas the scars of war were healing by 1926 and society showed substantial restoration by 1928.[135]

As students of society have long recognized, whatever affects the principles of a society, its customs, mores, or ethics, affects the society far more fundamentally than mere material destruction or superficial institutional change. Periods of peace reinforce mores which make for greater co-operation, and create attitudes that promote social welfare. World war required the inculcation of principles contradictory to such philosophic underpinnings of progressivism as humanitarianism, the social gospel, faith in the generality of man, respect for the individual, and democracy itself. Inevitably this affected society in ways which could not be immediately reversed at the signing of the armistice.

The election of 1920 did not halt the Progressive Movement; nor does calling it progressivism's graveyard seem appropriate. The election simply demonstrated that progressivism had been temporarily submerged during the war in the new war-brought social climate which neither produced nor supported progressive leaders.

The failure of progressives to analyze more completely the probable results of the war explains more than anything else the collapse of their movement. Many of them had advocated the war as a means of realizing their dreams of a better world; but, instead, the war meant injury to many of the elements of civilization and produced conditions antithetical to progressivism. Years of restoration were necessary before the movement of humanitarian reform could be resumed.

NOTES

CHAPTER I

1. Henry Allen to Hermann Hagedorn, February 18, 1919, Chauncey S. Baker interview, May 17, 1929, Leonard Wood to Frederick M. Alger, September 17, 1919, Hermann Hagedorn Papers, Library of Congress; William Howard Taft to Horace D. Taft, February 7, 1920, William Howard Taft Papers, Library of Congress; Hermann Hagedorn, *Leonard Wood* (New York, 1931), 326-7, 345.

2. Hagedorn, *Wood*, 331-2; *Presidential Campaign Expenses: Hearings before a Subcommittee of the Committee on Privileges and Elections, United States Senate* (Printed pursuant to Senate Resolution No. 357, 66 Cong., 2 Sess., for the use of the Committee on Privileges and Elections), 2 vols. (Washington, 1921) 285-98, (hereinafter cited as *Campaign Expenses*); Sumner S. Williams to Hagedorn, April 10, 1920, Hagedorn Papers; *New York Post*, December 10, 1919, January 31, 1920; *New York Tribune*, November 9, 1919; Taft to John C. Vivian, December 2, 1919, Taft Papers; William Allen White to Frederick Moore, January 6, 1920, William Allen White Papers, Library of Congress.

3. William Allen White, *A Puritan in Babylon* (New York, 1938), 179-80; Hagedorn, *Wood*, 337; Wood Diary, May 9, May 24, 1920, Peter Norbeck interview, February 1, 1929, Hagedorn Papers; *New York Post*, March 8, 1920; *New York Tribune*, March 15, 1920; *New York American*, February 23, 1920; *New York World*, March 23, 1920; Harry M. Daugherty to Ray Baker Harris, October 9, 1939, Ray Baker Harris Deposit of Warren G. Harding Materials, Library of Congress.

4. Baker interview, May 17, 1929, Hagedorn Papers; *Campaign Expenses*, 175, 484; Hagedorn, *Wood*, 338.

5. Hagedorn, *Wood*, 331-2, 339; Edward B. Clark interview, December 19, 1928, Henry L. Stimson to Wood, December 16, 1919, Albert R. Brunker interview, March 28, 1929, Hagedorn Papers; *New York Post*, January 31, 1920; Taft to Horace Taft, February 7, 1920, Isaac M. Ullman to Taft, March 31, 1920, Taft Papers; A. W. Page, "The Meaning of What Happened at Chicago," *World's Work*, 40 (August, 1920), 370; *New York Tribune*, February 3, 4, 1920.

6. *Campaign Expenses*, 176-7; Frederick Moore interview, February 8, 1929, Clark interview, December 19, 1928, Hagedorn Papers; Louise Overacker, *Presidential Primaries* (New York, 1926), 119.

7. *Campaign Expenses*, 175-7, 485; Clark interview, December 19, 1928, Hagedorn Papers; Overacker, *Primaries*, 119; *Cleveland Plain Dealer*, May 1, 1920.

8. Hagedorn, *Wood*, 341-5; *New York Post*, October 18, 1919; *Leslie's Illustrated Weekly Newspaper*, February 28, 1920; *New York Times*, February 25, March 21, May 13, June 10, 1920; Wood to Hiram Johnson, September 20, 1919, Hagedorn Papers; *New York Tribune*, February 12, 1920.

9. Wood to Mrs. Robinson, December 5, 1919, Hagedorn Papers; Wood to White, July 31, 1919, December 1, 1919, January 24, 1920, White to Wood, December 26, 1919, White Papers; *New York Times*, February 25, 1920.

10. White to Frederick Moore, December 1, 1919, White to J. E. House, February 23, 1920, White Papers; William E. Borah to C. C. Covanah, March 10, 1920, William E. Borah Papers, Library of Congress; H. J. Allen to Hagedorn, February 18, 1929, Hagedorn Papers; *New York Post*, February 11, 1920; Wash-

ington *Star,* February 26, 1920; Chicago *Tribune,* March 13, 1920; Willis F. Johnson, *George Harvey* (New York, 1929), 275.

11. "Truth about Leonard Wood," *Nation,* 110 (May 29, 1920), 714; *New York Post,* June 5, 1920.

12. "Leonard Wood," *New Republic,* 22 (March 17, 1920), 78-80.

13. New York *Tribune,* December 11, 1919; *New York Times,* May 24, 1920; MacChesney interview, November 27, 1928, Clark interview, December 19, 1928, Frederick Moore interview, February 8, 1929, Hagedorn Papers.

14. Taft to H. D. Taft, February 7, 1920, C. D. Hilles memorandum, April 17, 1920, Taft Papers; New York *Tribune,* March 6, 1920; *Campaign Expenses,* 14; Clark interview, December 19, 1928, Wood Diary, March 8, 24, April 4, 1920, Wood to Proctor, April 18, 1920, Brunker interview, March 30, 1929, E. H. Van Valkenburg interview, January 30, 1929, Hagedorn Papers; *New York Times,* April 21, 1920; New York *World,* March 10, 1920.

15. Brunker interview, March 26, 1929, Wood Diary, March 24, May 9, 1920, General William MacChesney interview, November 27, 1928, Hagedorn Papers; New York *Tribune,* March 6, April 27, 1920.

16. Washington *Star,* February 26, 1920; C. O. Johnson, *Borah of Idaho* (New York, 1936), 236; White to Chester H. Rowell, March 13, 1920, White Papers; *New York Post,* March 16, April 5, 1920; New York *Tribune,* April 11, 1920; *Nation,* 110 (May 19, 1920), 368.

17. *New York Post,* March 31, April 3, May 1, 1920; *New York Times,* March 3, 1920; New York *Tribune,* May 1, 1920; White to Rowell, March 13, 1920, White Papers.

18. *New York Post,* May 1, June 8, 1920; White to Rowell, March 13, 1920, White Papers; Overacker, *Primaries,* 117; George E. Mowry, *The California Progressives* (Berkeley, 1951), 286-7.

19. *New York Post,* January 12, March 27, April 3, 1920; New York *Tribune,* November 9, 1919, March 17, 1920; Overacker, *Primaries,* 123; *Campaign Expenses,* 39-43; *New York Times,* May 1, 1920; Washington *Star,* April 7, 1920.

20. Overacker, *Primaries,* 27, 62-70, 157; *New York Post,* May 27, 1920; New York *Tribune,* May 30, June 2, 1920.

21. *New York Post,* May 22, June 8, 1920; New York *Tribune,* June 2, 3, 5, 8, 1920; Taft to Robert Taft, June 5, 1920, Taft Papers.

22. Washington *Star,* January 4, 1920; Chicago *Tribune,* April 4, 1920; William T. Hutchinson, *Lowden of Illinois* (Chicago, 1957), passim; Walter Lippmann, "The Logic of Lowden?" *New Republic,* 22 (April 14, 1920), 206; James M. Cox, *Journey Through My Years* (New York, 1946), 100; Nicholas M. Butler, *Across the Busy Years* (New York, 1939), 391; Mark Sullivan, *The Twenties,* (New York, 1935), 41; Harold L. Ickes to White, June 24, 1920, White Papers.

23. New York *Tribune,* January 13, 1919; *New York Post,* March 11, 1919, January 14, 1920; Washington *Star,* January 25, 1920.

24. New York *Tribune,* January 6, April 14, 1920; *New York Times,* May 1, June 5, 1920; *New York Post,* December 23, 1919, June 5, 1920; *Sioux Falls Press,* March 19, 1920; Chicago *Tribune,* February 18, April 4, 1920; Washington *Star,* January 4, 1920; Hutchinson, *Lowden,* 435-6.

25. *New York Post,* January 12, February 7, March 27, May 1, 1920; Lippmann, "The Logic of Lowden?" 204; *New York Times,* June 3, 1920; Washington *Star,* January 25, 1920; New York *Tribune,* January 25, 1920.

26. *Campaign Expenses,* 57-8, 66; Overacker, *Primaries,* 124; Washington *Star,* March 3, 1920; *New York Times,* March 3, 1920; *New York Post,* February 7, April 12, 1920; New York *Tribune,* April 22, 1920.

27. *New York Post,* May 21, June 3, 1920; Washington *Star,* February 8, April 23, May 13, 1920; *Campaign Expenses,* 63; New York *Tribune,* March 18, May 31, June 2, 6, 7, 1920; Chicago *Tribune,* April 19, 1920; Taft to D. R.

Williams, May 4, 1920, Taft to G. J. Karger, May 27, 1920, Taft Papers; Hutchinson, *Lowden,* 441, 449.

28. Chicago *Tribune,* April 4, 18, 1920; New York *Tribune,* November 9, 1919, January 27, March 29, May 31, 1920; New York *World,* April 10, 1920; *Literary Digest,* 65 (June 5, 1920), 24.

29. New York *Tribune,* March 28, June 3, 5, 1920; *New York Times,* June 3, 1920; *New York Post,* June 3, 1920; Hutchinson, *Lowden,* 454-5.

30. New York *Tribune,* June 6, 7, 1920; *New York Times,* June 5, 1920.

31. The most available work on Harding is Samuel H. Adams, *The Incredible Era: the Life and Times of Warren G. Harding* (New York, 1939). More valuable are Harold F. Alderfer, *The Personality and Politics of Warren G. Harding* (Washington, D.C., 1939), and the Ray Baker Harris Deposit of Warren G. Harding Materials in the Library of Congress.

32. *New York Post,* January 23, 1920.

33. James W. Wadsworth to Harris, June 13, 1933, Harris Deposit; *New York Post,* May 1, 1920.

34. Adams, *Incredible,* passim.; Harry M. Daugherty, *The Inside Story of the Harding Tragedy* (New York, 1932), 6; Daugherty to Harris, June 7, 1938, Harris Deposit.

35. White, *Puritan,* 204.

36. Daugherty, *Harding Tragedy,* 14-20.

37. Harding to John L. Von Blon, December 22, 1919, Warren G. Harding Letters, Library of Congress; Chicago *Tribune,* January 29, 1920; *New York Times,* May 9, 1920; *New York Post,* May 1, 1920; *Campaign Expenses,* 267; New York *Tribune,* February 23, 1920.

38. New York *Tribune,* January 7, March 19, November 9, 1919; *New York Post,* March 13, 1919; Thomas B. Love to William Gibbs McAdoo, November 13, 1919, William Gibbs McAdoo Papers, Library of Congress.

39. New York *Tribune,* January 15, 20, 1920.

40. Washington *Star,* March 14, 1920; *Campaign Expenses,* 279.

41. *New York Times,* November 22, 1924.

42. New York *Tribune,* April 29, 1920; *Cleveland Plain Dealer,* May 1, 1920; *New York Times,* May 9, 16, June 2, 1920; *New York Post,* May 1, 1920; Washington *Star,* May 5, 1920; *Springfield* (Mass.) *Republican,* May 2, 1920; Brunker interview, March 26, 1929, Hagedorn Papers.

43. Sullivan, *Twenties,* 35; Daugherty to Taft, December 8, 1919, Taft to John C. Vivian, January 28, 1920, Taft Papers; *New York Times,* March 8, 1920; White, *Puritan,* 204; Henry L. Stimson to Wood, December 6, 1919, Hagedorn Papers; *New York Post,* February 7, 1920.

44. *Campaign Expenses,* 276-7, 763-4; Taft to Hilles, February 16, 1920, Taft Papers.

45. Daugherty to Taft, December 8, 1919, Taft to Vivian, January 28, 1920, Taft Papers.

46. Daugherty to Harris, June 29, 1938, Harris Deposit.

47. *New York Times,* February 21, 1920.

48. *New York Post,* March 13, 1920.

49. "Hoover," *Weekly Review,* 2 (January 31, 1920), 98; "Fighting for Hoover," *New Republic,* 22 (March 3, 1920), 4; R. Herrick, "For Hoover," *Nation,* 110 (June 5, 1920), 750-1.

50. Josephus Daniels, *The Wilson Era* (Chapel Hill, 1946), 322; Washington *Star,* January 24, 1920; *New York Post,* September 30, October 3, 1919, February 18, May 14, April 2, 1920; New York *Tribune,* March 10, 19, 1920; Hoover to Woodrow Wilson, November 19, 1919, Woodrow Wilson Papers, Library of Congress.

51. Daniels, *Wilson Era,* 322; *New York Post,* December 11, 1919, January 24, 1920; New York *Tribune,* January 25, 1920.

52. Roosevelt to Hugh Gibson, January 2, 1920, Franklin D. Roosevelt Papers, Franklin D. Roosevelt Library, Hyde Park, N. Y.; Taft to H. D. Taft, February 7, 1920, Taft Papers; Mrs. Antionette Funk to Daniel C. Roper, February 27, 1920, McAdoo Papers.

53. *New York Post,* December 11, 1919, January 7, 1920; New York *World,* January 21, 1920; Daniels, *Wilson Era,* 323; Taft to Robert Taft, February 7, 1920, Taft Papers; Eugene Lyons, *Our Unknown Ex-President* (New York, 1948), 200-1; *Literary Digest,* 65 (June 12, 1920), 20; New York *Tribune,* April 23, 1920.

54. Homer S. Cummings memorandum, undated but filed in Box 3, Series 1, Ray Stannard Baker collection of Woodrow Wilson Materials, Library of Congress.

55. Ibid. Josephus Daniels tells of a dinner to which Hoover was invited for the purpose of conferring with Democratic leaders. Hoover did not appear, but sent Julius Barnes as his spokesman. Talk of Hoover as the Democratic nominee was exploded by Barnes's "What in the hell are you gentlemen talking about? Herbert Hoover is a Republican and would not accept a Democratic nomination"; cf. Daniels, *Wilson Era,* 324.

56. "Hoover and the Rest," *Independent,* 102 (May 29, 1920), 297; Herbert Hoover, "Inside Harding's Cabinet," *Collier's,* 128 (September 29, 1951), 35; *New York Post,* April 3, 1920. A biographer said that Hoover wanted only to become a member of the cabinet, and thought that the best way to get a cabinet post was to let the presidential boom develop; cf. Lyons, *Unknown,* 199-200.

57. *Campaign Expenses,* 96-9, 447, 789-90, 798-807; Lyons, *Unknown,* 200-1; *New York Post,* May 5, 1920; "Johnson and the Chicago Convention," *Weekly Review,* 2 (May 15, 1920), 504; *Cleveland Plain Dealer,* May 6, 1920.

58. *New York Post,* September 30, January 6, 1919; "Concerning Mr. Hoover," *New Republic,* 22 (May 12, 1920), 326; Taft to Robert Taft, April 5, 1920, Taft Papers; New York *Tribune,* April 17, 1920. Denying that the wealthy classes were behind Hoover, Warren Gregory said that it was, rather, the "intelligent class"; cf. *Campaign Expenses,* 804.

59. Calvin Coolidge, *Autobiography* (New York, 1929), 141; Claude M. Fuess, *Calvin Coolidge* (Boston, 1940), 238-9; *New York Post,* December 23, 1919.

60. Coolidge, *Autobiography,* 143-4; Karl Schriftgiesser, *The Gentleman from Massachusetts: Henry Cabot Lodge* (Boston, 1944), 353; New York *Tribune,* December 3, 1919; Washington *Star,* January 4, 1920.

61. Coolidge, *Autobiography,* 145-6; Fuess, *Coolidge,* 257.

62. New York *Tribune,* January 26, 1920; Coolidge, *Autobiography,* 144-5; Fuess, *Coolidge,* 245; *Campaign Expenses,* 322; *New York Post,* June 5, 1920.

63. Schriftgiesser, *Gentleman,* passim; New York *World,* June 1, 1920.

64. *New York Times,* June 3, April 12, 1920.

65. New York *Tribune,* February 24, 1920; Michael J. Ryan to Borah, April 23, 1920, Borah Papers; Hilles to Taft, May 3, 1920, Taft Papers; *New York Times,* April 12, 1920; Daugherty to Harris, May 24, 1934, Harris Deposit; John King to Harding, June 15, 1920, copy, Thomas J. Walsh Papers, Library of Congress. Daugherty thought that Lowden was Penrose' choice early in the race; cf. Daugherty to Harris, May 24, 1934, Harris Deposit.

66. *New York Times,* June 3, 5, 6, 7, 1920; New York *Tribune,* June 5, 1920.

67. *New York Times,* May 29, June 5, 7, 1920; New York *Tribune,* May 17, June 5, 10, 1920; *New York Post,* June 8, 1920.

68. Allen to White, November 4, 1919, White Papers; *New York Post,* June 5, 1920; Wood Diary (copy), March 24, 1920, MacChesney interview, November 27, 1928, Hagedorn Papers.

69. *Campaign Expenses,* 243; Butler, *Across,* 390.

70. Taft to Judge William C. VanFleet, December 8, 1919, Taft Papers.
71. *New York Post,* March 8, 10, 16, 1920; New York *Tribune,* May 30, 1920.
72. *New York Post, March* 21, 24, 25, 1920; Overacker, *Primaries,* 124, 238; New York *Tribune,* December 3, 1919, April 5, 6, 1920; Clark interview, December 19, 1928, Hagedorn Papers; Hagedorn, *Wood,* 356-9; Johnson to Borah, February 23, 1920, Borah Papers; *New York Times,* March 3, 1920; New York *American,* March 4, 1920.
73. *New York Post,* April 3, 5, 1920; Overacker, *Primaries,* 238, 62; *Literary Digest,* 65 (April 17, 1920), 36.
74. *New York Post,* April 12, 14, 1920; MacChesney interview, November 27, 1928, Hagedorn Papers; New York *Tribune,* April 22, 1920; Overacker, *Primaries,* 238; Chicago *Tribune,* April 15, 1920.
75. *Campaign Expenses,* 367-81; New York *Tribune,* May 27, 1920.
76. New York *Tribune,* April 27, 1920; *New York Post,* May 1, 4, 1920.
77. *Campaign Expenses,* 7, 214; New York *Tribune,* January 15, 16, 20, 1920; E. W. Edwards to Miles Poindexter, March 11, 1920, Miles Poindexter Papers, Library of the University of Virginia; Washington *Star,* March 14, 1920; *Cleveland Plain Dealer,* February 26, 1920; *New York Post,* April 28, May 1, 1920.
78. *New York Post,* April 28, 1920; *New York Times,* May 4, 1920; Washington *Star,* April 25, 1920.
79. P. A. Stanton to Taft, May 9, 1920, Taft Papers; *New York Times,* May 1, 4, 1920; New York *Tribune,* April 11, May 1, 1920; *New York Post,* May 13, 1920.
80. Overacker, *Primaries,* 27, 68-9, 70, 238.
81. New York *Tribune,* June 6, 1920; Overacker, *Primaries,* 238.
82. New York *American,* February 23, 1920; New York *World,* March 23, 1920; *New York Times,* March 23, 30, 1920; New York *Tribune,* March 27, 1920.
83. *Campaign Expenses,* 501; Overacker, *Primaries,* 153. This refers only to the expenses of the national and state committees—expenditures of local committees and other groups and individuals could not be traced.
84. *New York Times,* June 2, 3, 6, 1920; *Campaign Expenses,* 66; New York *Tribune,* June 2, 3, 1920.
85. *New York Times,* May 27, 1920; Wood to Bishop Charles H. Brent, July 29, 1920, Hagedorn Papers.

CHAPTER II

1. *Nation,* 106 (January 31, 1918), 105; *New York Times,* June 21, 1918, July 20, August 1, 1919; New York *World,* May 16, 1920; New York *Tribune,* September 22, 1919; R. W. Woolley to Joseph R. Tumulty, August 19, 1919, Baker Collection.
2. Homer Cummings, Comments on the Recent Congressional Election, November 7, 1918, Wilson Papers; New York *Tribune,* February 23, 1919; *New York Times,* April 26, 1919; *New York Post,* May 28, 1919; New York *World,* July 7, 1919.
3. New York *Tribune,* March 1, September 22, 1919; *New York Times,* March 2, September 22, 1919; *New York Post,* September 16, 1919.
4. New York *World,* December 4, 1919, January 8, 1920; Edith B. Wilson, *My Memoir* (Indianapolis, 1938), 296-7; told by Bernard Baruch to Allan Nevins, Nevins to author, 1948.
5. Lodge to Root, September 29, 1919, Elihu Root Papers, Library of Congress; New York *World,* November 22, 24, December 18, 1919.

6. John M. Blum, *Joe Tumulty and the Wilson Era* (Boston, 1951), 233-4; notes in Wilson's handwriting undated, filed with October, 1920, papers, Wilson Papers.

7. New York *Tribune,* January 9, 1920.

8. New York *Tribune,* January 9, 10, 11, 1920; Chicago *Tribune,* January 9, 1920; *New York Post,* January 9, February 14, 1920; New York *World,* January 8, 1920.

9. Taft wrote that Wilson was determined to carry the treaty into the campaign and intended to run himself; cf. Taft to H. D. Taft, March 23, 1920, Taft Papers. Tumulty advised Wilson in February that if the Democrats ratified the treaty with the Lodge reservations "the Democratic party might as well not hold a convention this year"; cf. Blum, *Tumulty,* 238.

10. New York *Tribune,* April 23, 1920; New York *World,* May 10, 11, 1920.

11. New York *World,* May 18, 1920; Thomas A. Bailey, *Woodrow Wilson and the Great Betrayal* (New York, 1945), 383-4.

12. Irwin H. Hoover, *Forty-Two Years in the White House* (New York, 1934), 95-9; Edmund W. Starling as told to Thomas Sugre, *Starling of the White House* (New York, 1946), 137-8; George Creel, *Rebel at Large* (New York, 1947), 224; Wilson's illness was cerebral thrombosis—the blocking of an artery in the brain with consequent destruction of part of the brain. This illness may last for many years, punctuated by attacks as additional arteries close, and may have varying effects on personality and character. Some frequent (though not invariable) effects of the illness are that the patient becomes irascible, suspicious, morose, over emotional, loses physical and mental abilities, and may become somewhat psychopathic with moral changes; cf. Walter C. Alvarez, "Cerebral Arteriosclerosis," *Geriatrics,* 1 (1946), 189-216.

13. New York *World,* September 27, 1919; Hoover, *Forty-Two Years,* 101-2.

14. New York *World,* October 8, 1919; Joseph R. Wilson to Tumulty, October 14, 1919, Wilson Papers; Wilson, *Memoir,* 298; Starling, *Starling,* 155; Creel, *Rebel,* 225, 228; Cummings memorandum, May 31, 1920, Baker Collection.

15. Rixey Smith and Norman Beasley, *Carter Glass* (New York, 1939), 205; David F. Houston, *Eight Years with Wilson's Cabinet* (New York, 1926), 70; Daniels Diary, May 11, 1920, Daniels Papers; Blum, *Tumulty,* 312; Hoover, *Forty-Two Years,* 95-6; David Lawrence, *The True Story of Woodrow Wilson* (New York, 1924), 282. Irritated when cars passed him on the road, Wilson would order the Secret Service to overtake and arrest their drivers, and he asked the attorney general if the president did not have the powers of a magistrate; cf. Starling, *Starling,* 157; Wilson to A. Mitchell Palmer, September 9, 1920, Wilson Papers. Wilson's illness and third-term receptivity afford a point of departure for re-examination of some of the more obscure aspects of the last years of his administration, such as his peremptory dismissal of Secretary of State Robert Lansing in February, 1920, and his abrupt break with Colonel House after House urged Wilson to renounce a third term in order to secure ratification of the treaty.

16. Blum, *Tumulty,* 242; *New York Post,* March 26, 1920; *Cleveland Plain Dealer,* March 27, 1920.

17. *Literary Digest,* 65 (June 12, 1920), 20.

18. Cary T. Grayson, *Woodrow Wilson* (New York, 1960), 116-7.

19. Joseph P. Tumulty, *Woodrow Wilson as I Knew Him* (Garden City, 1921), 493-6; Daniels Diary, February 20, 1920, Daniels Papers; Funk to Roper, February 27, 1920, McAdoo Papers.

20. Carter Field, *Bernard Baruch* (New York, 1944), 192-4; Cummings memorandum, undated, filed in Box 3, Series 1, Baker Collection; card of the Postmaster General, Vol. 25, Item 4007, Albert S. Burleson Papers, Library of Congress.

21. New York *World,* June 18, 20, 1920; Blum, *Tumulty,* 243.

22. Chicago *Tribune,* June 19, 1920; *New York Post,* June 22, July 1, 1920;

New York *Tribune,* June 19, 20, 1920; New York *World,* June 20, 23, July 1, 1920; New York *American,* June 19, 1920.

23. Cummings memorandum, undated, filed in Box 3, Series 1, Baker Collection; Wilson to Edwin T. Meredith, June 14, 1920, Wilson Papers.

24. Glass Diary, June 19, 1920, Carter Glass Papers, Library of the University of Virginia.

25. Colby to Wilson, June 18, 1920, Baker to Wilson, June 10, 1920, Wilson Papers; Burleson to Daniels, October 23, 1934, Daniels Papers; Wilson to Baker, June 11, 1920, Newton D. Baker Papers, Library of Congress.

26. *New York Post,* June 19, 1920; *Chicago Tribune,* June 22, 25, 1920; *Washington Star,* June 23, 27, 1920; New York *World,* June 27, 1920.

27. *New York Post,* June 28, 1920; New York *World,* June 28, 1920.

28. *Campaign Expenses,* 354.

29. William Gibbs McAdoo, *Crowded Years* (Boston, 1931), passim.

30. *Literary Digest,* June 12, 1920.

31. McAdoo letters, December, 1919, McAdoo Papers; New York *Tribune,* January 11, 1920; New York *World,* December 30, 1919; Washington *Star,* January 4, 1920.

32. *New York Post,* February 21, 1920; McAdoo to Morris Shafroth, February 2, 1920, McAdoo Papers.

33. McAdoo to Claude G. Bowers, January 24, 1920; McAdoo to Thomas B. Love, February 7, 1920, McAdoo Papers.

34. McAdoo to F. W. Hazelhurst, February 13, 1920, McAdoo to Grayson, February 14, 1920, McAdoo Papers.

35. McAdoo to M. S. Bell, February 17, 1920, Wilson Papers; Tumulty to McAdoo, February 20, 1920, Funk to McAdoo, February 18, 1920, McAdoo Papers.

36. McAdoo to Frank B. Niles, February 27, 1920, McAdoo to Coleman C. Vaughan, March 12, 1920, McAdoo to Mrs. Janet A. Fairbanks, March 31, 1920, McAdoo Papers; New York *Tribune,* March 7, 1920; McAdoo to the Secretary of the Commonwealth of Pennsylvania, April 8, 1920, copy, Wilson Papers.

37. McAdoo to "Whitford," March 24, 1920, copy, Wilson Papers; Daniels Diary, March 2, 1920, Daniels Papers; McAdoo to Franklin Houston, March 19, 1920, McAdoo to Jouett Shouse, May 3, 1920, McAdoo Papers.

38. Copy of farm journal article, McAdoo Papers; New York *Tribune,* March 5, April 26, 1920.

39. McAdoo to Roper, December 8, 1919, Palmer to Tumulty, May 10, 1920, McAdoo Papers; New York *Tribune,* January 1, April 19, June 26, 1920; McAdoo to Tumulty, May 14, 1920, Wilson Papers; New York *World,* June 28, 1920.

40. McAdoo to J. H. O'Neil, December 30, 1919, McAdoo to Roper, January 15, 1920, McAdoo Papers; Daniels Diary, March 2, 1920, Daniels Papers; New York *Tribune,* March 5, April 26, 1920; New York *World,* March 30, 1920.

41. Funk to McAdoo, March 13, 1920, McAdoo Papers; *Campaign Expenses,* 357. McAdoo wrote a paragraph to the effect that there was no organization in his behalf but only voluntary activity, and that he would accept if nominated; cf. McAdoo to Funk, April 19, 1920, McAdoo Papers.

42. Zach Lamar Cobb to McAdoo, April 14, 1920, Claude Kitchin to McAdoo, June 4, 1920, Robert Woolley to McAdoo, April 24 and June 16, 1920, Burleson to McAdoo, May 16, 1920, McAdoo Papers; New York *Tribune,* June 20, 1920; *New York Post,* June 15, 1920; *New York Times,* June 20, 1920.

43. *New York Times,* June 23, 26, 1920; *Chicago Tribune,* June 26, 1920.

44. New York *American,* May 19, 27, 1920; Funk to McAdoo, March 13, 1920, McAdoo Papers; *Campaign Expenses,* 250.

45. *New York Times,* June 19, 1920.

NOTES

46. *New York Times,* June 19, 22, 1920; *New York Post,* July 1, 1920.

47. McAdoo telegrams to Love, June 18, 19, 1920, Love telegram to McAdoo, June 19, 1920, Roper telegram to Love, June 22, 1920, McAdoo telegram to Burris Jenkins, June 22, 1920, McAdoo Papers; New York *Tribune,* June 19, 1920.

48. *New York Post,* June 19, 1920; Funk telegram to McAdoo, June 20, 1920, Shouse to McAdoo, June 19, 1920, Woolley telegram to McAdoo, June 19, 1920, Ray Baker telegram to McAdoo, June 21, 1920, McAdoo Papers; New York *Tribune,* June 19, 1920.

49. Glass Diary, June 19, 1920, Glass Papers; New York *Tribune,* June 20, 1920; Chicago *Tribune,* June 21, 1920.

50. Smith, *Glass,* 206-7.

51. Funk to McAdoo, June 21, 1920, C. M. Brown telegram to McAdoo, June 21, 1920, McAdoo Papers; New York *Tribune,* June 24, 1920.

52. Washington *Star,* June 23, 1920; McAdoo to Baruch, June 23, 1920, Roper telegram to William D. Jamieson, June 24, 1920, McAdoo Papers; New York *Tribune,* June 24, 1920.

53. *New York Times,* June 24, 1920; New York *Tribune,* June 24, 26, 28, 1920; McAdoo telegram to Funk, June 24, 1920, Funk telegram to McAdoo, June 25, 1920, Grayson to McAdoo, June 28, 1920, McAdoo telegram to Cone Johnson, June 28, 1920, McAdoo telegram to A. W. McLean, June 29, 1920, McAdoo to B. F. Irvine, June 28, 1920, McAdoo Papers; Washington *Star,* June 23, 1920.

54. New York *World,* September 28, 1919; New York *Tribune,* January 1, 1920; O. G. Villard, "Ordeal by Dinner," *Nation,* 110 (January 17, 1920), 69; *New York Post,* January 9, 1920.

55. New York *Tribune,* March 2, 1920; Daniels Diary, February 20, 1920, Daniels Papers; Tumulty, *Wilson* 495-6; New York *World,* June 23, 1920.

56. New York *Tribune,* March 2, April 23, 1920; New York *World,* March 15, 1920; Mark Sullivan, "Your Move Democracy," *Collier's,* 65 (June 19, 1920), 18; *Cleveland Plain Dealer,* April 7, 1920; *New York Times,* May 18, 19, 1920.

57. New York *World,* May 2, 10, 19, 1920; New York *Tribune,* March 5, April 19, May 10, 1920; *New York Post,* May 15, 1920.

58. New York *World,* May 17, June 5, 23, 1920; *New York Post,* May 28, 1920; *Nation,* 110 (June 12, 1920), 789-91.

59. *New York Times,* June 20, 1920; New York *Tribune,* June 25, 1920.

60. James M. Cox, *Journey through My Years* (New York, 1946), passim; *New York Times,* July 11, 1920; Letter from Roy Roberts After a Ten-Day Visit in Ohio, 1920, White Papers.

61. Villard, "Ordeal by Dinner," 68; *Cleveland Plain Dealer,* January 25, February 19, 25, March 3, 1920; New York *World,* February 1, 1920; *Campaign Expenses,* 70-1; *New York Post,* May 5, 1920; Moore to Glass, April 13, 1920, Glass Papers.

62. *New Republic,* 23 (July 21, 1920), 216; New York *World,* May 12, 1920; James M. Cox, "Campaign Issues," *New York Times,* May 23, 1920; *New York Post,* May 20, 29, 1920.

63. *New York Times,* May 14, 19, June 2, 27, 1920; *Nation,* 111 (July 10, 1920), 29; *New York Post,* June 30, 1920.

64. Cox, "Campaign Issues."

65. *New York Times,* May 19, June 15, 20, July 25, 1920.

66. New York *Tribune,* June 23, 1920.

67. New York *World,* April 17, 1920; *Cleveland Plain Dealer,* May 3, 25, 1920; New York *Tribune,* June 23, 1920.

68. New York *Tribune,* December 19, 1919; *New York Post,* December 31, 1919.

176   THE ROAD TO NORMALCY

69. New York *Tribune,* January 9, 1920; Daniels Diary, January 8, 1920, Daniels Papers; *Springfield* (Mass.) *Republican,* January 9, 1920; *New York Post,* January 9, 1920.

70. New York *Tribune,* January 13, 16, March 21, April 30, 1920; *New York Times,* May 11, 1920.

71. New York *World,* May 1, June 7, 1920; *Literary Digest,* 65 (June 12, 1920), 20-1; New York *Tribune,* January 7, 18, March 14, 1920; Bryan to Edwin T. Meredith, May 15, 1920, McAdoo Papers.

72. New York *World,* June 24, 1920; New York *Tribune,* April 20, 24, June 19, 1920.

73. *New York Times,* May 23, 1920.

74. New York *Tribune,* May 21, June 15, 1920; New York *World,* May 24, June 16, 25, 1920.

CHAPTER III

1. *New York Post,* June 4, 9, 1920; *New York Times,* June 7, 1920; Washington *Star,* June 8, 1920.

2. Johnson telegram to Borah, June 3, 1920, Borah Papers; *New York Times,* June 1, 5, 6, 7, 1920; New York *Tribune,* June 6, 1920.

3. *New York Times,* May 11, 12, June 6, 9, 1920; Johnson telegram to Borah, June 3, 1920, Borah Papers; Claude Bowers, *Beveridge and the Progressive Era* (New York, 1932), 516.

4. Speeches and procedure, unless otherwise noted, are taken from the *Official Report of the Proceedings of the Seventeenth Republican National Convention* (New York, 1920).

5. *New York Post,* June 8, 1920; *New York Times,* June 9, 11, 1920; W. Murray Crane to Hilles, copy, July 3, 1920, copy of plank to Taft, July 19, 1920, Taft to C. S. Yost, June 19, 1920, Taft to Miss Helen Taft, June 3, 1920, Taft Papers; Lodge to Root, May 17, 1920, Root Papers.

6. Taft to Yost, June 19, 1920, Taft Papers; New York *Tribune,* June 11, 1920; *New York Times,* June 11, 1920; Baltimore *Sun,* June 11, 1920; *Springfield* (Mass.) *Republican,* June 11, 1920.

7. *New York Post,* June 12, 1920.

8. New York *Tribune,* June 12, 1920; William Allen White, *Autobiography* (New York, 1946), 583, 588.

9. *New York Post,* June 11, 1920; *New York Times,* June 12, 1920; New York *Tribune,* June 12, 1920.

10. *New York Times,* June 12, 1920. Of Wheeler's speech Irvin S. Cobb wrote: "Many present—fair-minded judges too, and persons of experience in such matters besides—went so far as to say that in many respects this was the worst speech that ever was"; cf. New York *World,* June 12, 1920.

11. *New York Times,* June 12, 1920. According to Mark Sullivan, Willis' was one of the most "orotund" voices in America and to have heard it roll out "four years ago" was to "get the combined enjoyments of oratory, grand opera, and hog calling"; cf. Sullivan, *Twenties,* 51.

12. *New York Times,* June 2, 1920; Clark interview, December 19, 1928, Hagedorn Papers; *New York Post,* June 9, 1920; New York *Tribune,* June 10, 1920; Chicago *Tribune,* June 10, 1920.

13. Chicago *Tribune,* June 6, 7, 9, 1920.

14. *New York Times,* June 6, 7, 1920; Chicago *Tribune,* June 8, 1920; Butler, *Across,* 279; Daugherty, *Harding Tragedy,* 33-37; Daugherty to Harris, June 29, 1928, Harris Deposit.

15. *New York Times,* June 12, 1920; New York *Tribune,* June 12, 1920.

16. *New York Times,* June 12, 1920; New York *Tribune,* June 12, 1920; Sullivan, *Twenties,* 57, 58, 359-60; Hagedorn, *Wood,* 359.

17. *New York Times,* June 12, 1920; New York *Tribune,* June 12, 1920.

18. *New York Times,* June 13, 1920; H. J. Allen interview, February 18, 1929, Wood Diary, copy, September 30, 1920, MacChesney interview, November 27, 1928, Hagedorn Papers.

19. Allen interview, February 18, 1929, Dorey interview, January 4, 1930, Hagedorn Papers. A number of physicians urged Wood to accept the vice-presidential nomination because, judging from Harding's appearance, the possibility of his living out his term was extremely dubious; cf. MacChesney interview, November 27, 1928, Hagedorn Papers.

20. Chicago *Tribune,* June 12, 1920; Adams, *Incredible,* 158.

21. Karl Schriftgiesser, *This was Normalcy* (Boston, 1948), 4; William E. Dodd, *Woodrow Wilson and His Work* (New York, 1932), 423; Harvey Thomas to Captain Osmen, July 27, 1920, Hagedorn Papers; White, *Autobiography,* 178, 584.

22. Taft to Hilles, February 17, 1920, Taft Papers; New York *Tribune,* June 5, 1920; Baker interview, May 17, 1929, Hagedorn Papers.

23. Taft to Hilles, February 17, 1920, Taft Papers; Baker interview, May 17, 1929, Law interview, May 28, 1929, Hagedorn Papers; *Editor and Publisher,* LX (August 13, 1927), 8; *Leases upon Naval Oil Reserves: Hearings before the Committee on Public Lands and Surveys, United States Senate* (Washington, 1924), 2933-3002, 3165 ff. Hamon died before Harding was inaugurated, but his son was reported to have told lawyers that he had been promised a one-third interest in the Teapot Dome lease; cf. J. G. Bennett to Walsh, February 25, 1924, Walsh Papers.

24. White, *Puritan,* 205; James E. Watson, *As I Knew Them* (Indianapolis, 1932); p. 222, Daugherty to Harris, May 24, 1934, J. W. Wadsworth to Harris, May 21, 1933; Harris Deposit; *New York Post,* June 10, 12, 1920.

25. Jacob Wood interview, September 23, 1928, Hagedorn Papers; Alderfer, *Harding,* 45-7.

26. *New York Post,* June 12, 1920; Johnson, *Harvey,* 274-5, and the Introduction by Calvin Coolidge.

27. Fuess, *Coolidge,* 256; Johnson, *Harvey,* 276; *New York Post,* June 15, 1920; Sullivan, *Twenties,* 29; *New York Times,* June 12, 13, 1920; James W. Wadsworth to Harris, October 8, 1932, William M. Calder to Harris, August 2, 1933, Joseph R. Grundy to Harris, May 24, 1934, Harris Deposit; Watson, *As I Knew Them,* 220.

28. Grundy to Harris, May 24, 1934, Calder to Harris, June 20, 1938, Harris Deposit; Watson, *As I Knew Them,* 220.

29. Wadsworth to Harris, October 8, 1932, Harris Deposit; Sullivan, *Twenties,* 59. Smoot in 1939 approved a draft account depreciating the role of the Smoke-filled Room in the nomination of Harding; cf. Smoot to Harris, August 11, 1939, Harris Deposit.

30. Johnson, *Harvey,* 276-7; Henry J. Haskell interview, 1931, Hagedorn Papers; Sullivan, *Twenties,* 61; White, *Puritan,* 206.

31. Haskell interview, 1931, Hagedorn Papers.

32. Alice Roosevelt Longworth, *Crowded Hours* (New York, 1933), 311.

33. Adams, *Incredible,* 151, 153; *New York Times,* June 12, 1920.

34. Walter Brown interview, November 19, 1930, Hagedorn Papers; Daugherty, *Harding Tragedy,* 44.

35. Washington *Star,* July 28, 1920; Wood Diary, copy, September 30, Hagedorn Papers; *New York Times,* June 12, 1920; Chicago *Tribune,* June 13, 1920; *New York Post,* June 15, 1920; Sullivan, *Twenties,* 63.

36. Dr. George T. Harding to Harris, July 26, December 13, 1937, Harris Deposit.

37. *New York Times,* June 12, 1920; New York *Tribune,* June 12, 1920; Washington *Star,* June 12, 1920.

38. Chicago *Tribune,* March 14, June 10, 13, 1920; New York *World,* April 13, 1920; Johnson, *Harvey,* 276; Clark interview, December 19, 1928, Wood Diary, copy, June 13, 1920, Hagedorn Papers; *New York Post,* June 14, 1920.

39. Author's interview with Will Hays, August, 1949; *New York Post,* June 12, 1920.

40. White, *Puritan,* 208; White, *Autobiography,* 586-7; Wadsworth to Harris, October 8, 1932, Daugherty to Harris, June 30, 1939, Harris Deposit; Washington *Star,* June 12, 1920.

41. Daugherty, *Harding Tragedy,* 44; New York *Tribune,* June 19, 1920.

42. Sullivan, *Twenties,* 65; *New York Times,* June 13, 1920; Walter Lippmann, "Chicago 1920," *New Republic,* 23 (June 23, 1920), 108.

43. Isaac M. Ullman telegram to Taft, June 12, 1920, Taft Papers. Harding's Saturday accessions through the eighth ballot had been: Missouri 17½; Indiana 8; New York 6; Wyoming 6; 4 each from Alabama, Kansas and Texas; 3½ from Nevada; 3 each from Tennessee, North Carolina and West Virginia; plus a few scattered votes. Missouri, Indiana, New York, Wyoming, and the southern states were controlled by the old guard, while Kansas was taking instructions from Senator Charles W. Curtis and Governor Allen.

44. Brown interview, November 19, 1930, Hagedorn Papers; *New York Times,* June 13, 1920; New York *Tribune,* June 13, 1920; Daugherty to Harris, June 29, 1938, Harris Deposit.

45. Daugherty, *Harding Tragedy,* 47-8; Brown interview, November 19, 1930, Hagedorn Papers; *New York Times,* June 13, 1920.

46. Hagedorn, *Wood,* 364-5; Procter interview, undated, Hagedorn Papers; New York *Tribune,* June 13, 1920; Fuess, *Coolidge,* 259; Chicago *Tribune,* June 13, 1920.

47. Ullman memorandum, June 19, 1920, Taft Papers.

48. Sullivan, *Twenties,* 61; Washington *Star,* June 21, July 28, 1920; New York *Tribune,* June 29, 1920; Butler, *Across,* 277-78; Ullman memorandum, June 19, 1920, Taft Papers. "At one moment Harvey had the preposterous idea that Will Hays was within the range of possibility, an idea that Hays himself shared"; cf. Longworth, *Crowded,* 307.

49. Daugherty, *Harding Tragedy,* 48-9; *New York Times,* June 13, 1920; Daugherty to Harris, May 24, 1934, October 9, 1939, Harris Deposit. In an eighth ballot caucus, King, who carried Penrose' proxy, was alone in opposition to throwing the Connecticut delegation to Harding. Of Penrose' role, Daugherty said that it was important; but Penrose did not show his hand. Against Wood, he supported Lowden. Gradually moving closer to Harding, he was for him in "the final windup." Daugherty said that Penrose helped more than any other man except Lowden. Cf. Ullman memorandum, June 19, 1920, Taft Papers; Daugherty to Harris, May 24, 1934, Harris Deposit.

50. Daugherty, *Harding Tragedy,* 49-50; Daugherty to Harris, May 24, 1934, Harris Deposit; New York *Tribune,* June 13, 1930; Procter interview, undated, Hagedorn Papers; *New York Times,* June 13, 1920.

51. *New York Times,* June 13, 1920; White, *Puritan,* 210-1; E. D. Duffield to White, July 20, 1920, White to Frank Knox, July 12, 1920, White Papers; Washington *Star,* June 14, 1920; *New York Post,* June 23, 1920; White, *Autobiography,* 536-7; Chicago *Herald and Examiner,* June 14, 1920; Hagedorn, *Wood,* 367.

52. *New York Times,* June 13, 1920.

53. New York *Tribune,* June 16, 1920; Butler, *Across,* 279; Daugherty to Harris, October 9, 1939, Harris Deposit. Harding was not on the "inside" concerning his own nomination—Harry did not tell him all—"it was better that he not know," said Daugherty; cf. Daugherty to Harris, May 24, 1934, Harris Deposit.

NOTES   179

Despite the impressions of some writers, Mrs. Harding did not drive Harding to the presidency. Daugherty had some difficulty in winning her acquiescence to his plans. Happy in her position as a senator's wife, she probably felt, as did Harding, that a larger job was beyond his capacities. "Of course, now that he is in the race and wants to win I must want him to, but down in my heart I am sorry," she told reporters. "I can see but one word written over the head of my husband if he is elected, and that word is 'tragedy!' "; cf. Sullivan, *Twenties,* 73; *New York Times,* June 11, 1920.

54. Gordon Johnson interview, February 1, 1929, Brunker interview, March 26, 1929, Wood to Bishop Brent, July 29, 1920, Hagedorn Papers.

55. New York *Tribune,* June 24, 1920; *New York Post,* July 20, 1920.

56. *New York Times,* June 6, 1920; Butler, *Across,* 278; Sullivan, *Twenties,* 75; Calder to Harris, May 22, 1934, Wadsworth to Harris, May 21, 1934, Harry S. New memorandum, undated, Harris Deposit; White, *Puritan,* 203, 209.

57. *New York Times,* June 13, 1920; New York *Tribune,* June 13, 1920; Chicago *Tribune,* June 13, 1920; *Cleveland Plain Dealer,* June 13, 1920; Washington *Star,* June 14, 1920.

58. *New York Post,* June 17, 1920; Washington *Star,* June 21, July 28, 1920. Mark Sullivan said that after his article on the Smoke-filled Room, he noticed that Smoot and others who had been on the inside regarded him with a faint smile, which he took as a hint that Harvey had pulled his leg. He told Hagedorn in 1929 that he assumed that the story as told to him was fiction for the greater glory of George Harvey; cf. Sullivan interview, December 8, 1929, Brown interview, November 19, 1930, Hagedorn Papers.

59. White, *Puritan,* 203.

60. *New York Times,* June 2, 13, 1920; *New York Post,* June 23, 1920; Watson, *As I Knew Them,* 223-4.

61. Sullivan, *Twenties,* 78; Daugherty to Harris, October 9, 1939, Harris Deposit; *New York Times,* May 9, 1920; *New York Post,* June 5, 1920.

62. Fuess, *Coolidge,* 261-2.

63. *Ibid.*

64. White, *Puritan,* 214.

CHAPTER IV

1. Johnson to Borah, July 9, 1920, Borah Papers.

2. White, *Autobiography,* 590; Mrs. J. Borden Harriman, *From Pinafores to Politics* (New York, 1923), 333-4. Officials later admitted releasing forty barrels of whisky for the convention; cf. *New York Times,* October 7, 1920.

3. New York *Tribune,* June 1, 1920; *New York Post,* June 28, 29, 30, July 1, 1920; *New York Times,* June 30, 1920. Wilson had read the speech earlier with "great satisfaction," criticizing only the suggestion that he had been at the point of death; cf. Cummings memorandum, undated, filed in Box 3, Series 1, Baker Collection.

4. Walsh telegram to J. Bruce Kremer, June 15, 1920, Walsh Papers; *New York Post,* June 24, 1920; New York *World,* June 20, 1920; Wilson to Colby, June 19, 1920, Cummings code telegrams to Wilson, June 22, 23, 1920, Baker Collection.

5. Cummings code telegram to Wilson, June 27, 1920, Cummings memorandum, undated, filed in Box 3, Series 1, Baker Collection.

6. *New York Post,* July 1, 1920; Wilson code telegram to Cummings, June 24, 1920, Baker Collection; New York *American,* July 2, 1920.

7. Burleson to Roper, July 12, 1920, Burleson Papers; *New York Post,* July 1, 2, 1920; author's interview with Cummings, 1952.
8. Smith, *Glass,* 211-2; *New York Post,* June 30, 1920; *New York Times,* July 1, 3, 1920.
9. Chicago *Tribune,* July 3, 1920; Harriman, *Pinafores,* 332-3; Arthur F. Mullen, *Western Democrat* (New York, 1940), 184-5; *New York Post,* July 3, 1920; *New York Times,* July 3, 1920; New York *Tribune,* July 3, 4, 1920; Washington *Star,* July 3, 1920; New York *World,* July 3, 1920.
10. Chicago *Tribune,* July 3, 1920.
11. Harriman, *Pinafores,* 333.
12. *New York Times,* July 3, 1920; *New York Post,* July 3, 1920; *Cleveland Plain Dealer,* July 3, 1920; New York *World,* July 3, 1920; Bruce Bliven, "San Francisco," *New Republic,* 23 (July 14, 1920), 186.
13. *New York Times,* July 1, 1920.
14. *New York Times,* July 1, 1920; Alfred E. Smith, *Up to Now* (New York, 1929), 209-11; Salvatore A. Cotillo, "Democratic Convention," *Outlook,* 125 (July 28, 1920), 564.
15. *New York Times,* July 1, 1920; *New York Post,* July 1, 1920.
16. *New York Post,* June 30, 1920; *New York Times,* July 5, 1920; Chicago *Tribune,* June 29, July 5, 1920; New York *Tribune,* June 27, 28, 1920; Bruce Bliven, "San Francisco," 197.
17. Funk to McAdoo, July 6, 1920, McAdoo Papers; *New York Post,* June 28, 29, 1920; *New York Times,* July 1, 1920; Burleson to Roper, July 12, 1920, Roper telegram to Burleson, June 30, 1920, Burleson Papers.
18. *New York Post,* June 30, July 1, 1920; Washington *Star,* June 30, 1920; *New York Times,* June 26, July 1, 2, 1920; Chicago *Tribune,* June 30, 1920; New York *Tribune,* July 2, 1920.
19. Washington *Star,* June 28, 1920; Cox, *Journey,* 226-7.
20. Chicago *Tribune,* July 3, 1920; New York *World,* July 4, 1920.
21. Chicago *Tribune,* July 4, 1920.
22. Chicago *Tribune,* July 5, 1920; McAdoo to Durbin, December 29, 1919, Funk to McAdoo, April 5, 1920, McAdoo Papers.
23. Funk to McAdoo, July 6, 1920, McAdoo Papers; New York *Tribune,* July 7, 1920.
24. Daniels, *Wilson Era,* 557; Funk to McAdoo, July 6, 1920, McAdoo Papers.
25. *New York Post,* July 6, 1920.
26. *New York Times,* July 1, 1920.
27. Cox, *Journey,* 226.
28. New York *Tribune,* July 7, 1920; Funk to McAdoo, July 6, 1920, Kenneth McKeller to McAdoo, December 6, 1920, McAdoo Papers.
29. *New York Times,* July 3, 1920; Funk to McAdoo, July 6, 1920, McAdoo Papers.
30. *New York Post,* June 29, 30, 31, 1920; Chicago *Tribune,* June 25, 1920; New York *Tribune,* June 29, 1920.
31. Wilson code telegram to Cummings, June 15, 1920, Baker Collection; Blum, *Tumulty,* 246-7.
32. Burleson to Daniels, October 23, 1934, Daniels Papers; Burleson to Newton D. Baker, April 20, 1926, copy, Baker Collection; Burleson to Roper, July 13, 1920, Burleson Papers.
33. Colby to Wilson, July 2, 1920, Wilson Papers; Cummings memorandum, January, 1929, Baker Collection; *New York Times,* July 1, 1920.
34. Cummings memorandum, January, 1929, Baker Collection; Daniels, *Wilson Era,* 555-6.

35. Burleson code telegram to Wilson, July 3, 1920, Cummings code telegram to Wilson, July 3, 1920, Wilson code telegram to Cummings (July 4, 1920 [?]), Colby code telegram to Wilson, July 4, 1920, Baker Collection.
36. Cummings memorandum, July 26, 1920, Baker Collection; Blum, *Tumulty,* 246-7; Washington *Star,* July 4, 1920.
37. Colby code telegram to Wilson, July 4, 1920, Baker Collection.
38. Wilson code telegram to Cummings, July 5, 1920, Cummings memorandum, January, 1929, Baker Collection.
39. Hoover, *Forty-Two Years,* 107; James Kerney, *The Political Education of Woodrow Wilson* (New York, 1926), 457; Burleson to Daniels, October 23, 1934, Daniels Papers.
40. New York *Tribune,* June 29, 30, 1920; Chicago *Tribune,* June 29, July 5, 1920; *New York Times,* June 30, 1920; Frances Perkins, *The Roosevelt I Knew* (New York, 1946), 27; Harriman, *Pinafores,* 329.
41. Cox, *Journey,* 232; *New York Times,* July 7, 12, 1920; Mullen, *Western Democrat,* 254-5.
42. Editorials of July 7, 1920; *Nation,* 111 (July 10, 1920), 32; Bliven, "San Francisco," 196; H. J. Howland, "Jackass," *Independent,* 103 (July 17, 1920), 68.
43 *New York Times,* July 7, 10, 1920; *New York Post,* July 6, 1920; Funk to McAdoo, July 6, 1920, McAdoo Papers; New York *World,* July 7, 1920.

CHAPTER V

1. *New York Post,* December 15, 1919; New York *Tribune,* May 11, 1920; author's interview with Will Hays, August, 1949.
2. *New York Post,* July 16, 24, 1920; Sullivan, *Twenties,* 106; *New York Times,* July 8, 23, 1920.
3. *New York Times,* June 16, July 19, 20, 21, August 1, 1920.
4. *New York Times,* July 9, 29, August 8, 1920; New York *Tribune,* August 11, 1920.
5. *New York Post,* October 16, 1920; Washington *Star,* September 8, 1920; *New York Times,* September 12, 14, November 2, 1920.
6. *New York Times,* July 12, 28, October 29, 1920.
7. *New York Times,* July 28, 1920.
8. *New York Post,* August 23, 1920; Johnson, *Harvey,* Introduction by Calvin Coolidge; *New York Times,* June 23, 1920; Daugherty to Harris, July 28, 1934, Harris Deposit.
9. *New York Times,* September 22, October 2, November 2, 1920; Harding to Bryan, November 13, 1920, Bryan Papers.
10. *New York Post,* August 14, 21, 1920; *New York Times,* October 25, 31, 1920.
11. Will Hays to Borah, April 5, 1920, Borah Papers; author's interview with Hays, August, 1949.
12. Cox, *Journey,* 241-3; *New York Times,* July 14, 1920; Washington *Star,* July 20, 1920; *New York Post,* July 17, 1920.
13. *New York Times,* July 19, 1920; Cox, *Journey,* 241-2.
14. Cummings telegram to Wilson, July 10, Wilson telegram to Cummings, July 12, Cummings memorandum of interview with Wilson, July 26, 1920, Baker Collection; *New York Times,* July 8, 20, 1920; author's interview with Cummings, July, 1953; Washington *Star,* July 21, 1920; Cox, *Journey,* 238; New York *Tribune,* July 28, 1920.

15. Washington *Star,* July 21, 1920; *New York Post,* July 22, 1920; author's interview with Cummings, July, 1953.
16. *New York Times,* July 22, 1920; *New York Post,* July 22, 1920.
17. Cox, *Journey,* 265; *New York Times,* August 8, 1920.
18. *New York Times,* July 25, September 3, 1920; Roosevelt to Howard C. Robbins, July 24, 1920, Roosevelt Papers.
19. *New York Times,* August 16, September 13, 23, October 15, November 1, 1920; Cox, *Journey,* 270.
20. *New York Times,* November 1, 1920; Roosevelt to Ronald Campbell, October 9, 1920, Roosevelt Papers; Ernest K. Lindley, *Franklin D. Roosevelt* (Indianapolis, 1931), 199.
21. *New York Post,* September 22, 1920; McAdoo to Tumulty, October 2, 1920, Wilson Papers; *New York Times,* September 21, October 1, 2, 3, 31, 1920.
22. *New York Times,* July 29, August 1, September 4, 1920; Washington *Star,* September 2, 1920; Roosevelt memorandum for George White, September 6, 1920, Roosevelt Papers; Funk to McAdoo, September 15, 1920, McAdoo to Shouse, September 17, 1920, Shouse to McAdoo, September 20, 1920, McAdoo Papers.
23. Funk to McAdoo, September 30, October 2, 1920, McAdoo Papers; *New York Times,* October 2, 5, 27, 1920; *New York Post,* September 22, 1920; Washington *Star,* October 30, 1920.
24. *Campaign Expenses,* 537. George White announced that the Democrats would publicize all receipts but would not limit the size of contributions; cf. *New York Times,* July 23, 1920.
25. *New York Times,* September 19, 24, October 29, 1920, March 2, 1921; *New York Post,* August 30, September 22, 1920; Charles H. McCarthy to Roosevelt, October 18, 1920, Roosevelt Papers.
26. Ullman to Taft, September 16, 1920, Taft Papers; Washington *Star,* September 22, 24, October 13, 1920; *New York Times,* September 27, October 21, 1920; Cummings Diary, October 5, 1920, Wilson Papers.
27. *New York Post,* July 22, August 9, September 16, 1920; Washington *Star,* August 30, 1920; *New York Times,* July 11, September 22, 1920; Peter J. Hamilton to Wilson, October 24, 1920, Wilson Papers.
28. Ullman to Taft, August 16, 1920, Taft Papers; Washington *Star,* September 22, 24, October 24, 1920; *New York Post,* August 26, September 22, 1920; Letters to Thomas J. Walsh.
29. *New York Times,* August 13, September 19, October 28, 29, 1920; Taft to Ullman, October 24, 1920, Taft Papers; Chicago *Tribune,* September 1, October 3, November 10, 1920; New York *Tribune,* October 27, 1920; Sullivan, *Twenties,* 130; Cox, *Journey,* 268, 270; *New York Post,* October 2, 1920.
30. *New York Times,* October 9, 25, 29, 1920; Cox, *Journey,* 276-9, 282; McAdoo Personal Notebook 2, McAdoo Papers.
31. *New York Times,* August 15, 24, 26, 1920.
32. *New York Times,* August 27, 1920; Washington *Star,* August 27, 1920.
33. *New York Times,* August 27, 28, September 1, 4, 5, 10, 15, 1920.
34. *New York Times,* August 23, 25, 28, September 6, 1920.
35. *New York Times,* August 28, 1920; Washington *Star,* August 28, 1920; *New York Post,* September 11, 1920; author's interview with Hays, August, 1949.
36. *New York Post,* October 2, 1920; Washington *Star,* September 1, 1920; Irving Fisher to Taft, September 2, 1920, Taft Papers; Cummings Diary, October 5, 1920, Baker Collection; *New York Times,* September 6, 26, 1920. Cox later explained that the newspapers played up his fund charges too prominently, which "created some uneasiness in the East for a time"; cf. Cox, *Journey,* 268.
37. *New York Times,* June 19, July 15, 1920; New York *Tribune,* July 30, August 4, 1920.

38. *New York Times,* August 11, 15, 1920.

39. *New York Times,* June 19, July 8, 15, 1920.

40. *New York Times,* July 23, 1920; *New York Post,* August 14, 1920; New York *Tribune,* July 25, 1920.

41. *New York Times,* August 5, 17, 20, 27, 1920.

42. *New York Times,* August 8, 9, 10, 1920; New York *Tribune,* August 8, 9, 11, 1920; *New York Post,* August 11, 14, 1920.

43. Crane to Taft, July 19, 1920, Hilles to Taft, July 19, August 26, 1920, Herbert Parsons to Taft, August 25, 1920, Taft Papers; Hoover telegram to White (August, 1920 [?]), White to Hoover, August 28, 1920, Hoover telegram to White, August 27, 1920, White Papers; Phillip C. Jessup, *Elihu Root* (New York, 1938), 411-2.

44. *New York Times,* August 29, 1920.

45. *New York Post,* August 30, September 1, 1920; New York *Tribune,* August 29, 1920; *New York Times,* August 29, September 3, 6, 7, 29, 1920; Ullman to Taft, August 30, 1920, Taft telegram to Hilles, September 7, 1920, A. Lawrence Lowell to Taft, September 9, 1920, J. J. Spurgeon to Taft, August 31, 1920, J. L. Barton to Taft, September 23, 1920, Hilles to Taft, September 20, 1920, Taft Papers; White to Harding, September 10, 1920, White Papers.

46. *New York Times,* September 4, 6, 12, 18, 19, 21, 24, 30, 1920.

47. Hiram Johnson to Borah, July 27, 1920, Borah to Colonel Miller, October 3, 1920, Borah Papers; *New York Times,* September 30, October 1, 3, 4, 5, 6, 1920.

48. *New York Times,* October 8, 1920.

49. *New York Times,* October 8, 9, 16, 17, 21, 22, 1920; *New York Post,* October 8, 1920; Washington *Star,* October 8, 1920; Bowers, *Beveridge,* 522.

50. *New York Times,* October 9, 10, 18, 28, 1920.

51. Taft to "Dick," July 24, 1920, Ullman to Taft, September 22, 1920, Taft Papers; *New York Times,* June 24, October 10, 12, 1920; White to Mrs. Stevens, October 27, 1920, White Papers.

52. *New York Times,* October 15, 20, 1920; author's interview with Hays, August, 1949.

53. *New York Times,* October 17, 20, 24, 1920; Taft to Hilles, October 21, 1920, Taft Papers. The *New York Times* compared Taft to the professor who voted Republican because, as the party of intelligence, it would sooner or later see the absurdity of high tariffs.

54. *New York Times,* October 9, 1920.

55. *New York Times,* October 12, 16, 17, November 1, 1920.

56. *New York Times,* October 21, 22, 28, 1920.

57. Coolidge, *Autobiography,* 149; *New York Times,* October 19, 26, 29, September 17, 19, 1920; Hilles to Taft, November 1, 1920, Taft Papers; Harry S. New memorandum, undated, filed in Correspondence of Roosevelt Headquarters, Box 5, Roosevelt Papers.

58. *New York Times,* August 15, 18, 20, 29, September 24, 1920.

59. *New York Times,* September 4, 5, 9, 28, October 1, 2, 5, 1920.

60. *New York Times,* August 7, October 22, 27, 28, 1920; Steve Early to Louis Howe, August 11 and August 18, 1920, Roosevelt Papers.

61. *New York Post,* August 23, November 1, 1920; *New York Times,* August 30, September 9, 15, 1920.

62. *New York Times,* September 6, 8, 9, 14, 15, 1920; *New York Post,* August 25, September 14, 1920; New York *Tribune,* September 13, 1920; McAdoo to Meredith, September 15, 1920, McAdoo Papers.

63. Blum, *Tumulty,* 253; *New York Times,* September 30, October 4, 1920.

64. Blum, *Tumulty,* 254; Cummings Diary, October 4, 1920, Baker Collection.

65. *New York Times,* October 3, 6, 12, 19, 28, 1920; Tumulty, *Wilson,* 500; Daniels Diary, October 12, 1920, Daniels Papers; Houston, *Eight Years,* 92-4; Burleson interview, 1927, Baker Collection.

66. Walsh to Pat Harrison, September 2, 1920, Walsh Papers; Daniels Diary, September 21, 1920, Daniels Papers; *New York Post,* October 1, 1920; Cummings Diary, October 5, 1920, copy, Baker Collection; *New York Times,* October 5, 1920; Washington *Star,* October 7, 10, 1920.

67. *New York Times,* October 8, 9, 10, 12, 13, 15, 16, 1920.

68. *New York Times,* October 16, 17, 19, 20, 22, 1920.

69. *New York Times,* October 24, 1920.

70. W. L. Hill to Pat Harrison, September 25, 1920, Walsh Papers; *New York Times,* October 10, 21, 23, 24, 26, 27, 31, 1920.

71. *New York Times,* October 31, November 1, 2, 1920.

72. *New York Times,* August 10, 13, 29, October 12, 23, 1920; Lindley, *FDR,* 193.

73. McAdoo to Wilson, October 17, 1920, Wilson Papers; *New York Times,* September 12, 25, October 15, 16, 23, November 2, 1920.

74. Roosevelt to W. S. Cowles, October 11, 1920, Roosevelt Papers; *New York Times,* October 14, 22, 1920; Washington *Star,* October 17, 1920; McAdoo to Roper, October 18, 1920, McAdoo Papers.

75. McAdoo to E. M. O'Shea, April 21, 1920, McAdoo Papers; *New York Times,* July 25, August 1, 1920; *New York Post,* August 16, 21, 1920.

76. *New York Times,* August 8, 20, 28, September 7, October 15, 1920.

77. *New York Times,* August 27, October 29, 30, 1920.

78. *New York Times,* August 8, 22, September 12, 14, October 1, 1920.

79. *New York Times,* August 10, September 30, November 1, 1920.

80. *New York Times,* August 15, 19, September 29, 1920; *New York Post,* August 19, 1920; Ickes to White, June 24 and June 30, 1920, White Papers.

81. *New York Times,* July 23, August 31, October 4, 1920; White to Homer Hoch, July 12, 1920, White to Eugene Howe, September 4, 1920, White Papers.

82. *New York Times,* July 7, 23, September 7, 9, October 2, 7, 22, 1920.

83. *New York Times,* July 19, 23, August 4, September 1, 7, 12, 26, October 10, 15, 25, 28, 1920.

84. *New York Times,* July 23, September 7, 1920.

85. Johnson to Bryan, September 14, 1920, William Jennings Bryan Papers, Library of Congress; Washington *Star,* October 5, 6, 1920; *New Republic,* 23 (June 30, 1920), 137; Daniels Diary, October 7, 1920, Daniels Papers.

86. Steve Early to Louis Howe, August 12, 1920, Roosevelt Papers; *New York Post,* October 16, 1920; Franklin K. Lane, *The Letters of Franklin K. Lane* (New York, 1922), 356-9.

87. New York *Sun,* March 2, 4, 1920; *New York Times,* July 1, 8, 19, 23, September 10, 15, October 1, 14, 31, 1920.

88. *New York Times,* August 15, September 25, October 1, 26, 1920; Steve Early to Louis Howe, August 18, 1920, Roosevelt Papers.

89. *New York Times,* July 16, 23, October 26, 1920; *New York Post,* August 26, 1920.

90. *New York Times,* July 18, August 31, October 26, 1920; *New York Post,* August 21, September 2, 1920; McAdoo Personal Notebook 2, McAdoo Papers; Daniels Diary, September 5, 1920, Daniels Papers.

91. *New York Times,* July 21, 24, August 1, 6, 14, 27, 1920.

92. *New York Times,* October 11, 19, 22, 27, 1920; *New York Post,* October 13, 1920; Washington *Star,* October 28, 1920.

93. Adams, *Incredible*, 179-81; *New York Times*, October 17, 23, 30, November 1, 1920; Wilson, *Memoir*, 305-6; Sullivan, *Twenties*, 131.

94. Washington *Star*, October 30, 1920; *New York Times*, October 30, 31, November 1, 1920; Adams, *Incredible*, 184-5.

95. *New York Times*, August 28, September 7, 10, 29, October 3, 1920.

96. *New York Times*, June 24, September 24, October 8, 1920.

97. Daniels Diary, September 12, 1920, Daniels Papers; Funk to McAdoo, September 30, 1920, McAdoo Papers; *New York Post*, October 2, 1920.

98. *New York Times*, October 17, 1920.

99. *New York Times*, September 30, 1920.

100. *New York Times*, September 5, 1920; *New York Post*, October 11, 1920.

101. *New York Times*, July 11, September 6, 1920.

102. *New York Post*, June 5, September 7, October 25, 1920.

103. *New York Times*, August 4, September 7, October 31, 1920; Washington *Star*, October 5, 1920.

104. Franklin D. Roosevelt to Ronald Campbell, October 9, 1920, Roosevelt Papers; *New York Times*, September 21, 24, 28, 1920; *New York Post*, September 21, 1920; W. L. Hill to Pat Harrison, September 25, Walsh Papers; Blum, *Tumulty*, 254.

105. President's Research Committee on Social Trends in the United States, *Recent Social Trends in the United States* (New York, 1933), 859, 222; George Soule, *Prosperity Decade* (New York, 1947), 84-6.

106. *New York Times*, July 22, 1920; *Springfield* (Mass.) *Republican*, November 1, 1920.

107. Washington *Star*, October 5, 28, 1920; *New York Times*, September 10, 1920.

108. *New York Times*, August 1, September 26, 1920; New York *Tribune*, August 11, 1920; W. L. Hill to Harrison, September 25, 1920, Walsh Papers.

109. Washington *Star*, October 4, 31, 1920; *New York Times*, October 31, 1920.

110. *New York Times*, August 5, 12, 16, 1920.

111. *New York Times*, August 15, October 29, 1920.

112. *New York Times*, October 21, 26, 22, November 2, 1920; Fuess, *Coolidge*, 273; Taft speech at Salt Lake City, October 25, 1920, Taft Papers.

113. Washington *Star*, October 29, 1920; Sullivan to Walsh, September 17, 1920, Walsh Papers; *New York Times*, October 1, November 2, 1920; New York *Tribune*, October 31, 1920; Chicago *Tribune*, November 2, 1920.

114. Daniels Diary, August 10, 1920, Daniels Papers; Creel, *Rebel*, 229; Houston, *Eight Years*, 92-3; Blum, *Tumulty*, 254; Lindley, *FDR*, 198; *New York Post*, November 3, 1920.

115. *New York Times*, July 10, October 30, 31, November 2, 1920.

116. The states in which Republicans made the largest percentile gains were Maryland, Michigan, Wisconsin, Minnesota, Nebraska, North Dakota, Colorado, Wyoming, Montana, Utah, Idaho, Washington, and California. The Democrats best held their own, outside of the South and border states, in Connecticut, New Jersey, Delaware, West Virginia, Indiana, Kansas, and Oregon; cf. *New York Times*, March 6, 1921; Edgar E. Robinson, *The Presidential Vote, 1896-1932* (Stanford, Calif., 1934).

117. *New York Post*, November 3, 4, 1920; Borah to Johnson, November 15, 1920, Borah Papers; New York *American*, November 3, 1920; Chicago *Tribune*, November 3, 4, 6, 1920; Washington *Star*, November 4, 1920; *Cleveland Plain Dealer*, November 3, 1920; New York *Tribune*, November 4, 1920.

118. *New York Post*, November 3, 1920; New York *Tribune*, November 3, 1920; Chicago *Tribune*, November 4, 1920. Other papers attributing the result primarily to accumulated resentments at the Wilson administration were the Kansas

City *Star,* Washington *Star, Springfield* (Mass.) *Republican, St. Louis Post-Dispatch,* Philadelphia *Public Ledger, New Yorker Staats-Zeitung,* and Baltimore *Sun.*

119. *New York Post,* November 4, 1920; McAdoo to Wilson, November 4, 1920; Baruch to Wilson (November 4, 1920 [?]), Wilson Papers; Taft to Mabel T. Boardman, November 3, 1920, Taft Papers; Cox to McAdoo, November 8, 1920, McAdoo Papers; Coolidge, *Autobiography,* 154; Roosevelt to Mrs. Anna K. Henderson, November 9, 1920, Roosevelt Papers; author's interview with Hays, September, 1950.

120. Newton Baker to Wilson, November 3, 1920, Wilson Papers.

121. White, *Autobiography,* 465, 482; George E. Mowry, *Theodore Roosevelt and the Progressive Movement* (Madison, 1946), 10; Charles A. Beard, *The Rise of American Civilization,* Vol. II (New York, 1930), 565-6.

122. Creel, *Rebel,* 197; Harold Stearns, *Liberalism in America* (New York, 1919), 3-4, 99-100; Merle E. Curti, *Growth of American Thought* (New York, 1943), 684-5.

123. John Chamberlain, *Farewell to Reform* (New York, 1933), 295-6, 260; Lane, *Letters,* 263. Wilson told Josephus Daniels that "Every reform we have won will be lost if we go into this war"; cf. Daniels interview, 1929, Baker Collection.

124. Oswald G. Villard, *Fighting Years* (New York, 1939), 373; Harry Elmer Barnes, "Woodrow Wilson," *American Mercury,* 1 (April, 1924), 479; George E. Mowry, "The First World War and American Democracy," *War as a Social Institution,* edited by J. D. Clarkson and T. C. Cochran for the American Historical Association (New York, 1941), 177-8; Lane, *Letters,* 313; Mowry, *Roosevelt and the Progressive Movement,* 320-79; Harold L. Ickes, *The Autobiography of a Curmudgeon* (New York, 1943), 224-32.

125. Charles Evans Hughes described Palmer's tactics as "violations of personal rights which savor of the worst practices of tyranny"; cf. *New York Post,* May 28, 1920. Among newspapermen a story circulated that Palmer had confidentially told some of them that he put forth stories of revolution in order to be able to combat a certain radicalism in the labor movement; cf. Clinton W. Gilbert, *Behind the Mirrors* (New York, 1922), 43-4. Stearns, *Liberalism,* 5-6, 200-1; Mowry, "War and American Democracy," 179.

126. *New York World,* January 9, 1920; Curti, *American Thought,* 684; Parke R. Kolbe, *The Colleges in Wartime and After* (New York, 1919), 120-2.

127. Mowry, "War and American Democracy," 179.

128. *Recent Social Trends,* 586, 1163-4, 1154-5; *Encyclopedia of Social Sciences,* IV, 566.

129. Curti, *American Thought,* 710-1; *Recent Social Trends,* 415-22.

130. *Recent Social Trends,* 398, 427-8; Mowry, "War and American Democracy," 173-5; White, *Puritan,* 186; William W. Sweet, *The Story of Religions in America* (New York, 1939), 511-2; Kolbe, *Colleges in Wartime,* 120-2.

131. Mowry, "War and American Democracy," 173-4; White, *Autobiography,* 597; Vernon L. Parrington, *Main Currents in American Thought* (New York, 1941), 347-73, 392-3.

132. Mowry, "War and American Democracy," 180-2.

133. *New York World,* July 7, 1920; Ray S. Baker, *American Chronicle* (New York, 1945), 261; White to Baker, December 28, 1920, White Papers; White, *Autobiography,* 496; Hiram Johnson to Bryan, September 14, 1920, Bryan Papers.

134. Lincoln Steffens, *Autobiography* (New York, 1931), 831; Samuel Gompers, *Seventy Years of Life and Labor* (New York, 1925), Vol. 2, 501; Chamberlain, *Farewell to Reform,* 260, 304-5; Richard Hofstadter, *The Age of Reform* (New York, 1955), 270-80.

135. *Recent Social Trends,* 1126, 1154-5, 1158-9, 422-3, 398, 427-8; Mowry, "War and American Democracy," 180-1.

SELECTED BIBLIOGRAPHY

PRIMARY SOURCES

Manuscripts

Newton D. Baker Papers, Library of Congress.
Ray Stannard Baker Collection of Woodrow Wilson Material, Library of Congress.
William E. Borah Papers, Library of Congress.
William Jennings Bryan Papers, Library of Congress.
Albert S. Burleson Papers, Library of Congress.
Josephus Daniels Papers, Library of Congress.
Carter Glass Papers, Library of the University of Virginia.
Leonard Wood Papers, Hermann Hagedorn Papers, Library of Congress.
Warren G. Harding Letters, Library of Congress.
Ray Baker Harris Deposit of Warren G. Harding Materials, Library of Congress.
Cordell Hull Papers, Library of Congress.
William Gibbs McAdoo Papers, Library of Congress.
Miles Poindexter Papers, Library of the University of Virginia.
Franklin D. Roosevelt Papers, Franklin D. Roosevelt Library, Hyde Park, New York.
Elihu Root Papers, Library of Congress.
William Howard Taft Papers, Library of Congress.
Thomas J. Walsh Papers, Library of Congress.
William Allen White Papers, Library of Congress.
Woodrow Wilson Papers, Library of Congress.

Party Publications

Official Report of the Proceedings of the Democratic National Convention, 1920. Indianapolis: Bookwalter-Ball Printing Co., 1920.

Official Report of the Proceedings of the Seventeenth Republican National Convention. New York: Tenny Press, 1920.

Government Publications

Presidential Campaign Expenses: Hearings before a Subcommittee of the Committee on Privileges and Elections, United States Senate. Printed pursuant to Senate

Resolution No. 357, 66 Congress, 2 Session, for the use of the Committee on Privileges and Elections. 2 vols. Washington, 1921.

Leases upon Naval Oil Reserves: Hearings before the Committee on Public Lands and Surveys, United States Senate. Printed pursuant to Senate Resolutions Nos. 282, 294, and 434, 67 Cong., 4 Sess., and No. 147, 68 Cong., 1 Sess., for the use of the Committee on Public Lands and Surveys. 3 vols. Washington, 1924.

Memoirs

Baker, Ray S. *American Chronicle.* New York: Charles Scribner's Sons, 1945.

Bryan, William J. *The Memoirs of William Jennings Bryan.* Philadelphia: John C. Winston Co., 1925.

Butler, Nicholas M. *Across the Busy Years.* New York: Charles Scribner's Sons, 1939.

Coolidge, Calvin. *Autobiography.* New York: Cosmopolitan Book Corp., 1929.

Cox, James M. *Journey Through My Years.* New York: Simon & Schuster, 1946.

Creel, George. *Rebel at Large.* New York: G. P. Putnam's Sons, 1947.

Daniels, Josephus. *The Wilson Era.* Chapel Hill: University of North Carolina Press, 1946.

Daugherty, Harry M. *The Inside Story of the Harding Tragedy.* New York: Churchill Co., 1932.

Gompers, Samuel. *Seventy Years of Life and Labor.* 2 vols. New York: E. P. Dutton & Co., 1925.

Grayson, Cary T. *Woodrow Wilson: An Intimate Memoir.* New York: Henry Holt & Co., 1960.

Harriman, Mrs. J. Borden. *From Pinafores to Politics.* New York: Henry Holt & Co., 1923.

Hoover, Irwin H. *Forty-Two Years in the White House.* Boston and New York: Houghton Mifflin Co., 1934.

Houston, David F. *Eight Years with Wilson's Cabinet.* New York: Garden City Publishing Co., 1926.

Hull, Cordell. *Memoirs.* New York: Macmillan Co., 1948.

Ickes, Harold L. *Autobiography of a Curmudgeon.* New York: Reynal & Hitchcock, 1943.

Longworth, Alice Roosevelt. *Crowded Hours.* New York: Charles Scribner's Sons, 1933.

McAdoo, William G. *Crowded Years.* New York: Houghton Mifflin Co., 1931.

Mullen, Arthur F. *Western Democrat.* New York: Wilfred Funk, 1940.

Perkins, Frances. *The Roosevelt I Knew.* New York: Viking Press, 1946.

Smith, Alfred E. *Up To Now.* New York: Viking Press, 1929.

Starling, Edmund W. *Starling of the White House.* New York: Simon & Schuster, 1946.

Steffens, Lincoln. *Autobiography.* New York: Harcourt, Brace & Co., 1931.

Stimson, Henry L. *On Active Service.* New York: Harper & Brothers, 1947.

Tumulty, Joseph P. *Woodrow Wilson as I Knew Him.* Garden City: Doubleday, Page & Co., 1921.

Villard, Oswald G. *Fighting Years: Memoirs of a Liberal Editor.* New York: Harcourt, Brace & Co., 1939.

Watson, James E. *As I Knew Them.* Indianapolis: Bobbs-Merrill Co., 1932.

White, William Allen. *Autobiography.* New York: Macmillan Co., 1946.

Wilson, Edith B. *My Memoir.* Indianapolis: Bobbs-Merrill Co., 1938.

Secondary Works

Adams, Samuel H. *The Incredible Era: the Life and Times of Warren G. Harding.* New York: Houghton Mifflin Co., 1939.

Alderfer, Harold F. *The Personality and Politics of Warren G. Harding.* Washington, D. C., 1939. Photographic reproduction of dissertation in Library of Congress.

Allen, Frederick L. *Only Yesterday.* New York: Harper & Brothers, 1931.

Bailey, Thomas A. *Woodrow Wilson and the Great Betrayal.* New York: Macmillan Co., 1945.

Beard, Charles A. and Mary R. *The Rise of American Civilization.* Vol. II, New York: Macmillan Co., 1930.

Blum, John M. *Joe Tumulty and the Wilson Era.* Boston: Houghton Mifflin Co., 1951.

Bowers, Claude G. *Beveridge and the Progressive Era.* New York: Literary Guild, 1932.

Chafee, Zechariah. *Free Speech in the United States.* Cambridge, Mass.: Harvard University Press, 1941.

Chamberlain, John. *Farewell to Reform.* New York: John Day Co., 1933.

Curti, Merle E. *The Growth of American Thought.* New York: Harper & Brothers, 1943.

Dodd, William E. *Woodrow Wilson and His Work.* New York: Peter Smith, 1932.

Field, Carter. *Bernard Baruch.* New York: McGraw-Hill Book Co., 1944.

Fleming, David F. *The United States and the League of Nations, 1918-1920.* New York: G. P. Putnam's Sons, 1932.

Fuess, Claude M. *Calvin Coolidge,* Boston: Little, Brown & Co., 1940.

Gilbert, Clinton W. *Behind the Mirrors.* New York: G. P. Putnam's Sons, 1922.

Hagedorn, Hermann. *Leonard Wood.* New York: Harper & Brothers, 1931.

Hofstadter, Richard. *The Age of Reform.* New York: Alfred A. Knopf, 1955.

Hutchinson, William T. *Lowden of Illinois.* Chicago: University of Chicago Press, 1957.

Jessup, Phillip C. *Elihu Root.* New York: Dodd, Mead & Co., 1938.

Johnson, Claudius O. *Borah of Idaho.* New York: Longmans, Green & Co., 1936.

Johnson, Willis F. *George Harvey*. New York: Houghton Mifflin Co., 1929.

Kerney, James. *The Political Education of Woodrow Wilson*. New York: The Century Co., 1926.

Kolbe, Parke R. *The Colleges in Wartime and After*. New York: D. Appleton & Co., 1919.

Lane, Franklin K. *The Letters of Franklin K. Lane*. New York: Houghton Mifflin Co., 1922.

Lawrence, David. *The True Story of Woodrow Wilson*. New York: George H. Doran & Co., 1924.

Lindley, Ernest K. *Franklin D. Roosevelt*. Indianapolis: Bobbs-Merrill Co., 1931.

Lodge, Henry Cabot. *The Senate and the League of Nations*. New York: Charles Scribner's Sons, 1925.

Lyons, Eugene. *Our Unknown Ex-President*. New York: Doubleday & Co., 1948.

McKay, Kenneth C. *The Progressive Movement of 1924*. New York: Columbia University Press, 1947.

Moos, Malcolm. *The Republicans*. New York: Random House, 1956.

Mowry, George E., "The First World War and American Democracy," *War as a Social Institution*. Edited by J. D. Clarkson and T. C. Cochran for the American Historical Association. New York: Columbia University Press, 1941.

——. *The California Progressives*. Berkeley: University of California Press, 1951.

——. *Theodore Roosevelt and the Progressive Movement*. Madison: University of Wisconsin Press, 1946.

Overacker, Louise. *Presidential Primaries*. New York: Macmillan Co., 1926.

Palmer, James E. *Carter Glass*. Roanoke: Institute of American Biography, 1938.

Parrington, Vernon L. *Main Currents in American Thought*. New York: Macmillan Co., 1941.

Paxson, Frederick L. *Normalcy, 1919-1923*. Berkeley: University of California Press, 1948.

President's Research Committee on Social Trends in the United States. *Recent Social Trends in the United States*. New York: McGraw-Hill Book Co., 1933.

Schriftgiesser, Karl. *The Gentleman from Massachusetts: Henry Cabot Lodge*. Boston: Little, Brown & Co., 1944.

——. *This was Normalcy*. Boston: Atlantic Monthly Press–Little, Brown & Co., 1948.

Smith, Rixey and Norman Beasley. *Carter Glass*. New York: Longmans, Green & Co., 1939.

Soule, George. *Prosperity Decade*. New York: Rinehart & Co., 1947.

Stearns, Harold. *Liberalism in America*. New York: Boni & Liveright, 1919.

Sullivan, Mark. *The Twenties*. Our Times, Vol. VI. New York: Charles Scribner's Sons, 1935.

Sweet, William W., "*The Story of Religions in America*. New York: Harper & Brothers, 1939.

Synon, Mary. *McAdoo*. Indianapolis: Bobbs-Merrill Co., 1924.

INDEX

Adams, John F., 83
Adamson Act, 17
Addams, Jane: in social work, 15; predicts war would bring reaction, 163
administration Democrats: 78, 109, 113, 127, 128, 134; for McAdoo, 63; for Hoover, 67; split by Palmer, 73, 116; challenged by Democratic bosses, 75; oppose Bryan, 78; control convention, 102, 112-113; paralyzed by Wilson's receptivity, 112; divided on candidates, 113, 116-117; want Cox to concentrate on League, 133; hold aloof from the campaign in the West, 130-131; pleased by Cox's acceptance, 135; charge big business with causing recession, 156
Alabama, 68, 115
Alaska, in Democratic platform, 105
aliens: Republican platform on, 81; deported, 164
Allen, Henry: as Wood supporter, 31, 48, 82, 86; boom for, 48; permits Kansas to vote for Harding, 95; opposed by labor, 89, 100; promised vice-presidential nomination, 95, 100; presented for vice-president, 101
American Federation of Labor: 45; condemns Republican platform, 81-82; for Cox, 155
American Legion, 22, 26
American Mercury, 165
American Peace Society, 19
Amidon, Samuel B.: 114, 115; McAdoo convention leader, 111
Ansbury, Timothy T., presents Franklin D. Roosevelt, 121
Antisaloon League: 151; endorses McAdoo, 64
Anti-Semitism, 164
Arkansas, support for Palmer, 73
Armenia, in Democratic platform, 105
Article X: 137, 139, 144, 145, 146, 153; Lodge on, 80; Harding on, 135, 140; Lodge-Wilson difference on, 55-56; compromise move, 57; Wilson on, 143
Asiatic exclusion: in Republican platform, 81; in Democratic platform, 106
Associated Press, report of Smoke-filled Room, 91
association of nations: 80, 103, 160; Harding on, 136, 137, 138, 141; League to Enforce Peace condemns, 137; Hoover on, 139; Cox on, 144

Atlanta Journal, 44
Atterbury, William W., a Wood manager, 48
Austrian-Americans, shift to Republicans, 161

Babson, Roger, backs Cox on league, 138
Bailey, Joseph W., 142
Baker, Newton D.: Wilson urges to attend convention, 62; in campaign, 129, 146; on reaction, 161-162
Baker, Ray S.: McAdoo supporter, 69; switches support to Palmer, 69, 70; in conference on nominating Wilson, 119; war ruined progressivism, 166
Baltimore American, on Harding nomination, 99
Baltimore *Sun,* on Republican league plank, 81
Barnes, Julius, Hoover supporter, 43, 171n
Baruch, Bernard: 57, 60, 70, 102, 120; urges Wilson to compromise on league, 55; works for McAdoo, 64, 68; cancels San Francisco reservations, 69; wants Cox to take dry stand, 151
Bassett, John S., on Cox campaign, 132
Bellamy, Edward, 15
Berger, Victor, barred from Congress, 164
Beveridge, Albert J., 79
Bickett, Thomas W., for Hoover, 43
Bigelow, John H., presents Palmer, 110
Bismarck (Nebraska), 155
Blackstone Hotel, 85, 86, 87, 97
Bliss, Tasker H., Lodge reservations would not cripple league, 57
Bliven, Bruce: on Bryan, 111; on Cox nomination, 122
Bolshevism: 22, 81, 161, Democratic platform on, 106. *See also* reds book publication, decline after war, 165, 167
Borah, William E.: Johnson supporter, 80, 81, 84, 135; on Wood's militarism, 29; on Wood's financing, 52-53, 85; supported for permanent chairman, 79; in Smoke-filled Room, 88; accepted Lenroot, 100; in campaign, 125; threatens bolt, 137-138; says election defeat for league, 160; on reaction, 161-162
Boston police strike, 45

191

INDEX

Boston *Post,* on Harding acceptance speech, 135
Bourne, Randolph, war caused reaction, 162
Brandegee, Frank B.: 80, 87, 139; in Smoke-filled Room, 88; active for Harding, 89; move to stop Harding with Hays, 94
Brennan, George R.: 61; opposes McAdoo, 68
Britain, 45, 140, 153, 154
Brittain, Nan, 90
Brown, C. M., McAdoo wants withdrawal disregarded, 70
Brown, Walter: Harding leader, 90; objects to Saturday adjournment, 92; on Smoke-filled Room, 98
Bryan, William Jennings: 19, 24, 60, 76, 78, 88, 111, 118, 119, 125, 128, 163; opposes making league issue, 56, 77, 106-108; opposes third term, 57; opposes Cox, 75; supports league, 76-77; preconvention campaign, 72, 76-78; on issues, 77; strength in convention, 102; backs Walsh for chairman, 104; in resolutions committee, 104; challenges platform, 106-109; no part in campaign, 129; on reaction, 150, 161-162; calls election repudiation of Wilson, 161
Bryn Mawr, 138
Burleson, Albert S.: 60, 102, 111, 127; thought Wilson wanted third term, 62; urged by Wilson to attend convention, 62; backs McAdoo, 68, 111, 112; opposed Volstead Act, 105; opposed nomination of Wilson, 118-119; Wilson's displeasure at, 119, 120; alienated labor, 155; predicts defeat, 159
business: Republican platform on, 81; Harding agent of, 101; Harding program for, 149; Cox praises, 147
business, big: 132-133; opposes International Labor Organization, 21; Johnson denounces, 32, 50; Hoover favored, 45; at Republican convention, 85-87, 99; Cox attacks, 147; La Follette says controls both parties, 148; charged with recession, 156; for conservative government, 161
business, small, threatened by trusts, 15
Butler, Nicholas M.: for Lowden, 34; boom for, 48-49; presented, 83; in balloting, 84; on attempt to stop Harding, 94; on Penrose' role, 97; signs Declaration of Thirty-One Proleague Republicans, 139
Byllesby, Henry M.: backs Wood, 26; at Republican convention, 86

Calder, William M.: on Smoke-filled Room, 88; on Penrose' role, 97; seconds Lenroot, 100
California: 31, 68, 82, 92, 112, 153; primary, 44-45, 51-52, 66
campaign fund investigation: 52-53; supported by old guard, 28; effect on Lowden, 86
campaign funds: 41, 50, 88, 104, 107; publicity for, 17. *See also* Cox, slush fund charges
Campbell, James E., 112
Carlin, C. C., 72, 113
Carnegie, Andrew, 19
censorship: opposed by Harding, 37; by Wilson administration, 163
Chadbourne, Thomas L.: backs McAdoo, 64; cancels San Francisco reservations, 69; wants Cox to take dry stand, 151
Chamberlain, John, war ruined progressivism, 166
Chancellor, William Estabrook, 153
charitable contributions, decline after war, 166
Chevy Chase Club, 60
Chicago, 145, 153
Chicago convention. *See* Republican National Convention.
Chicago *Tribune:* sued by Henry Ford, 22; on Johnson's Illinois vote, 51; on a third term, 63, 117; on McAdoo, 70; on Lowden, 83; reports conference to select uninstructed delegates, 91; on Harding nomination, 99; on Colby speech, 109; on Cox nomination, 121; on Cox as campaigner, 131; predicts landslide, 158, says election league defeat, 160
child labor: restricted, 16; Republican platform on, 81; Democratic platform on, 106
China, 139
Christianity and the Social Crisis, 15
church, fights bosses, 15. *See also* social gospel
Cincinnati Enquirer, 73
Clark, Champ: wants Wilson to withdraw, 59; receptive to nomination, 78; suggested by Wilson for vice-president, 118
Clayton Antitrust Act, 17
Cleveland *News,* 40
Cleveland *Plain Dealer:* 59, 76; on Democratic platform, 109; on Cox nomination, 121; says election a victory for league, 160
Cobb, Frank, 163
Cobb, Irvin: 82; receives votes for Democratic nomination, 115

INDEX 193

Cockran, Bourke: debates Bryan on platform, 107; proposes wet plank, 109; presented Smith, 110; in campaign, 129
Cohen, John S., 44
Colby, Bainbridge: 102; visits Wilson, 62-63; urged by Wilson to go to convention, 63; backed by Wilson for permanent chairman, 104; on resolutions committee, 104; debates Bryan on platform, 109; sentiment for his nomination, 114, 116; move to nominate Wilson, 118; as vice-presidential possibility, 121; in campaign, 129, 142, 146
Cole, W. L., 41
Columbia University, 48
Columbus Dispatch, for Wood, 40
Communism. *See* reds
compulsory arbitration: 89, 149; Allen for, 100; Democratic platform opposes, 106
Congress: 18, 73, 81, 83; election results, 159
Congress Hotel, 87, 93
Connecticut: 128; delegation resisted move to stop Harding with Hays, 94
conscientious objectors, Harding favors exemption, 37
conservation: 16, 17; Harding opposed, 37, 149; Republican platform on, 81; Franklin D. Roosevelt on, 148
Coolidge, Calvin: 89; preconvention campaign, 45-46, 51; presented to convention, 83; on George Harvey's influence, 88; nominated for the vice-presidency, 100-101; campaign tour, 124-125, 142; as speaker, 125; on Cox as campaigner, 131; position on league, 140; attacks Wilson, 150, 157; predicts landslide victory, 158
Coolidge, Mrs. Calvin, 101
Cornwell, John J., presents Davis, 111
corrupt practices laws, 16, 17, 133
cost of living: 32, 156; Republican platform on, 81
Cowley, Malcolm, 165
Cox, James M.: 77, 78, 88, 111, 112, 119, 136; on Lowden, 34; Wilson opposed, 62; relations with McAdoo, 66, 114; sketch, 73-74, 76; preconvention campaign, 73-76; on league, 73, 75, 127, 131, 132, 133, 134, 135-136, 138, 140, 141-146, 156; as a progressive, 73, 74, 75, 146-149; on prohibition, 74, 151-152; feared Wilson nomination, 76; as campaigner, 76, 131, 132; presented, 110; strengthened by Harding nomination, 112; convention strategy, 112, 115; in balloting, 112-116; encouraged by Mc-Adoo withdrawal, 114; second choice of McAdoo leaders, 114; nominated, 116; protests Glass statement that he was unacceptable to the administration, 119; picks Franklin D. Roosevelt, 121; press reaction to nomination, 121-122; visit to Wilson, 127; acceptance ceremonies, 128, 135; campaign tour, 128-129; asks Moore to take charge, 130; slush fund charges, 131-134; asks Wilson's help, 143; calls Harding a liar, 144; believed victory possible, 146, 159; on Russia, 148; William Allen White on, 148; hurt by Wilson's unpopularity, 150; rejects materials maintaining Harding had Negro blood, 153; and Irish-Americans, 153-154; and German-Americans, 154; loses labor support, 155; press does not report his offer to accept reservations, 156; vote received, 159; blames defeat on war, 161
Cox and Roosevelt Independent League, 146
Crane, W. Murray: presents proleague plank, 80; in Smoke-filled Room, 88; protests Harding's position on league, 136
creativity, decline after war, 165
Creel, George: shocked at Wilson's appearance, 58; works for McAdoo, 67
crime wave, 163-164, 167
Cuba, 25, 30, 82
Cummings, Homer S.: 60, 102; interview with Hoover, 44; on causes of 1918 defeat, 54; on Wilson's mental condition, 58; visit to White House; 62; keynote address, 103-104; puts Colby on resolutions committee, 104; presented to convention, 111; in balloting, 112-116; hoped for nomination, 116; blocks nomination of Wilson, 118-119; removed as national chairman, 127; in campaign, 129-142; refused to make senate race, 130; advised Wilson to stay out of campaign, 143; urged more emphasis on league, 144
Curtis, Charles W.: in Smoke-filled Room, 88, works for Harding, 89; predicts Harding nomination, 92; told Kansas to vote for Harding, 95
cynicism, after the war, 163-165

Daniels, Josephus: 60, 102, 171n, 186n; for Hoover, 43; on Colby, 114; opposed nomination of Wilson, 118-119; in campaign, 129, 142, 146
Daugherty, Harry M.: on Wood, 26, 40, 96, 101; sketch, 38; manages Har-

194 INDEX

ding's preconvention campaign, 39-42; wooed Jake Hamon, 41-42, 86-87; defeated as delegate-at-large, 51; convention strategy, 84, 92, 93; relations with Penrose, 87, 95; credited with Harding nomination, 97, 99; accepted Lenroot, 100; influence on Harding campaign, 124-125, 136; says Wilson unpopularity decisive, 157

Davis, John W.: 78, 119; presented to convention, 111; in balloting, 112-116; campaign for league, 146

Dayton Evening News, 73

Debs, Eugene, 17

Declaration by Thirty-One Proleague Republicans, 139, 140, 146

Democratic administration. *See* Wilson administration

Democratic bosses: 15, 78, 115, 122; oppose McAdoo, 68; challenge Wilson Democrats for control, 75; back Cox, 75, 117; strength in convention, 102; back Thomas J. Walsh for resolutions chairman, 104; urge Cox to take wet position, 151; gain control of party, 163

Democratic National Committee: 44, 54, 72, 129; Atlantic City meeting, 64; favored Palmer, 67, 71; decides delegate contests, 102; wants to continue Cummings as chairman, 127

Democratic National Convention: 60, 67, 70; delegate contests, 102; setting, 103; resolutions committee, 104, 110; candidates presented, 110-111; platform 105-109, 121, 135

Democrats: 43, 67, 76, 81, 88, 123; political tides against, 23; move to nominate Hoover, 43-44; hoped Wilson would run on league, 54, 56; urged Wilson to renounce a third term, 59; few want Bryan, 77; move to right, 122; finances, 130; campaign conference, 130; defeat in Maine, 142; lose labor support, 155; charge that the press is unfair, 155

Department of Labor, 17

Des Moines (Iowa), Harding speech, 137-139

dictatorship, wartime, 18

disarmament, Cox for, 145-147

Dodge, Cleveland, 151

Doheny, Edward L.: 26; at Republican convention, 86

DuPont, T. Coleman: at Republican convention, 86; Cox denounces, 144

Early, Steve: advance man for Franklin D. Roosevelt, 129; on Wilson's unpopularity, 150

education: supported by progressives, 16; federal aid to, 18; Cox on, 75; Republican platform on, 81; Democratic platform on, 106; Franklin D. Roosevelt on, 148

Edwards, Edward I.: 77, 78, 122; in Michigan primary, 72; presented, 111; in balloting, 112

Eighteenth Amendment, 18, 75, 89, 151. *See also* prohibition

election of 1904, 16

election of 1910, 37

election of 1912, 17, 23, 28, 31, 37, 49, 64, 73, 100, 161

election of 1914, 37, 83

election of 1916, 18, 23, 74, 155, 161

election of 1918, 20, 21, 23, 74; Cummings on cause of Democratic defeat, 54

election of 1920: importance, 13, 22; returns, 159-160

Emmerton, Louis, announced Lowden candidacy, 34

Espionage Act, 162

exports, 19, 156

Fall, Albert B., visits Wilson, 58

Farm Loan Banks, 17, 64, 67

farmers: 50, 134, angry at Wilson administration, 23; Harding on, 37, 149; oppose Hoover, 45; Cox on, 75, 147; Democratic platform on, 106; income drops, 156; alienated from Democrats, 157; in progressive movement, 162

Federal Reserve System: 17, 64, 133, 147; Democratic platform on, 106

Field, Carter, predicts Harding's nomination, 39

Fisher, Irving, campaign for league, 146

flood control, Democratic platform on, 106

Florida, for McAdoo, 68

Folk, Joseph W., 76

Ford, Henry, sues Chicago *Tribune,* 22

Fourteen Points, 20, 154

France, 143, 144

Frankfurter, Felix, attacks Palmer, 73

free enterprise, threatened by trusts, 14

free speech: restricted by war, 18, 162; McAdoo for, 67; Democratic platform on, 106; Cox for, 148

Frelinghuysen, Joseph S., in Smoke-filled Room, 88

French Lick Springs (Indiana), 76

Funk, Mrs. Antionette: works for McAdoo, 66, 67-68, 69, 70-71, 114, 117; agrees on Franklin D. Roosevelt, 121; on Cox's nomination, 122; complains about campaign, 130

INDEX

Gary, Elbert M., at Republican convention, 86
Georgia: 113, 115, 142; resolution against third term, 59; Democratic primary, 65-66, 71, 72
Georgia delegation: 102; for Palmer, 73
Gerard, James W.: advocated Hoover, 44; presented to convention, 111; chairman Democratic finance committee, 129
German-American Citizenship League, 154-155
German-Americans: oppose Versailles Treaty, 21, 23; support Johnson, 33, 50, 51; Cox on, 74; in campaign, 154; Harding on, 154; shift to Republicans, 160
Germany: 80, 167; popular hatred of, 20; looks to the league for justice says Roosevelt, 146
Gillette, F. H., election a victory for the league, 140
Ginn, Edwin, 19
Glass, Carter: 60, 78; says Wilson's mind was affected, 58; quotes Wilson on candidates, 62; predicts McAdoo, 68; supported by Shouse, 69; refuses to co-operate with McAdoo, 70; took Wilson's platform ideas to convention, 102, 104; suppressed Wilson's prohibition plank, 105; debates platform with Bryan, 109; presented to convention, 111; in balloting, 112-116; hoped for nomination, 116-117; opposes move to nominate Wilson, 118-120
Gompers, Samuel: on police strike, 45; backs Democrats, 155; on progressivism's failure, 166
government corruption, 164, 167
Grand Central Palace, 129
Grayson, Dr. Cary T.: 59, 60, 65-66; cancels Wilson's September tour, 58; told of Wilson's third term plans, 60; says nomination would kill Wilson, 62
Gregory, Warren: 171n; headed Hoover clubs, 45
Grundy, Joseph R., in Smoke-filled Room, 88
Guffey, Joseph, 115

Hague Tribunal, 136, 141
Hale, Matthew, progressive bolter to Cox, 148
Hamon, Jake: for Lowden, 35, 83, 87; Daugherty seeks his support, 41-42; sketch, 86; controlled delegates, 86-87; seeks deal with Wood, 87; said he spent a million dollars to nominate Harding 87
Hanna, Dan R.: backed Wood, 26; at Republican convention, 86
Harding, Warren G.: 24, 28, 32, 34, 74, 101, 128, 131; for normalcy, 23, 158; preconvention campaign 25, 36-42, 51, 52; rumor that he had Negro blood, 36, 90, 153; sketch, 36-37; on socialism, 37; on the league, 37, 134-140, 142, 144, 146, 147; Penrose' support for, 38, 47, 95, 97; urged to run by Daugherty, 39; liked by old guard and Wall Street, 40-41; and Butler, 49; helped by campaign fund investigation, 53; presented to convention, 82-83; considered out of the race, 40-41, 83; convention strategy, 84; convention organization, 84; in balloting, 84-96; offers Johnson vice-presidency, 85, 90; backed by Smoked-filled Room, 88-91; addresses Ohio caucus, 90; predicts nomination, 91; gets Lowden's support, 95; nominated, 96; nomination analyzed, 98-99; press reaction to nomination, 99-100; antithesis of Wilson, 101; acceptance speech, 123-124, 135, 136; campaign tour, 124; campaign style, 125, 126; answers slush fund charges, 133; rebuked by Wilson, 143; Ickes on, 148; on progressivism, 149; attacks Wilson, 150; on prohibition, 151-152; on Irish-Americans, 154; on German-Americans, 154; gets labor support, 155; confident of victory, 158-159; vote received, 159; death predicted by doctors, 177n; did not know real story of his nomination, 178n
Harding, Mrs. Warren G.: 40, 91, 95, did not urge Harding to run, 179n
Harding scandals, origin in convention, 97
Harmon, Judson: 112; defeats Harding for governor, 37; suggested by Wilson for vice-president, 118
Harrison, Francis B., presented, 111
Harrison, Pat: 104, 115, 116, 154; favored Colby for vice-president, 121; chairman of Democratic speakers' bureau, 129
Harvey, George: associated with big business, 86; sketch, 87-88; in Smoke-filled Room, 87-91, 98; attempt to block Harding with Hays, 94; credited with Harding nomination, 97; not decisive in Harding nomination, 99; helps Harding prepare league speech, 125, 136
Have Faith in Massachusetts, 46

Hays, Will: 87, 89, 131-133, 155; endorsed by Wood, 31; predicted Harding's nomination, 40; defends delegate contest decisions, 79; on Smoke-filled Room, 91; agrees to weekend recess, 93; sketch, 123; continued as national chairman, 123; influence in campaign, 125; soft-pedals league, 134; on Declaration by Thirty-One Proleague Republicans, 139; predicts landslide victory, 158; says election was repudiation of Wilson, 161
Hearst, William Randolph: 131; supports Johnson, 32; says election a defeat for the league, 160
Herrick, Myron T.: consents for Harding to adjournment, 92-93; seconds Lenroot nomination, 100
Hert, Alvin T.: 84, 93; used Lowden to stop Wood, 83; predicts dark horse, 86; fed votes to Harding, 91; moves adjournment, 92; conferences with Procter, 93-94; throws Kentucky to Harding, 95, seconded Lenroot, 100
highways, federal aid to: 18; Bryan on, 77; Republican platform on, 81; Democratic platform on, 106
Hill, W. L., says election decided by unpopularity of Wilson, 157
Hilles, Dewey, proleague pressure on Harding, 136
Hitchcock, Frank H.: Wood manager, 30; split with Procter, 30-31; success in winning delegates, 31
Hitchcock, Gilbert M.: favors Hoover, 43; defeated by Bryan, 77; presented to convention, 111; hoped for nomination, 116
Hitchcock Reservations, 55, 134
Hofstadter, Richard, war ruined progressivism, 166
Holt, Hamilton, backs Cox, 138
Hoover, Herbert: 24, 35, 72; sketch, 42; preconvention campaign, 42-45; political record, 43; supported league, 43, 52, 136, 139; Democratic move to nominate, 43-44, 67; announced he was a Republican, 44; in primaries, 44, 49-52; finances, 45; criticism of, 45; managers, 45; supported by Robert A. Taft, 49; regarded as progressive, 51; presented to convention, 82; in campaign, 125; protests Harding's league position, 136
Hoover, Irving, H., on Wilson's illness, 58-59
House, Col. Edward M.: urged Wilson to compromise on league, 57; Wilson breaks with, 173n
Houston, David F.: 60; predicts Democratic defeat, 159

Howe, Louis, accompanied Franklin D. Roosevelt, 129
Hudson tubes, 64
Hughes, Charles Evans: 16, 18, 137; as a candidate, 49; opposed by the New York organization, 89; campaigns, 125; signed Declaration by Thirty-One Proleague Republicans, 139
Hull, Cordell: Wilson proposes for vice-presidency, 118; in conference on third nomination, 119-120
Humphreys, Benjamin C., urged Wilson to withdraw, 59
hyphenated Americans: 161; Wilson attack on, 58; Republican appeal to, 126; shift to Republicans, 159-160. *See also* German-Americans; Irish; Italian - Americans; Austrian - Americans

Ickes, Harold L.: on Lowden, 34; on Harding nomination, 148; opposes league, 148; bolts to Cox, 148; discouraged by reaction, 163
Illinois, 33, 51, 76, 83, 111, 113, 115
immigration: effect of war on, 30; Republican platform on, 81. *See also* Asiatic exclusion
In His Steps, 15
The Independent, on Cox's nomination, 122
Indiana: 68, 73, 76, 91, 103, 111, 113, 115, 126; primary, 34, 36, 38-39, 52. *See also* Thomas Taggart
individual income, 156
industry, growth: 13-14, 19; Democratic platform on, 106
inflation. *See* cost of living
initiative and referendum: progressives adopt, 16; Bryan for, 77
intellectuals, desert cause of reform, 165
International Labor Organization, opposed by businessmen, 21
International Workers of the World, 164
Interstate Commerce Commission, 16
intolerance: effect of war on, 18; Democratic platform on, 106
Iowa, 67, 113
Irish: oppose treaty, 21; support Johnson, 32, 50; Democratic platform on, 105; against Democrats, 130; Cox on, 153-154; Harding on, 154
irreconcilables: 80, 136, 138, 139, 161; displeased with Lowden, 34; threaten Lodge, 57; welcome Wilson's refusal to compromise, 57. *See also* Hiram Johnson; William E. Borah
L'Italia, 155

Index

Italian-Americans: oppose treaty, 21, 23; support Johnson, 32; in campaign, 155; shift to Republicans, 160

Jackson Day Dinner, 43, 55, 57, 64, 71
Japan, 139
Japanese excluded, 164
Jenkins, Burris: 114; asked to nominate McAdoo, 68; McAdoo asks him not to nominate, 69; presents McAdoo, 110-111
Jennings, Al, on Harding-Hamon deal, 87
Johnson, Cone, seconds Franklin D. Roosevelt, 121
Johnson, Hiram: 34, 35, 39, 48, 81, 86, 98, 135; as a progressive, 16, 23, 31, 32; preconvention campaign, 28, 31-33; sketch, 31; opposes red hunts, 32; supported by hyphenated Americans, 32; denounces intervention in Russia, 32, 50; delegates unreliable, 32, 79, 85; on league, 32, 137, 138; as orator, 33; handicapped by record as bolter, 39; threatens to enter Ohio, 40; in primaries, 45, 50-52; on prohibition, 51; initiates campaign fund investigation, 53, 85; backs Borah for permanent chairman, 79; presented to convention, 82; attempts adjournment, 84; in balloting, 84, 92, 96; sought for vice-presidency, 85, 90, 93; condemns Smoke-filled Room, 96-97; no chance for nomination, 100; threatens split in party, 137; Harding on, 140; on postwar reaction, 150, 166; predicts landslide victory, 158
Johnson, James G., presents Cox, 110
Julian, W. A., 112
juvenile delinquency, 164

Kansas, 48
Kansas City *Post*, 68
Kansas City Star: informed of Smoke-filled Room decision, 89; says election was league defeat, 160
Kansas delegation: 85, 92; moves votes to Harding, 91; defection, body blow to Wood, 95
Kealing, Joseph B. marshal of unpledged delegates, 91
Kelsey, Clarence H., protests Harding's league position, 136
Kentucky: 39, 76, 103, 113, 128, 158; delegation moves to Harding, 95-96; Republican campaign emphasis on, 126
Kenyon, William S.: backed Johnson, 32; headed campaign fund investigation, 53, 132

King, John: 27, 95, 163; sketch, 26; manages Wood's campaign, 26; breaks with Wood, 27; backs Lowden to stop Wood, 83; Wood attempts reconciliation with, 83; holds Penrose' proxy, 87; marshal of unpledged delegates, 91; opposed Harding, 178n
Kitchen, Claude: wants Wilson to withdraw, 59; predicts McAdoo's nomination, 68
Knox, Frank, backs Wood, 26, 50
Knox, Philander C.: 89; endorsed by Penrose, 47
Ku Klux Klan, 22, 164, 167
Kuhn, Otto H., 26

La Follette, Robert M.: 16, 17; in balloting, 84, 96; on candidates, 148; predicts war will bring reaction, 163
labor: 82, 134, 155, 157; progressivism favors, 14, 16, 17, 163; Wilson opposes after war, 18, 163, 164; strikes of 1919, 18; hurt by inflation, 23; opposed Wood, 29, 34; opposition to, 30, 100; supported Johnson, 32, 50; attitude toward Lowden, 34-35; backed McAdoo, 64; opposed Palmer, 72; Cox on, 74, 147; Republican platform on, 81; opposed Allen, 89, 100; Coolidge on, 101; Democratic platform on, 106; Franklin D. Roosevelt on, 148; Harding program for, 149; in the campaign, 155; alienated by Burleson, 155; unemployment rises, 156
Lamont, Thomas W., backs Cox on league, 138
Lane, Franklin K.: favors Hoover, 43; on Wilson's unpopularity, 150; predicts war will bring reaction, 163
Lansing, Robert, fired by Wilson, 23, 173n
Lardner, Ring, receives votes for presidential nomination, 115
Lawrence, David, 39, 45, 59, 70, 98, 131, 150, 157, 158
League of Nations: 33, 60, 79, 111, 119, 121, 125, 131, 132, 152, 153, 154; election of 1920 decisive, 13; woven into the treaty, 21; made partisan issue, 21, 55; defeat in Senate, 21, 55-56, 57; threat to Republican unity, 23; Johnson on, 31-32, 137-138; liberals on, 32; Lowden on, 34; Hoover support, 43, 52, 136, 139; Lodge wants referendum, 46; Taft support, 49, 80; and the question of a third term, 54; pressure for compromise on, 55, 56, 60, 77-78; Wilson calls for referendum on, 56,

61, 127, 143; effect of Lodge Reservations on, 57; Cox on, 73, 75, 127, 131-136, 138, 140-146, 156; Bryan on, 76-77, 106-108; Marshall on, 78; Lodge on, 80, 140; Republican platform on, 61, 80-81, 134-135; Harvey fight on, 88; Lenroot on, 101; Cummings on, 103; Democratic platform on, 104-105; Colby on, 109; Glass on, 109; Harding on, 37, 134-142, 144, 146, 147; Hays and Penrose want to soft pedal, 134; proleague Republicans, 139-140, 146; Coolidge on 140; Republican speakers' committee on, 140; as a vote-getter, 142; Cox offers to accept reservations, 145, 156; Franklin D. Roosevelt on, 145-146; Davis on, 146; Gompers supports, 155; as the issue of the election, 160-161. See also association of nations; Article X; Lodge Reservations; Versailles Treaty; Wilson
League of Women Voters, 152
League to Enforce Peace: 19, says Harding's association proposal is impractical, 137-138
Lenroot, Irvine L.: proposed for vice-president, 100; in balloting, 101
Lippmann, Walter: on Wood, 29-30; on Lowden, 34
Literary Digest, poll, 44, 59, 64, 77
Lodge, Henry Cabot: 24, 82, 89, 109, 145; leads fight on league, 21, 32, 37, 47; offer to nominate Wood, 26; and Coolidge, 46; presidential aspirations, 46-47, 56; wants referendum on league, 56; permanent chairman, 79; keynote address, 79-80; opposes proleague plank, 80; Friday night adjournment, 84-85; in Smoke-filled Room, 88-89; Saturday afternoon adjournment, 92-94; attempt to block Harding nomination, 94; notification speech, 123; endorses association of nations, 140; in Maine, 142; denounced by Cox, 144
Lodge Reservations: 134-135, 139; Wilson refuses to accept, 21; favored by Wood, 29; Harding voted for, 37; compared to Hitchcock Reservations, 55; on Article X, 55; effect on league assayed, 57; administration leaders want Wilson to accept, 60; Bryan on, 107-108
Long, Breckenridge, 142
Longworth, Alice Roosevelt: 27; on Smoke-filled Room's choice of Harding, 89-90
Looking Backward, 15
Los Angeles Express, 45
Los Angeles Times, 45

Louisiana, 113, 116, 152
Love, Thomas B., McAdoo supporter, 69, 71, 114
Lowden, Frank O.: 28, 32, 39, 41, 49, 88, 89, 98; preconvention campaign, 24-25, 33-36; sketch, 33-34; on league, 34; on reds, 34; in primaries, 34-35, 50-52; financing, 34-35, 53, 85; hostility to Wood, 35; handicaps, 35; charged with corruption, 35, 53; used to stop Wood, 36, 83; in poll, 40; encouraged by Penrose, 47; delegates, 79; presented to convention, 82; opposition to, 83; in balloting, 84, 92, 96; offers Johnson vice-presidency, 85; during Smoke-filled Room session, 86; conference with Wood and Procter, 93-94; attempted weekend recess, 93-95; withdraws in favor of Harding, 95-96
Lowell, A. Lawrence: on Lodge Reservations, 57; displeased with Harding's league position, 137; signed Declaration of Thirty-One Proleague Republicans, 139
loyalty oaths, 164
Lusk Laws, 164
lynching, postwar increase in, 164, 167

McAdoo, Mrs. Eleanor Wilson: 71, opposes McAdoo's seeking presidency, 65
McAdoo, William Gibbs: 72, 74, 77, 78, 96, 102, 118, 119, 128; boom, 24, 63-71; in *Literary Digest* poll, 44, 59, 64; fears that Wilson seeks a third term, 60, 64-66, 69; June 18 withdrawal, 61-62, 68-69, 114, 116-117; sketch, 64; refuses to speak at Jackson Day Dinner, 64; avoids appearance of seeking nomination, 65-66; would accept if nominated, 65-66, 69-71, 112; on issues, 66-67; relations with Cox, 66, 114; fights Palmer, 67; opposes Hoover, 67; bosses against, 68; finances, 68; proposes to back Glass, 70; report that he has tuberculosis, 70; presented to convention, 110-111; leaders' convention strategy, 111-112; Burleson for, 68, 111-112; in balloting, 112-116; leaders confer with Palmer, 113-114; no manager at convention, 117; backers approve of Roosevelt, 121; in campaign, 129-131, 146; on Cox campaign, 132; on contest between reaction and progress, 147; for prohibition, 151; says election was repudiation of Wilson administration, 161

McCamant, Wallace, nominates Coolidge, 100-101
McCarthy, Charles H., in Roosevelt headquarters, 129
McCormick, Medill: 80-81, 84; communicated with Penrose, 87; in Smoke-filled Room, 88; active for Harding, 89; proposed Lenroot, 100
McCormick, Vance C.: 60, 104; favors Hoover, 43; Palmer manager, 60; in conference on third term, 119-120
Mack, Normal E., predicts third term, 54
McKinley, William C., 36, 38, 83, 101, 124
McNary, Charles L., backs Johnson, 32
Madison Square Garden, 132, 144
Mahoney, Jeremiah T., 120
Maine election, 142
Marburg, Theodore, backs Cox on league, 138
Marion (Ohio), 123-125
Marion *Star,* 36-37, 128
Marsh, Wilbur W.: 72; opposes Cummings for chairman, 127; Democratic treasurer, 129
Marshall, Thomas R.: receptive to nomination, 78; on resolutions committee, 104; in balloting, 112; in campaign, 129; supports league, 146
Maryland, 51, 124
Massachusetts: 115; primary, 46, 51; delegation told by Lodge not to vote for Harding, 94
Mencken, Henry L., 165
merchant marine: Wood favors, 29; Democratic platform on, 106; Harding for, 149
Meredith, Edwin T.: 102; favorite son for McAdoo, 67; presented to convention, 111; in balloting, 112; vice-presidential possibility, 121
Metropolitan Magazine, 26
Mexico: 58, 82, 87, 103, 104; Republican platform on, 81; Democratic platform on, 106
Michigan: primary, 34, 44, 50, 66, 72; delegation, 68
middle class: in progressive movement, 14-15, 162, support of progressivism undermined, 18
Miles, Nelson A., bolted Cox on league, 142
militarism: 103, 162; in Republican platform, 81; in Wilson administration, 163
military service: advocated by Wood, 28; Bryan's plank on, 107
Miller, David H., on Lodge Reservations, 57
Miller, Nathan L., presents Hoover, 82

Minneapolis State Fair, 124
Minnesota, 73, 116
Mississippi, 68, 110, 113, 128
Missouri: Harding strength in, 41; votes loaned to Lowden, 84; shifts to Harding, 91-92; Republican campaign emphasizes, 126
mob violence, 162
Monell, Ambrose: backs Wood, 26; at Republican convention, 86
Monroe Doctrine, 137
Montana, 51, 68
Moore, Edmund H.: 114; fights McAdoo, 68; opposes administration on Reed, 102; convention strategy, 112, 115; conference with Palmer, 113; on causes of Cox nomination, 116; against continuing Cummings, 127; objected to Cox visit to Wilson, 127; opposed for national chairman, 127-128; against prohibition, 128; against making league the campaign issue, 128; asked to take charge of campaign, 130; on Irish, 154
moral decline, 163-165
Morgan, J. P.: 13, 26; and Republican convention, 86
Moses, George H., 79
muckrakers, 15
Mullen, Arthur F., 114
Mulvane, David W., gave votes to Harding, 91
Murphy, Charles F.: 112; thinks Wilson wants third term, 61; opposes McAdoo, 68; likes Marshall, 68; agrees to Roosevelt, 121

Nation: attacks Wood, 29; backs Johnson, 32; opposes treaty, 32; attacks Palmer, 73; on Harding nomination, 100
national bulletin: proposed by Bryan, 77, 106, 107; Colby on, 109
national debt, Republican platform on, 81
National Italian-American Republican League, 155
nationalism: in Republican platform, 81; in Democratic platform, 106
Nebraska: 116; primary, 49, 51; delegation 77
Negro: 30; Harding on, 152; Democrats on, 152-153
Nevada, 68
New, Harry S.: supports Harding, 39; says Penrose not a factor, 97
New Freedom, 88, 163
New Hampshire primary, 44, 50, 142
New Jersey: 78, 103, 111; primary, 51; against prohibition, 76; votes for

Cox, 113; Republican campaign emphasis on, 126
New Republic: 109; on Wood movement, 29; for Johnson, 32; against treaty, 32; for Hoover, 43; on Harding nomination, 100; on Cox nomination, 122
New York: 68, 78, 103, 111, 114, 128, 159; votes for Butler, 49, 84; support for Palmer, 73; against prohibition, 76; shifts votes to Lowden, 84; opposed Hughes, 89; for Saturday adjournment, 92; goes to Cox, 113; Harding in, 124
New York *American:* says millionaires back Wood, 26; ignored Harding, 40; exposed Wood spending, 52; says millionaires back McAdoo, 68; on Democratic league plank, 105; says election a defeat for league, 160
New York Assembly: expells socialists, 22, 37; denounced by Harding, 37; passes Lusk Laws, 164
New York *Herald,* election defeat for league, 160
New York *Post:* on Hoover, 44; on third term, 59, 63, 117; for compromise on league, 57; calls Smoke-filled Room story "melodrama," 98; on Harding nomination, 99; on Cummings keynote, 104; on Democratic platform, 109; on Harding's Des Moines speech, 138; urges Democrats to emphasize the league, 144; says press is unfair to Democrats, 156; calls election a repudiation of Wilson, **160**
New York *Sun and Herald,* on Harding nomination, 99
New York Times: ignored Harding, 40; says Harding is Penrose' candidate, 47; advocates Davis, 78; on league plank, 81; predicts Smoke-filled Room, 83; on Smoke-filled Room, 98; on Harding nomination, 99; on Democratic platform, 109; on the Democratic candidates, 121; on Cox's campaign, 128, 132; on Cox's slush fund charges, 133; on Harding acceptance, 135; on Harding's league position, 136; on Taft and the league, 139; says unpopularity of Wilson will decide the election, 158; predicts Republican landslide, 158
New York *Tribune:* predicts Harding, 39; ignores Harding, 41; on Hoover, 43; on third term, 55; on McAdoo withdrawal, 61, 70; on Cox strength, 76; on Bryan's chances, 77; on Republican league plank, 80; on Smoke-filled Room, 91; on Harding nomination, 99; on Cox nomination, 121; on Harding's acceptance, 135; on Harding's Des Moines speech, 138; predicts Republican victory in Maine, 142; predicts Republican landslide, 158; says election repudiation of Wilson, but victory for the league, 160
New York *World:* charges millionaires back Wood, 26, 52; ignored Harding, 41; for Hoover, 44; praises Coolidge, 46; mocks Lodge, 47; on third term, 54-55; calls for compromise on treaty, 56, 57; calls for truth on Wilson's illness, 58; Seibold-Wilson interview, 60-61; Wilson in good health, 63; attacks Palmer, 73; on Harding nomination, 99; on Democratic platform, 109; says election repudiation of Wilson, 160; condemns Lusk laws, 164
New Yorker Staats-Zeitung, says election defeat for league, 160
Newbury scandal, 50
Nineteenth Amendment, 18, 89, 152, 160
Nonpartisan League, backs Johnson, 32, 51
Norbeck, Peter, backs Wood, 26, 50
Norris, George W., 17
North American Review, 87
North Carolina: 158; primary, 52, 67; for McAdoo, 68, 71; support for Palmer, 73; Republican campaign in, 126
North Dakota, 50

Oberlin College, 138
O'Brien, Charles F. S., presents Edwards, 111
Ohio: 83, 88, 111, 113, 152; Harding campaign in, 40; against prohibition, 76; Republicans emphasize campaign in, 126; primary, 36, 51
Ohio Central College, 36
Ohio Republican delegation: 74, 110; seventh ballot demonstration, 92; desertions from Harding, 90, 92; Friday midnight caucus, 90; membership, 112
Ohio State Journal, 40
oil: 128; at Republican convention, 86-87; credited with Harding nomination, 97; Democratic platform on, 106; paid Republican deficit, 126; Harding for securing foreign supplies, 149
Oklahoma: support for Palmer, 73; Republican delegation controlled by Hamon, 86-87
old guard: 35, 37, 84, 96; pushes favorite sons into primaries, 28;

backs campaign fund investigation, 28; nullifies Johnson's primary victories, 33; uses Lowden to stop Wood, 35-36, 92; liked Harding, 39, 51, 100; encouraged Johnson to enter Indiana primary, 52; forced adjournment, 85; Smoke-filled Room conference, 87-91; Saturday afternoon conference, 94-95; gained control of Republican party, 163
Omaha World-Herald, on Bryan's comeback, 77
Oregon, 68, 100; primary, 34, 48, 52
Oriental exclusion. *See* Asiatic exclusion
Owens, Robert L.: presented to convention, 14; in balloting, 112-116

Palmer, A. Mitchell: 24, 60, 65, 74, 76, 102, 109, 111, 112, 128; red hunt, 18, 22, 72, 155, 164; alienated labor, 23; on third term, 54, 72; seeks Wilson's permission to run, 60; Wilson opposed, 62; rift with McAdoo, 67; favored by national committee, 64; gets Baker's support, 69; sketch, 71; Jackson Day address, 71; preconvention campaign, 71-73; condemned on red hunt by liberals and lawyers, 72, 73; delegates, 73; accused of corruption, 73; presented, 110; in balloting, 112-116; conference with Moore, 113; confers with McAdoo leaders, 113-114; releases delegates, 115; split administration, 116; aloof from campaign, 129; urged emphasis on league, 144; home bombed, 164
Panama Canal tolls, Republican platform on, 81
Paris Peace Conference, 19, 20-21, 57
Parker, Alton B., presented, 16
Parker, John J., 126
Parker, John M., progressive bolter, 148
Parsons, Herbert: proleague pressure on Harding, 136; bolts Republican party, 138; campaign for league, 146
Patents, fewer after war, 165, 167
peace movement, 19-21
Pennsylvania: 47-48, 66, 85, 89, 111, 113, 115, 116, 128; Wood-Sproul agreement, 31; McAdoo strength in, 68; Palmer controls delegation, 73; against prohibition, 76; votes for Sproul, 84; delegation seeks word from Penrose, 87; goes to Harding, 95, 96; Harding in, 124
Pennsylvania Railroad, 48
Penrose, Boise: 26, 71; fought by Johnson, 32; encouraged labor, 35, 47; encouraged Harding, 38, 47; against Hoover, 43; endorsed Knox, 47; sketch, 47; and Wood, 47, 57; endorses Sproul, 48; communication with convention, 87; illness, 87; role in Harding nomination, 95, 97, 99; on Cox nomination, 122; objects to porch campaign, 124; on slush fund, 133; wants to soft-pedal league, 134; says labor for Cox, 155; says unpopularity of administration decisive, 157
pensions for mothers, 16
Pershing, John J., pushed into primaries, 28, 49, 51
Philippines: 154; Democratic platform on, 105
Phipps, Lawrence C., in Smoke-filled Room, 88
physical education, Republican platform on, 81
Pinchot, Gifford: against Hoover, 45; backed Harding, 148
Plattsburg group, supported Wood, 26
Poindexter, Miles: in primaries, 28; presented to convention, 83
poll, congressional, on Republican candidates, 40
Pomerene, Atlee W., 112
Populist party, 14
Pound, Roscoe, attacks Palmer, 72
preparedness, 82
Prichard, Jeter C., 83
primaries, Republican, 49-52; *See also individual states and candidates*
Princeton, 128
Procter, William Cooper: becomes Wood's manager, 27; campaign methods, 27-31; financial contributions to Wood, 30, 53; split with Hitchcock, 30-31; fights Harding in Ohio, 39-40; offers Harding Ohio deal, 40; invades Illinois, 50-51; conferences with Lowden, 93-94; betrayed by Hert, 95
profiteering: 82, 156; Bryan on, 77, 107; Robinson on, 104; Cox on, 132, 147; Harding on, 149
Progressive party, 31, 43, 48, 73, 79
progressives: 31, 44; oppose treaty, 21; shift to Republicans, 23, 24, 159-160; introduce primary, 49; support Harding, 148-149; Republican, bolt to Cox, 148
progressivism: 13-18, 122, 132, 161-162; importance of election for, 13; undermined by war, 18, 163; opposed by Wood, 29; Republican convention hostile to, 85; Harding nomination defeat for, 100; in Democratic platform, 106, 109; White says main issue, 134; Cox says league expansion of, 141; in Cox campaign, 146-149; McAdoo says election a contest for, 147; Franklin D. Roosevelt on, 148;

Harding campaign on, 149; defeat of, 161-167
prohibition: 51, 68, 73, 74, 78, 117, 121, 128; Eighteenth Amendment ratified, 18; untimely, 22; Cox on, 75, 110; big cities wet, 76; Bryan on, 77, 108, 111; Wilson for wet plank, 105; Bryan's dry plank, 106; Glass on, 109; Colby on, 109; as campaign issue, 151-152; bearing on election result, 160. *See also* Volstead Act
Puerto Rico, Democratic platform on, 105
Pullman Company, handicap to Lowden, 33, 35

race issue: 132, 152; Cox and Wilson reject, 153
race violence, 163-164
radicalism: 43, 82, 125; among workers, 15; Republican platform on, 81; Coolidge against, 101; Cox on causes of, 147-148; in postwar period, 164; progressives on, 162
radicals: Palmer's war on, 18; deported, 22; administration action against, 116
railroads: 32, 43, 124; progressives regulate, 16; Wood favors private ownership, 29; Republican platform on, 81; McAdoo suggests government ownership, 67; Cox on, 147; Democratic platform on, 106
Rauschenbusch, Walter, 15
reaction: Lodge on, 79-80; Harding nomination an expression of, 101; Cox nomination an expression of, 121-122; McAdoo on contest against, 147; Cox's warning of, 147-148; Roosevelt calls campaign a contest against, 148; Sullivan, Lawrence, Bryan, and Johnson on, 150; Gompers on, 155; described, 161-167; analysis of causes of, 165-167
realism, 165
recession, 156-157
reds: 29, 45, 72, 81, 82, 110; red hunts, 32, 155, 163-164; Communist party organized, 22; attacked by Wood, 28; war psychology on, 30; Lowden on, 34; Harding favors suppression, 149-150; deported, 164; red scare declines, 167. *See also* A. Mitchell Palmer; radicalism
Reed, James F.: rejected as delegate, 102; backs Cox, 135; praised by Harding, 140; deserted Cox, 142
religion. *See* church; social gospel movement
Remmel, H. L.: seconded Lenroot, 100; seconded Coolidge, 101

Republican campaign: finances, 126, 130, 132-134, 143; organization, 126
Republican National Convention: 53, 79-103; platform, 33, 61, 80-82, 135; delegate contests, 79; nominating speeches, 82-83; balloting, 84-85, 92, 96; hostile to progressivism, 85. *See also individual candidates*
Republican party: progressive under Theodore Roosevelt, 16, 24; unity threatened by league issue, 23; bosses, 82, 85; advantageous position, 23, 123; bolters, 138
Review of Reviews, 42
Rexall Drug Store poll, 159
Robinson, Mrs. Corinne Roosevelt, seconds Wood, 82
Robinson, Joseph T.: Democratic permanent chairman, 104; opposes Colby's move to nominate Wilson, 118-119; in campaign, 129
Roosevelt, Franklin D.: 128; for Hoover, 43; seconds Smith, 110; sketch, 120; "first fight," 120; fight against unit rule, 120; chosen vice-presidential candidate, 120-121; press reaction to nomination, 121; visit to Wilson, 127; campaign tour, 129, 142; complains of campaign inertia, 130; on league, 145-146; on progressive issues, 148; predicts defeat, 159; attributes defeat to war, 161
Roosevelt, Mrs. Franklin D., on campaign tour, 129
Roosevelt, Theodore: 16, 17, 20, 23, 25, 26, 28, 29, 31, 32, 37, 46, 50, 51, 54, 76, 82, 83, 100; moves to right during war, 163
Roosevelt, Theodore Jr., in campaign, 125, 142
Root, Elihu: 19, 137; backed Wood, 26; urged Wood to fire King, 27; urged Wood to resign from the army, 29; drafted Republican league plank, 80; protests Harding's position on league, 136; signed Declaration of Thirty-One Proleague Republicans, 139; campaigned for Harding, 139
Roper, Daniel C.: 102; on McAdoo withdrawal, 69, 70; works for McAdoo, 67; rebukes Burleson, 112; says McAdoo would accept, 112
Roraback, J. Henry, resisted pressure for Hays, 94
roughriders, 25
Russia: 20, 103, 167; U. S. intervention in, 32; Cox on, 148

Sacco and Vanzetti, 22
Sacramento Union, 45

St. Lawrence seaway: Democratic platform on, 106; Cox on, 147
Salt Lake City, anti-third-term conference, 63
San Francisco, 87
San Francisco *Bulletin,* 45
San Francisco *Chronicle,* 121
San Francisco Civic Auditorium, 102
San Francisco convention. *See* Democratic National Convention
San Francisco *News,* 45
Scripps, Robert, 153
Seattle general strike, 164
Seibold, Louis: interview with Wilson, 60-61; on the cause of McAdoo's withdrawal, 69
Senate: sent committee to interview Wilson, 58; Roosevelt says could not ignore mandate, 146; election result, 159
Senate cabal, in Harding nomination, 97, 99
Senate Finance Committee, 47
Senate Judiciary Committee, investigated Bolshevism, 22
Seventeenth Amendment, 17
Sharp, William G., bolts Cox on league, 142
Sheldon, Charles M., 15
Sherman, Lawrence Y., on third term, 54-55
Shouse, Jouett: 113; leaves McAdoo for Glass, 69; complains about White's campaign, 130
Simmons, F. M.: drafts compromise on Article X, 57; favorite son for McAdoo, 67; presented to convention, 111
Sinclair, Harry F.: backs Wood, 26; at Republican convention, 86
Sixteenth Amendment, 17. *See also* taxes, income
Slemp, Bascom, 83
Smith College, 138
Smith, Al: 61; favorite son, 78; presented to convention, 110; in balloting, 112; seconds Roosevelt, 121; in campaign, 129; defeated, 159
Smith, Hoke, in Georgia primary, 72
Smoke-filled Room: 92, 94, 113; Daugherty predicts, 42; *New York Times* predicts, 83; Smoot predicts, 85; participants in, 88; Grundy on, 88; Calder on, 88; credited with Harding nomination, 97; role assessed, 98-99; Smoot on, 177n; Sullivan on, 179n
Smoot, Reed: 80, 82; arranged adjournment, 84-85; predicts Smoke-filled Room, 85; in Smoke-filled Room, 88;
active for Harding, 89; attempt to block Harding with Hays, 94
social gospel movement: contribution to progressivism, 15, 162; declined during war, 165, 167. *See also* church
social workers, contribution to progressivism, 15
socialism: as component of progressivism, 15; Harding on, 37
Socialists: vote in 1912, 17; expelled from New York legislature, 22, 37
South: 32, 151: shifts votes to Lowden, 84; McAdoo strength in, 112; voted against Wilsonism, 117; Republican campaign in, 126; nominated Cox, 148; Harding wins states in, 159
South Carolina: support for McAdoo, 68; support for Palmer, 73
South Dakota: convention, endorses third term, 55; primary, 34, 35, 50
Southerland, Howard: 83; West Virginia delegation for, 52
Southern Pacific Railway, 31
Spencer, Selden P.: 143; in Smoke-filled Room, 88
Springfield Republican: on Republican league plank, 81; on Cox nomination, 122
Sproul, William C.: 49, 89; agreement with Wood, 31, 48; preconvention campaign, 47-48; endorsed by Penrose, 48; presented to convention, 83; in balloting, 84
Standard Oil, 13
Starling, Edmund W., on Wilson illness, 59
Stearns, Frank W., for Coolidge, 46
Stearns, Harold, on effects of war, 162
Steffens, Lincoln, war ruined progressivism, 166
Stimson, Henry L.: urged Wood to fire King, 27; told Wood Harding movement was dangerous, 41; signed Declaration by Thirty-One Proleague Republicans, 139
Stone, Harlan, signed Declaration by Thirty-One Proleague Republicans, 139
strikes of 1919. *See* labor
Sullivan, Mark, 41, 42, 46, 69, 97, 104, 117, 124, 128, 132, 150, 155, 158, 179n
Sullivan, Roger C., 72
Swen, Charles L., on Wilson's illness, 59

Taft, Robert, for Hoover, 49
Taft, William Howard: 16-17, 36, 49, 51, 83, 92, 135, 137; president of League to Enforce Peace, 19; on Wood, 26, 27; on Harding, 37, 41;

as a candidate, 49; on league, 49, 59, 80; on Saturday recess attempt to block Harding, 94; campaigned for Harding, 125, 138-139; on Cox as a campaigner, 131; protests Harding league position, 136; Harding on, 140; Cox charges him with duplicity, 144; predicts victory, 158; says election repudiation of Wilson, 161
Taggart, Thomas: 112; opposes McAdoo, 68; urges Cox to take dry stand, 151
Tammany: 122; opposes Bryan, 78. *See* Charles F. Murphy
tariff: 17, 147, 157; Wood for protective, 29; Harding on, 37, 149; Republican platform on, 81; Democratic platform on, 106
taxes: 33; McAdoo for reduction, 67; McAdoo for, on unearned incomes, 67; Republican platform on, 81; Democratic platform on, 106
taxes, corporation, 16, 17, 18
taxes, excess profits: Wood for repeal, 29; Cox wants repeal, 75, 147; Harding against, 149
taxes, gross sales, Cox advocates, 147
taxes, income: 16, 17, 18; Harding opposed, 37, 149; Cox opposed, 75
Taylor, Alf, 126
teachers, fired if socialistic, 164
Teapot Dome, 164, 177n
Tennessee: 113, 115, 128, 152, 158; compact to vote for Davis, 116; Republican campaign in, 126; goes to Harding, 159
Texas: Wood strength in, 31; for McAdoo, 64, 68
Theory of the Leisure Class, 15
Third International, 22. *See also* reds
Third term. *See* Woodrow Wilson
Thompson, William B.: 26; supports Johnson, 32; fought Lowden, 83; at Republican convention, 86
Treaty of Versailles. *See* Versailles Treaty
trusts, 15-17
Tumulty, Joseph P.: 60, 72, 118; urged Wilson to compromise on league, 56-57; urged Wilson to withdraw, 59, 62; promoted Seibold interview, 61; approved McAdoo's attitude, 66; denied Wilson had expressed opposition to Cox, 119; opposed Colby's move to nominate Wilson, 119; on Cox's campaign, 132; said election could not be referendum, 143; urged more emphasis on league, 144; said press unfair to Democrats, 156; predicts defeat, 159
Turkey, 103

Ullman, Frederick: 139; predicts Harding's nomination, 92; on Cox as a campaigner, 131
Underwood, Oscar: says Wilson makes league issue of the election, 57; in campaign, 129
Underwood Tariff, 71
unions. *See* labor
United States Constitution, 75, 137
University of Tennessee, 64
Upham, Frederick W., 133

Vanderbilt, Cornelius, at Republican convention, 86
Vassar, 138
Vauclain, Samuel, at Republican convention, 86
Veblen, Thorstein, 15
Vermont, 152
Versailles Treaty: 21, 55, 60, 154, 162; opposed by hyphenated Americans, 23; liberals oppose, 32; becomes a partisan issue, 55; defeat in Senate, 57; Democratic platform on, 105. *See also* League of Nations
veterans' bonus, in Democratic platform, 105-106
Viereck, George S., 154, 155
Villard, O. G., attacks Wood, 29
violence, upsurge after the war, 18, 163-164
Virginia: 68, 78, 115, 116; Republican campaign in, 127
Virginia platform, 104
Volstead Act, 75, 78, 105, 151

Wadsworth, James W.: on Harding, 38; in Smoke-filled Room, 88-89; says Penrose not in control, 97
Wall Street: 88, 111; betting odds, 35, 61-62, 71, 73, 91, 123, 159; liked Harding, 40
Walsh, David I., 104, 130
Walsh, Frank P., Irish plank defeated, 105
Walsh, Thomas J.: anti-Wilson candidate for permanent chairman, 104; league plank adopted, 104-105; urges more emphasis on league, 143
War: 20, 103, 165; injured Democrats, 23; brought intolerance, 18; aroused hatreds, 29-30; undermined progressivism, 18, 162-163, 166-167; made idealistic peace unpopular, 162
War Industries Board, 55
War Risk Insurance, 64
Warren, Charles B., 84, 95, 96
Washington *Herald,* says election victory for league, 160

Index

Washington *Star,* 63, 70, 99, 121, 131, 144, 160
Watson, James E., 80, 87, 88, 100
Watson, Thomas, in Georgia primary, 72, 142
Weeks, John W.: 100, 136; in Smoke-filled Room, 88
West Virginia: 39, 52, 68, 78, 83; moves votes to Harding, 91; Republicans emphasize campaign in, 126
wets, 78, 122, 148. *See also* prohibition; Volstead Act
Wheeler, Charles Stetson, presents Johnson, 82
White, George: 112, 154; becomes Democratic national chairman, 128; sketch, 128; manages campaign, 129-131; says progressivism main issue, 134; denies use of race material, 153
White, Henry, on effect of Lodge Reservations, 57
White, William Allen: 26, 81, 103; opposes Wood's militarism, 29; alienated by Johnson's league stand, 32; launched Allen boom, 48; says big business dominated Republican convention, 86; on Penrose, 97-98; says Harding nomination not a plot, 99; Cox nomination signified reaction, 122; proleague pressure on Harding, 136, 139; signed Declaration of Thirty-One Proleague Republicans, 139; campaigned for Harding, 148-149; on war and reaction, 161-163, 166
Willis, Frank B.: 74, 93, 100; nominates Harding, 82-83
Wilson, Joseph, calls for truth on Wilson's illness, 58
Wilson, Woodrow: 16, 17, 19-23, 27, 42, 46, 72, 73, 74, 75, 76, 78, 101-103, 122, 128, 132, 145, 148, 154; predicts reaction, 163
—administration: 63; progressive accomplishments, 17, 18, 24, 147; reaction after war, 18, 163-164; unpopularity of, 23, 49, 65, 150-151, 157-158; endorsed, 59; handicap to McAdoo, 112; Cox's nomination a defeat for, 121-122; resented by Democratic bosses, 68; Republicans attack, 150; handicap to Cox, 151; alienated hyphenated Americans, 154; alienated labor, 155, 164; election a repudiation of, 160-161. *See also* administration Democrats
—illness: 21, 23, 24, 55, 57-59; Creel shocked at appearance, 58; Glass says mind affected, 58; Cummings on mental condition, 58; resumes cabinet meetings, 58-59; Irving Hoover says illness changed Wilson, 58-59; Swem says he was incompetent, 59; Starling says illness changed Wilson, 59; pictures show him looking well, 61; Grayson says nomination would kill him, 62; Seibold interview emphasizes recovery, 61; tour of Washington bathing beaches, 63; Cummings says sacrificed himself, 103
—league fight: October, 1918, appeal, 21, 43; September, 1919, speaking tour, 21, 31, 55, 58; calls for referendum on league, 21, 55-57; resists compromise, 21, 55, 57; defeated by Lodge, 47; wrote Hitchcock Reservations, 55; urged to compromise, 57, 60; says Republican platform accepts referendum idea, 61; attacked by Bryan for not yielding, 56, 77; berated by Lodge, 80; urged more campaign emphasis on league, 144
—third-term bid: Wilson thought to be receptive to third nomination, 24, 54, 55, 60, 63, 65, 66, 69, 76, 117; overshadowed other Democrats, 24; support for a third term, 54, 59, 64; Wilson promotes his candidacy, 54-63, 104; opposition to a third nomination, 59, 63; Wilson says he might have to run again, 60; opposes other candidates, 61, 62, 72; causes McAdoo withdrawal, 69, 112; in the balloting, 114; third-term bid in convention, 116-120; platform instructions, 118; suggests vice-presidential candidates, 118
—in the campaign: on prohibition, 105; Cox-Roosevelt visit, 127; urged Cummings to stay as national chairman, 127; role in campaign, 129, 142-143; confident of victory, 143, 159; rejects race issue, 153
Wilson, Mrs. Woodrow: 57, 58, 61, 63, 119; says Wilson might run, 60
Wilsonian Democrats. *See* administration Democrats.
Wisconsin, votes for La Follette, 84
Wise, Stephen S., in campaign, 129
woman suffrage: 151-152; Democratic platform on, 106; Bryan on, 111; not significant in election result, 160. *See also* Nineteenth Amendment
women's rights, Democratic platform on, 81
Wood, Leonard: 24, 25, 32-36, 39, 40, 46, 48, 84, 86, 88, 89, 90, 91, 95, 98, 99, 164; preconvention campaign, 25-31; break with the regulars, 25, 27; support for, 26-27; relations with John King, 26-27, 83; on the league, 26, 28-29; as a speaker, 28-29; on

reds, 29; militarism, 28-29; on progressive issues, 29; as leader of a radical jingo sect, 29-30; inexpert in politics, 30; acquires Hitchcock, 30; relations with Allen, 31, 48, 95; in primaries, 35, 39, 40, 49-52; secures delegates, 31, 79; endorses Hays, 31; hostility to Lowden, 35; in poll, 40; finances, 40, 52-53, 85; alliance with Sproul, 48; presented to convention, 82; convention strategy, 83, 85-86, 93-95; in balloting, 84-85, 93, 96; offers Johnson vice-presidency, 85; rejects Hamon oil deal offer, 87; rejects Penrose offer, 87; confers with Lowden in effort to stop Harding, 93-95; fury at defeat, 96; urged by doctors to take vice-presidency under Harding, 177n

Woolley, Robert W.: works for McAdoo, 67; on McAdoo withdrawal, 69

workman's compensation laws, 16

World Court, 136

World War I: 74, 79-80, 165; undermines progressivism, 18, 163; Johnson on, 150; and Democratic defeat, 161

World War II, Roosevelt predicts that America would enter, 146

Wyoming, 91, 116

youth, in revolt, 22

THE JOHNS HOPKINS UNIVERSITY STUDIES IN HISTORICAL AND POLITICAL SCIENCE

✓ ✓ ✓

SEVENTY-NINTH SERIES (1961)

1. Enterprise and Anthracite: Economics and Democracy in Schuylkill County, 1820-1875

    By CLIFTON K. YEARLEY, JR.

2. Birth Rates of the White Population in the United States, 1800-1860: An Economic Study

    By YASUKICHI YASUBA

✓ ✓ ✓

THE JOHNS HOPKINS PRESS
BALTIMORE

THE JOHNS HOPKINS UNIVERSITY STUDIES IN HISTORICAL AND POLITICAL SCIENCE

A subscription for the regular annual series is $5.00. Single numbers may be purchased at special prices. A complete list of the series follows.

FIRST SERIES (1883)—Bound Volume.. O. P.
1. Introduction to American Institutional History, An. By E. A. Freeman..... .75
2. Germanic Origin of New England Towns. By H. B. Adams.......... O. P.
3. Local Government in Illinois. By Albert Shaw. Local Government in Pennsylvania. By E. R. L. Gould...... O. P.
4. Saxon Tithingmen in America. By H. B. Adams........................ .75
5. Local Government in Michigan and the Northwest. By E. W. Bemis.... .75
6. Parish Institutions of Maryland. By Edward Ingle.................... 1.00
7. Old Maryland Manors. By John Hemsley Johnson .... O. P.
8. Norman Constables in America. By H. B. Adams..................... .75
9-10. Village Communities of Cape Ann and Salem. By H. B. Adams....... 1.25
11. Genesis of a New England State. By A. Johnston .... O. P.
12. Local Government and Schools in South Carolina. By B. J. Ramage... 1.00

SECOND SERIES (1884)—Bound Volume O. P.
1-2. Method of Historical Study. By H. B. Adams....................... O. P.
3. Past and Present of Political Economy. By R. T. Ely.................... 1.00
4. Samuel Adams, the Man of the Town Meeting. By James K. Hosmer..... 1.00
5-6. Taxation in the United States. By Henry Carter Adams............... 1.25
7. Institutional Beginnings in a Western State. By Jesse Macy............... .75
8-9. Indian Money in New England, etc. By William B. Weedon............ O. P.
10. Town and Country Government in the Colonies. By E. Channing......... O. P.
11. Rudimentary Society Among Boys. By J. Hemsley Johnson............... O. P.
12. Land Laws of Mining Districts. By C. H. Shinn..................... O. P.

THIRD SERIES (1885)—Bound Volume. O. P.
1. Maryland's Influence Upon Land Cessions to the U. S. By H. B. Adams.. 1.5
2-3. Virginia Local Institutions. By E. Ingle .... O. P.
4. Recent American Socialism. By Richard T. Ely....................... O. P.
5-6-7. Maryland Local Institutions. By Lewis W. Wilhelm................ 2.0
8. Influence of the Proprietors in Founding New Jersey. By A. Scott....... .7
9-10. American Constitutions. By Horace Davis .... O. P.
11-12. City of Washington. By J. A. Porter .... O. P.

FOURTH SERIES (1886)—Bound Volume O. P.
1. Dutch Village Communities on the Hudson River. By I. Elting....... O. P.
2-3. Town Government in Rhode Island. By W. E. Foster. The Narragansett Planters. By Edward Channing...... O. P.
4. Pennsylvania Boroughs. By William P. Holcomb 1.0
5. Introduction to Constitutional History of the States. By J. F. Jameson.... O. P.
6. Puritan Colony at Annapolis, Maryland. By D. R. Randall............. O. P.
7-8-9. Land Question in the United States. By S. Sato .... O. P.
10. Town and City Government of New Haven. By C. H. Levermore....... 1.5
11-12. Land System of the New England Colonies. By M. Egleston.......... O. P.

FIFTH SERIES (1887)—$8.00
1-2. City Government of Philadelphia. By E. P. Allinson and B. Penrose....... O. P.
3. City Government of Boston. By James M. Bugbee....................... O. P.
4. City Government of St. Louis. By Marshall S. Snow................... .7
5-6. Local Government in Canada. By John George Bourinot............. O. P.

7. Effect of the War of 1812 Upon the American Union. By N. M. Butler.. O. P.
8. Notes on the Literature of Charities. By Herbert B. Adams.............. .75
9. Predictions of Hamilton and De Tocqueville. By James Bryce.......... O. P.
10. Study of History in England and Scotland. By P. Fredericq............ .75
11. Seminary Libraries and University Extension. By H. B. Adams......... .75
12. European Schools of History and Politics. By A. D. White............ 1.00

SIXTH SERIES (1888)
History of Co-operation in the United States O. P.

SEVENTH SERIES (1889)—Bound Vol. O. P.
1. Arnold Toynbee. By F. C. Montague 1.25
2-3. Municipal Government in San Francisco. By Bernard Moses.......... 1.25
4. Municipal History of New Orleans. By William W. Howe............. .75
5-6. English Culture in Virginia. By William P. Trent................ O. P.
7-8-9. River Towns of Connecticut. By Charles M. Andrews.............. O. P.
10-11-12. Federal Government in Canada. By John G. Bourinot.............. O. P.

EIGHTH SERIES (1890)—Bound Vol... O. P.
1-2. Beginnings of American Nationality. By A. W. Small................... 2.00
3. Local Governments in Wisconsin. By D. E. Spencer..................... .75
4. Spanish Colonization in the Southwest. By F. W. Blackmar............... O. P.
5-6. Study of History in Germany and France. By P. Fredericq.......... 2.00
7-9. Progress of the Colored People of Maryland. By J. R. Brackett....... 2.00
10. Study of History in Belgium and Holland. By P. Fredericq............ O. P.
11-12. Seminary Notes on Historical Literature. By H. B. Adams and Others... 2.00

NINTH SERIES (1891)—Bound Volume O. P.
1-2. Government of the United States. By W. W. and W. F. Willoughby... O. P.
3-4. University Education in Maryland. By B. C. Steiner. The Johns Hopkins University (1876-1891). By D. C. Gilman 1.00
5-6. Municipal Unity in the Lombard Communes. By W. K. Williams.... O. P.
7-8. Public Lands of the Roman Republic. By A. Stephenson................ 1.50
9. Constitutional Development of Japan. By T. Iyenaga.................... O. P.
10. History of Liberia, A. By J. H. T. McPherson .... O. P.

11-12. Indian Trade in Wisconsin. By F. J. Turner .... O. P.

TENTH SERIES (1892)—Bound Volume O. P.
1. Bishop Hill Colony. By Michael A. Mikkelsen .... O. P.
2-3. Church and State in New England. By Paul E. Lauer................. O. P.
4. Church and State in Maryland. By George Petrie.................... 1.00
5-6. Religious Development of North Carolina. By S. B. Weeks......... 1.00
7. Maryland's Attitude in the Struggle for Canada. By J. W. Black....... O. P.
8-9. Quakers in Pennsylvania. By A. C. Applegarth 1.50
10-11. Columbus and His Discovery of America. By H. B. Adams and H Wood 1.50
12. Causes of the American Revolution. By J. A. Woodburn............... O. P.

ELEVENTH SERIES (1893)
1. Social Condition of Labor. By E. R. L. Gould 1.00
2. World's Representative Assemblies of Today. By E. K. Alden.......... 1.00
3-4. Negro in the District of Columbia. By Edward Ingle.................. 2.00
5-6. Church and State in North Carolina. By Stephen B. Weeks.............. O. P.
7-8. Condition of the Western Farmers, etc. By A. F. Bentley............. 2.00
9-10. History of Slavery in Connecticut. By Bernard C. Steiner............. 1.50
11-12. Local Government in the South. By E. W. Bemis and Others......... 2.00

TWELFTH SERIES (1894)—Bound Vol. O. P.
1-2. Cincinnati Southern Railway. By J. H. Hollander.................... 2.00
3. Constitutional Beginnings of North Carolina. By J. S. Bassett.......... 1.25
4. Struggle of Dissenters for Toleration in Virginia. By H. R. McIlwaine... O. P.
5-6-7. Carolina Pirates and Colonial Commerce. By S. C. Hughson.......... O. P.
8-9. Representation and Suffrage in Massachusetts. By G. H. Haynes......... 1.25
10. English Institutions and the American Indian. By J. A. James............ .75
11-12. International Beginnings of the Congo Free State. By J. S. Reeves.. 2.00

THIRTEENTH SERIES (1895)
1-2. Government of the Colony of South Carolina. By E. L. Whitney........ 2.00
3-4. Early Relations of Maryland and Virginia. By J. H. Latané............ O. P.
5. Rise of the Bicameral System in America. By T. F. Moran.......... O. P.

6-7. White Servitude in the Colony of Virginia. By J. C. Ballagh........ O. P.
8. Genesis of California's First Constitution. By R. D. Hunt.............. 1.00
9. Benjamin Franklin as an Economist. By W. A. Wetzel................ O. P.
10. Provisional Government of Maryland. By J. A. Silver................... 1.00
11-12. Government and Religion of the Virginia Indians. By S. R. Hendren. O. P.

FOURTEENTH SERIES (1896) — Bound Volume .... O. P.
1. Constitutional History of Hawaii. By Henry E. Chambers................ .75
2. City Government of Baltimore. By Thaddeus P. Thomas .... .75
3. Colonial Origins of New England Senates. By F. L. Riley............ 1.25
4-5. Servitude in the Colony of North Carolina. By J. S. Bassett.......... O. P.
6-7. Representation in Virginia. By J. A. C. Chandler 1.50
8. History of Taxation in Connecticut (1636-1776). By F. R. Jones....... 1.25
9-10. Study of Slavery in New Jersey, A. By Henry S. Cooley............... 1.00
11-12. Causes of the Maryland Revolution of 1689. By F. E. Sparks.......... 2.00

FIFTEENTH SERIES (1897)
1-2. Tobacco Industry in Virginia Since 1860. By B. W. Arnold............ O. P.
3-5. Street Railway System of Philadelphia. By F. W. Speirs............. O. P.
6. Daniel Raymond. By C. P. Neill.... 1.00
7-8. Economic History of B. & O. R. R. By M. Reizenstein .... O. P.
9. South American Trade of Baltimore. By F. R. Rutter................... 1.50
10-11. State Tax Commissions in the United States. By J. W. Chapman......... 2.00
12. Tendencies in American Economic Thought. By S. Sherwood......... .75

SIXTEENTH SERIES (1898)
1-4. Neutrality of the American Lakes, etc. By J. M. Callahan............. 3.00
5. West Florida. By H. E. Chambers.. O. P.
6. Anti-Slavery Leaders of North Carolina. By J. S. Bassett.............. O. P.
7-9. Life and Administration of Sir Robert Eden. By B. C. Steiner............. 2.50
10-11. Transition of North Carolina from a Colony. By E. W. Sikes.......... 1.25
12. Jared Sparks and Alexis de Tocqueville. By H. B. Adams............. 1.00

SEVENTEENTH SERIES (1899)
1-2-3. History of State Banking in Maryland. By A. C. Bryan.... .... 2.50

4-5. Know-Nothing Party in Maryland. By L. F. Schmeckebier............. 2.00
6. Labadist Colony in Maryland. By B. B. James......................... .75
7-8. History of Slavery in North Carolina. By J. S. Bassett.............. O. P.
9-10-11. Development of the Chesapeake and Ohio Canal. By G. W. Ward.. 2.00
12. Public Educational Work in Baltimore. By Herbert B. Adams.............. 1.00

EIGHTEENTH SERIES (1900)
1-4. Studies in State Taxation. By J. H. Hollander.........Paper 3.00; Cloth 3.50
5-6. Colonial Executive Prior to the Restoration. By P. L. Kaye............ 1.50
7. Constitution and Admission of Iowa into the Union. By J. A. James.... 1.00
8-9. Church and Popular Education. By H. B. Adams..................... 1.50
10-12. Religious Freedom in Virginia: The Baptists. By W. T. Thom..... O. P

NINETEENTH SERIES (1901)
1-3. America in the Pacific and the Far East. By J. M. Callahan........... O. P.
4-5. State Activities in Relation to Labor. By W. F. Willoughby............. 1.50
6-7. History of Suffrage in Virginia. By J. A. C. Chandler.................. O. P.
8-9. Maryland Constitution of 1864. By W. S. Myers..................... 1.50
10. Life of Commissary James Blair. By D. E. Motley..................... .75
11-12. Governor Hicks of Maryland and the Civil War. By G. L. Radcliffe.. O. P.

TWENTIETH SERIES (1902) — Bound Volume .... O. P.
1. Western Maryland in the Revolution. By B. C. Steiner.................. 1.00
2-3. State Banks Since the National Bank Act. By G. E. Barnett............. 1.75
4. Early History of Internal Improvements in Alabama. By W. E. Martin. 1.50
5-6. Trust Companies in the United States. By George Cator................... O. P.
7-8. Maryland Constitution of 1851. By J. W. Harry...................... 1.50
9-10. Political Activities of Philip Freneau. By S. E. Forman............. O. P.
11-12. Continental Opinion on a Proposed Middle European Tariff Union. By G. M. Fisk....................... 1.00

TWENTY-FIRST SERIES (1903)—Bound Volume .... O. P.
1-2. Wabash Trade Route. By E. J. Benton .... O. P.
3-4. Internal Improvements in North Carolina. By C. C. Weaver........ 1.50

iv

5. History of Japanese Paper Currency. By M. Takai .... O. P.
6-7. Economics and Politics in Maryland, 1720-1750, and the Public Services of Daniel Dulany the Elder. By St. G. L. Sioussat .... O. P.
8-9-10. Beginnings of Maryland, 1631-1639. By B. C. Steiner........... O. P.
11-12. English Statutes in Maryland. By St. G. L. Sioussat................. O. P.

TWENTY-SECOND SERIES (1904)

1-2. Trial Bibliography of American Trade-Union Publications, A. By G. E. Barnett...................... 2.00
3-4. White Servitude in Maryland, 1634-1820. By E. I. McCormac......... O. P.
5. Switzerland at the Beginning of the Sixteenth Century. By J. M. Vincent. 1.00
6-7-8. History of Reconstruction in Virginia. By H. J. Eckenrode........ O. P.
9-10. Foreign Commerce of Japan Since the Restoration. By Y. Hattori..... 1.25
11-12. Descriptions of Maryland. By B. C. Steiner....................... 1.50

TWENTY-THIRD SERIES (1905)

1-2. Reconstruction in South Carolina. By J. P. Hollis................... O. P.
3-4. State Government in Maryland, 1777-1781. By B. W. Bond, Jr. .... O. P.
5-6. Colonial Administration Under Lord Clarendon, 1660-1667. By P. L. Kaye. 2.25
7-8. Justice in Colonial Virginia. By O. P. Chitwood...................... O. P.
9-10. Napoleonic Exiles in America, 1815-1819. By J. S. Reeves............. O. P.
11-12. Municipal Problems in Medieval Switzerland. By J. M. Vincent...... .75

TWENTY-FOURTH SERIES (1906)— Bound Volume .... O. P.

1-2. Spanish-American Diplomatic Relations Before 1898. By H. E. Flack.. O. P.
3-4. Finances of American Trade Unions. By A. M. Sakolski................ 2.25
5-6. Diplomatic Negotiations of the United States with Russia. By J. C. Hildt 2.50
7-8. State Rights and Parties in North Carolina, 1776-1831. By H. M. Wagstaff 2.25
9-10. National Labor Federations in the United States. By William Kirk.... 2.25
11-12. Maryland During the English Civil Wars. Part I. By B. C. Steiner.... 1.50

TWENTY-FIFTH SERIES (1907)—Bound Volume .... O. P.

1. Internal Taxation in the Philippines. By J. S. Hord.................... .75

2-3. Monroe Mission to France, 1794-1796. By B. W. Bond, Jr......... 1.75
4-5 Maryland During the English Civil Wars. Part II. By Bernard C. Steiner. 1.75
6-7. State in Constitutional and International Law. By R. T. Crane....... O. P.
8-9-10. Financial History of Maryland, 1789-1848. By Hugh S. Hanna.... 2.00
11-12. Apprenticeship in American Trade Unions. By J. M. Motley......... 2.00

TWENTY-SIXTH SERIES (1908)

1-3. British Committees, Commissions, and Councils of Trade and Plantations, 1622-1675. By C. M. Andrews. 2.25
4-6. Neutral Rights and Obligations in the Anglo-Boer War. By R. G. Campbell 2.25
7-8. Elizabethan Parish in Its Ecclesiastical and Financial Aspects. By S. L. Ware 1.75
9-10. Study of the Topography and Municipal History of Praeneste, A. By R. V. D. Magoffin................. 1.75
11-12. Beneficiary Features of American Trade Unions. By J. B. Kennedy.. O. P.

TWENTY-SEVENTH SERIES (1909)

1-2. Self-Reconstruction of Maryland, 1864-1867. By W. S. Myers....... 2.00
3-4-5. Development of the English Law of Conspiracy. By J. W. Bryan..... 2.50
6-7. Legislative and Judicial History of the Fifteenth Amendment. By J. M. Mathews 2.00
8-12. England and the French Revolution, 1789-1797. By W. T. Laprade...... O. P.

TWENTY-EIGHTH SERIES (1910) — Bound Volume .... O. P.

1. History of Reconstruction in Louisiana. (Through 1868). By J. R. Ficklen.. O. P.
2. Trade Union Label. By E. R. Spedden 1.75
3. Doctrine of Non-Suability of the State in the United States. By K. Singewald 2.00
4. David Ricardo: A Centenary Estimate. By J. H. Hollander................ O. P.

TWENTY-NINTH SERIES (1911)

1. Maryland Under the Commonwealth: A Chronicle of the Years 1649-1658. By B. C. Steiner..Paper 2.50; Cloth 3.00
2. Dutch Republic and the American Revolution. By Friedrich Edler..... 3.00
3. Closed Shop in American Trade Unions. By F. T. Stockton................. O. P.

THIRTIETH SERIES (1912)—Bound Volume .... O. P.

1. Recent Administration in Virginia. By F. A. Magruder................... 2.50

v

2. Standard Rate in American Trade Unions. By D. A. McCabe.
   Paper 2.50; Cloth 3.00
3. Admission to American Trade Unions. By F. E. Wolfe.................. 2.50

THIRTY-FIRST SERIES (1913)
1. Land System in Maryland, 1720-1765. By Clarence P. Gould.
   Paper 1.50; Cloth O. P.
2. Government of American Trade Unions. By T. W. Glocker..Paper 2.50; Cloth 3.00
3. Free Negro in Virginia, 1619-1865. By J. H. Russell.................. 2.50
4. Quinquennales: An Historical Study. By R. V. D. Magoffin.
   Paper .75; Cloth 1.00

THIRTY-SECOND SERIES (1914) — Bound Volume................... O. P.
1. Jurisdiction in American Building-Trades Unions. By N. R. Whitney.. 2.50
2. Slavery in Missouri, 1804-1865. By H. A. Trexler................... O. P.
3. Colonial Trade of Maryland. By M. S. Morriss........Paper 2.00; Cloth 2.50

THIRTY-THIRD SERIES (1915)
1. Money and Transportation in Maryland, 1720-1765. By Clarence P. Gould.
   Paper 2.25; Cloth 2.75
2. Financial Administration of the Colony of Virginia. By Percy Scott Flippin.
   Paper 1.25; Cloth 1.75
3. Helper and American Trade Unions. By John H. Ashworth.............. 2.00
4. Constitutional Doctrines of Justice Harlan. By Floyd Barzilia Clark.... 3.00

THIRTY-FOURTH SERIES (1916)
1. Boycott in American Trade Unions. By L. Wolman.................... 2.00
2. Postal Power of Congress. By Lindsay Rogers 2.50
3. Control of Strikes in American Trade Unions. By G. M. Janes.
   Paper 1.50; Cloth 2.00
4. State Administration in Maryland. By John L. Donaldson.Paper 2.00; Cloth 2.50

THIRTY-FIFTH SERIES (1917)
1. Virginia Committee System and the American Revolution. By J. M. Leake.
   Paper 2.00; Cloth 2.50
2. Organizability of Labor. By W. O. Weyforth........Paper 3.00; Cloth 3.50
3. Party Organization and Machinery in Michigan Since 1890. By A. C. Millspaugh...........Paper 2.50; Cloth 3.00

THIRTY-SIXTH SERIES (1918)
1. Standard of Living in Japan. By K. Morimoto .... O. P.
2. Sumptuary Law in Nurnberg. By K. R. Greenfield......Paper 2.00; Cloth 2.50
3. Privileges and Immunities of State Citizenship. By R. Howell.
   Paper 2.00; Cloth 2.50
4. French Protestantism, 1559-1562. By C. G. Kelly.......Paper 2.50; Cloth 3.00

THIRTY-SEVENTH SERIES (1919) — Bound Volume .... O. P.
1. Unemployment and American Trade Unions. By D. P. Smelser, Jr...... 2.25
2. Labor Law of Maryland. By M. H. Lauchheimer......Paper 2.25; Cloth 2.75
3. American Colonization Society, 1817-1840. By E. L. Fox.
   Paper 3.00, Cloth 3.50
4. Obligation of Contracts Clause of the United States Constitution. By W. B. Hunting..........Paper 1.50; Cloth 2.00

THIRTY-EIGHTH SERIES (1920) — Bound Volume .... O. P.
1. United States Department of Agriculture. By W. L. Wanlass.
   Paper 1.50; Cloth 2.00
2. Amalgamated Association of Iron, Steel and Tin Workers. By J. S. Robinson. 2.00
3. Employment of Plebiscite in Determination of Sovereignty. By J. Mattern. 3.00

THIRTY-NINTH SERIES (1921)
1. Capitalization of Goodwill. By Kemper Simpson...................... O. P.
2. Rise of the Cotton Mills in the South. By Broadus Mitchell............ O. P.
3. International Molders' Union of North America. By Frank T. Stockton..... 3.00

FORTIETH SERIES (1922)—Bound Volume .... O. P.
1. Presidential Campaign of 1832. By Samuel R. Gammon, Jr............. 2.50
2. Canadian Reciprocity Treaty of 1854. By C. C. Tansill................. 1.50
3. Recent Problems in Admiralty Jurisdiction. By Edgar T. Fell......... 2.00
4. Creation of the Presidency, 1775-1789: A Study in Constitutional History. By Charles C. Thach, Jr............... 2.50

FORTY-FIRST SERIES (1923) — Bound Volume .... O. P.
1. Paper Money in Maryland, 1727-1789. By Kathryn L. Behrens............ O. P.
2. Shop Committee in the United States. By Carroll E. French.............. 1.50

vi

3. Bavaria and the Reich: The Conflict Over the Law for the Protection of the Republic. By J. Mattern........... 1.75
4. James Henry Hammond, 1807-1864. By Elizabeth Merritt............... 2.00

FORTY-SECOND SERIES (1924)
1. Contemporary French Opinion on the American Civil War. By W. Reed West 2.00
2. Frederick Law Olmsted: A Critic of the Old South. By Broadus Mitchell. 2.00
3. Constitutional Doctrines of Justice Oliver Wendell Holmes. By Dorsey Richardson 1.50
4. Reformation in Poland: Some Social and Economic Aspects. By Paul Fox. 2.00

FORTY-THIRD SERIES (1925)
1. Agrarian Movement in North Dakota. By Paul R. Fossum................ 2.50
2. Virginia Frontier, 1754-1763. By Louis K. Koontz........................ O. P.
3. Ordinance Making Powers of the President of the United States. By James Hart .... Paper 3.50; Cloth 4.00

FORTY-FOURTH SERIES (1926)
1. Sumptuary Legislation and Personal Regulation in England. By F. Elizabeth Baldwin...... Paper 3.00; Cloth 3.50
2. Doctrine of Continuous Voyage. By H. W. Briggs 3.00
3. Wage Policies of Labor Organizations in a Period of Industrial Depression. By V. J. Wyckoff................. 1.50

FORTY-FIFTH SERIES (1927)
1. State as a Party Litigant. By R. D. Watkins 3.00
2. Relation of Thomas Jefferson to American Foreign Policy. By W. K. Woolery 1.75
3. Ecclesiastical Censure at the End of the Fifteenth Century. By W. K. Gotwald 1.00
4. Constitutional Status and Government of Alaska. By G. W. Spicer.
Paper 1.75; Cloth 2.25

FORTY-SIXTH SERIES (1928)
1. Mission of William Carmichael to Spain. By S. G. Coe.............. 1.50
2. Workers (Communist) Party and American Trade Unions. By D. M. Schneider 1.50
3. Virginia Constitutional Convention of 1901-1902. By R. C. McDaniel..... 2.50
4. Protection of Citizens Abroad by Armed Forces of the United States. By M. Offutt............................ 2.00

FORTY-SEVENTH SERIES (1929)
1. Congressional Investigating Committees. By M. E. Dimock............ 2.75
2. Study of Judicial Administration in the State of Maryland, A. By G. K. Reiblich 2.50
3. Financial History of Baltimore, 1900-26. By L. O. Rea................ 2.50
4. Franco-German Relations, 1878-1885. By R. H. Wienefeld.............. 2.75

FORTY-EIGHTH SERIES (1930)
1. Economic and Social Aspects of Federal Reclamation. By Dorothy Lampen. 2.00
2. Russo-American Relations, 1815-1867. By Benjamin Platt Thomas.......... 2.75
3. Maryland Legislature. By Harry Joseph Green........... Paper 1.00; Cloth 1.50
4. Southern Commercial Conventions, 1837-1860. By Herbert Wender.... 3.00

FORTY-NINTH SERIES (1931)
1. Departments of the American Federation of Labor. By Albert Helbing.. 2.00
2. State Legislative Committees: A Study in Procedure. By C. I. Winslow.... 2.25
3. French Opposition to the Mexican Policy of the Second Empire. By F. E. Lally............................ 2.25
4. Henry Charles Carey: A Study in American Economic Thought. By A. D. H. Kaplan 1.50

FIFTIETH SERIES (1932)
1. Hours of Labor. By Lazare Teper... 1.50
2. Some Presidential Interpretations of the Presidency. By Norman J. Small. 3.00
3. Governor of Maryland, The. By Charles J. Rohr .... Paper 2.50; Cloth 3.00
4. Yellow Dog Contract. By Joel I. Seidman 1.50

FIFTY-FIRST SERIES (1933)
1. Studies on Scipio Africanus. By Richard M. Haywood.................. 1.50
2. Right of Search and the Slave Trade in Anglo-American Relations, 1814-1862. By Hugh G. Soulsby........ 2.75
3. American Policy of Recognition Towards Mexico. By S. A. MacCorkle.. 1.50
4. Mathew Carey: A Study in American Economic Development. By K. W. Rowe 2.00
5. Hezekiah Niles as an Economist. By R. G. Stone....... Paper 2.00; Cloth 2.50

FIFTY-SECOND SERIES (1934)
1. Italy's Relations with England, 1896-1905. By J. L. Glanville.......... 2.50
2. Capital Issues Committee and War

Finance Corporation. By Woodbury Willoughby 2.00
3. Maryland Business Corporations, 1783-1852. By J. G. Blandi............ 2.00
4. American Doctrine of State Succession. By H. A. Wilkinson............... 2.25

FIFTY-THIRD SERIES (1935)
1. Juristic Status of Egypt and the Sudan. By Vernon A. O'Rourke........... O. P.
2. Workmen's Compensation in Maryland. By Evelyn Ellen Singleton.......... 2.00
3. Mutual Savings Banks in Baltimore. By Robert W. Thon, Jr............. 1.50
4. Contribution of the Ideologues to French Revolutionary Thought. By Charles H. Van Duzer............. 2.50

FIFTY-FOURTH SERIES (1936)
1. Movement for the Acquisition of All Mexico, 1846-1848. By John D. P. Fuller............................ 2.50
2. Gas Light Company of Baltimore. By George T. Brown.................. 2.00
3. Journeymen Barbers' International Union of America. By W. Scott Hall 2.00
4. Supreme Court and Political Questions. By C. G. Post.
Paper 1.25; Cloth 2.50

FIFTY-FIFTH SERIES (1937)
1. Germany and Morocco Before 1905. By Francis T. Williamson.......... 3.00
2. History and Development of the Fourth Amendment of the United States Constitution. By Nelson B. Lasson..... 2.00
3. Influence of Border Disorders on Relations Between the United States and Mexico, 1876-1910. By Robert Gregg 3.00
4. Floating Debt of the Federal Government, 1919-1936. By Edward Raguet Van Sant 1.50

FIFTY-SIXTH SERIES (1938)
1. Commercial Banking and the Stock Market Before 1863. By Joseph Edward Hedges 2.50
2. Industry and Commerce of the City of Rome (50 B. C.–200 A. D.). By Helen Jefferson Loane............. 2.50
3. Investment Value of Goodwill. By Lawrence N. Bloomberg............ 1.00
4. Historical Scholarship in the United States, 1876-1901: As Revealed in the Correspondence of Herbert B. Adams. By W. Stull Holt..Paper 3.50; Cloth 4.00

FIFTY-SEVENTH SERIES (1939)
1. History of Criminal Syndicalism Legislation in the United States, A. By Eldridge Foster Dowell............ 2.50

2. Wholesale Marketing of Fruits and Vegetables in Baltimore. By Robert G. Deupree 2.00
3. History of the Woman's Peace Party. By M. L. Degen...Paper 3.25; Cloth 3.75

FIFTY-EIGHTH SERIES (1940)
1. Malaria and Colonization in the Carolina Low Country, 1526-1696. By St. Julien Ravenel Childs.............. 3.75
2. Municipal Indebtedness: A Study of the Debt-to-Property Ratio. By Leroy Shattuck, Jr...................... 2.50
3. Security Affiliates of National Banks. By W. W. Peach.................. 2.75

FIFTY-NINTH SERIES (1941)
1. Investment Management. By John A. Loftus........................... 2.50
2. Baltimore 1870-1900: Studies in Social History. By C. Hirschfield......... 2.50
3. National Bituminous Coal Commission. By R. H. Baker............. 4.50

SIXTIETH SERIES (1942)
1. From Barter to Slavery: The Economic Relations of Portuguese and Indians in the Settlement of Brazil 1500-1580. By Alexander Marchant...... 2.50
2. Geopolitik: National Self-Sufficiency and Empire. By J. Mattern........ 2.25
3. Question of Expatriation in America Prior to 1907. By I-Mien Tsiang... 2.00
4. Public Trusteeship. By Norman Heaney 2.00

SIXTY-FIRST SERIES (1943)
1. Maryland During and After the Revolution. By Philip A. Crowl........ 2.50
2. Charles J. Bonaparte, Patrician Reformer. By Eric F. Goldman....... 2.25
3. Studies in the History of the English Feudal Barony. By S. Painter...... 3.00
4. Economic Thought of Woodrow Wilson. By W. Diamond.
Paper 2.00; Cloth 3.00

SIXTY-SECOND SERIES (1944)
1. Andrea Barbarigo, Merchant of Venice, 1418-1449. By Frederic C. Lane.... O. P.
2. Growth of German Historicism. By Friedrich Engel-Janosi.............. O. P.
3. Wheats of Classical Antiquity. By N. Jasny.......................... 2.50

SIXTY-THIRD SERIES (1945)
1. Henry Barnard's American Journal of Education. By Richard E. Thursfield.
Paper 4.00; Cloth 4.50
2. Roman Rhetorical Schools as a Preparation for the Courts Under the Early Empire. By E. Patrick Parks....... 1.50

3. Slave States in the Presidential Election of 1860. By Ollinger Crenshaw. Paper 4.00; Cloth 4.50

SIXTY-FOURTH SERIES (1946)
1. Great National Project: A History of the Chesapeake and Ohio Canal. By W. S. Sanderlin...Paper 4.00; Cloth 4.50
2. Richard Hildreth. By Donald E. Emerson 2.75
3. William Rufus Day: Supreme Court Justice from Ohio. By Joseph E. McLean 2.75

SIXTY-FIFTH SERIES (1947)
1. British Block Grants and Central-Local Finance. By Reynold E. Carlson.... 3.25
2. Landowners and Agriculture in Austria, 1815-1848. By Jerome Blum....... 4.00

SIXTY-SIXTH SERIES (1948)
1. French Freemasonry Under the Third Republic. By Mildred J. Headings.. 4.50
2. Science and Rationalism in the Government of Louis XIV, 1661-1683. By James E. King.................... O. P.

SIXTY-SEVENTH SERIES (1949)
1. Capitalism in Amsterdam in the 17th Century. By Violet Barbour....... O. P.
2. The Patent Grant. By Burke Inlow.. O. P.
3. Saint Mary Magdalene in Mediaeval Literature. By Helen Garth........ 2.00

SIXTY-EIGHTH SERIES (1950)
1. The Organization of State Administration in Delaware. By Paul Dolan... 2.50
2. The Theory of Inter-Sectoral Money Flows and Income Formation. By John Chipman........................ 2.50
3. Congressional Differences over Foreign Affairs, 1921-41. By George Grassmuck .... O. P.

Bound Volumes Discontinued Beginning with the Sixty-Ninth Series.

SIXTY-NINTH SERIES (1951)
1. Party and Constituency: Pressures on Congress. By Julius Turner........ O. P.
2. The Legates of Galatia From Augustus to Diocletian. By Robert K. Sherk.. 2.50

SEVENTIETH SERIES (1952)
1. Federal Examiners and the Conflict of Law and Administration. By Lloyd D. Musolf 3.00
2. The Growth of Major Steel Companies, 1900-1950. By Gertrude G. Schroeder ....Paper 4.00, Cloth 5.00

SEVENTY-FIRST SERIES (1953)
1. The Revolt of 1916 in Russian Central Asia. By Edward D. Sokol......... 3.25
2. Four Studies in French Romantic Historical Writing. By Friedrich Engel-Janosi 2.50

SEVENTY-SECOND SERIES (1954)
1. Price Discrimination in Selling Gas and Electricity. By Ralph Kirby Davidson ....Paper $3.00, Cloth 4.00
2. The Savings Bank of Baltimore, 1816-1866. By Peter L. Payne and Lance E. Davis ....Paper 3.00

SEVENTY-THIRD SERIES (1955)
The Paris Commune in French Politics, 1871-1880. By Jean T. Joughin.... Two vols. ....Paper 7.50
1. Volume I: The Partial Amnesty
2. Volume II: The Final Amnesty

SEVENTY-FOURTH SERIES (1956)
1. Robert Oliver, Merchant of Baltimore, 1783-1819. By Stuart Weems Bruchey. Paper 5.00
2. Political Theory and Institutions of the Khawārij. By Elie Adib Salem. Paper 3.00

SEVENTY-FIFTH SERIES (1957)
1. Britons in American Labor: A History of the Influence of the United Kingdom Immigrants on American Labor, 1820-1914. By Clifton K. Yearley, Jr. 4.00
2. The Location of Yamatai: A Case Study in Japanese Historiography. By John Young .... O. P.

SEVENTY-SIXTH SERIES (1958)
1. Trends in Birth Rates in the United States since 1870. By Bernard Okun. 3.50
2. The Dynamics of Supply: Estimation of Farmers' Response to Price. By Marc Nerlove..........Paper 4.00; Cloth 5.00

SEVENTY-SEVENTH SERIES (1959)
1. Republicans Face the Southern Question—The New Departure Years 1877-1897. By Vincent P. De Santis. Paper 4.00; Cloth 5.00
2. Money, Class, and Party: An Economic Study of Civil War and Reconstruction. By Robert P. Sharkey. Paper 4.00; Cloth 5.50

SEVENTY-EIGHTH SERIES (1960)
1. The Nobility of Toulouse—An Economic Study of Aristocracy in the Eighteenth Century. By Robert Forster. Paper 3.50; Cloth 5.00
2. The Union Pacific Railroad—A Case in Premature Enterprise. By Robert William Fogel.....Paper 3.00; Cloth 3.50

SEVENTY-NINTH SERIES (1961)
1. Enterprise and Anthracite: Economics and Democracy in Schuylkill County, 1820-1875. By Clifton K. Yearley, Jr. Cloth 5.00
2. Birth Rates of the White Population in the United States, 1800-1860: An Economic Study. By Yasukichi Yasuba. Paper 5.00